Sonic Art

Written by an active composer, performer and educator, *Sonic Art: An Introduction to Electroacoustic Music Composition* provides a clear and informative introduction to the compositional techniques behind electroacoustic music. It brings together theory, aesthetics, context and practical applications to allow students to start thinking about sound creatively, and gives them the tools to compose meaningful sonic art works.

In addition to explaining the techniques and philosophies of sonic art, the book examines over forty composers and their works, introducing the history and context of notable pieces, and includes chapters on how to present compositions professionally, in performance and online. The book is supported by an online software toolkit which enables readers to start creating their own compositions. Encouraging a 'hands-on' approach to working with sound, *Sonic Art* is the perfect introduction for anyone interested in electroacoustic music and crafting art from sounds.

Adrian Moore is Reader in Music at the University of Sheffield and Director of the University of Sheffield Sound Studios. He is an active composer and performer of electroacoustic music.

Sonic Art

An Introduction to Electroacoustic Music Composition

Adrian Moore

Routledge
Taylor & Francis Group

NEW YORK AND LONDON

First published 2016
by Routledge
711 Third Avenue, New York, NY 10017

and by Routledge
2 Park Square, Milton Park, Abingdon, Oxon, OX14 4RN

Routledge is an imprint of the Taylor & Francis Group, an informa business

©2016 Taylor & Francis

Library of Congress Cataloging in Publication Data
Names: Moore, Adrian, 1969– author.
Title: Sonic art : an introduction to electroacoustic
music composition / Adrian Moore.
Description: New York, NY; Abingdon, Oxon : Routledge, 2016. | "2016 |
Includes bibliographical references and index.
Identifiers: LCCN 2015036701 | ISBN 9781138925014 (hardback) |
ISBN 9781138925038 (paperback) | ISBN 9781315684024 (e-book)
Subjects: LCSH: Computer composition. | Electronic composition. |
Computer music–Instruction and study.
Classification: LCC MT56.M66 2016 | DDC 781.3/4–dc23LC record
available at http://lccn.loc.gov/2015036701

ISBN: 978-1-138-92501-4 (hbk)
ISBN: 978-1-138-92503-8 (pbk)
ISBN: 978-1-315-68402-4 (ebk)

Typeset in Sabon
by Out of House Publishing

Contents

Figures

Tables

Preface

This book was written for undergraduate and postgraduate students specialising in electroacoustic music composition and sonic art at the University of Sheffield Department of Music. Whilst the tools mentioned here are part and parcel of our teaching programme, they are very flexible and easy to use; there seemed no reason not to make both the tools and the book available to all.

This book was originally titled *Sonic Art: Recipes and Reasonings* with the subtitle being a play on words about cookbooks. I have made suggestions about what can be done with different sounds (recipes) and have described why various techniques may be appropriate (reasonings – a pun on seasoning in cookery). Well, nobody got it! Hence the now extended subtitle mentioning 'electroacoustic music', a term which also covers a multitude of approaches. Ultimately we are aiming to make something that could not be called 'music' in the traditional sense but which has 'musical' sensitivities: a sense of pace and style; phrasing; dynamic contrasts; pitched materials; percussive sounds; programmatic implications; new spaces; new sounds – all structured by listening and reacting.

Contemporary music using computers or other electronic devices has broken all of the barriers about what we think sonic art, electroacoustic music or whatever we may call it, actually is. I have tried to place sound – the enjoyment of working with it and the need to place the right sounds at the right times – at the heart of this book. The tradition behind this book is very Western European. It is a product of my experience and, in particular, my own musical education. To be all inclusive – to accept all music as worthy – would expose my lack of experience and would necessitate the removal of my name from the front cover. I doubt a book that said 'you can do this or you can do that, it does not really matter so long as you like it' would excite anyone. However, in revising the book over the last year, I hope to have been somewhat more inclusive, somewhat more open minded, whilst remaining sufficiently dogmatic to keep me interested and excited about influencing students studying electroacoustic music composition.

Please note that this is not a book that 'starts at the very beginning'. Indeed it assumes quite a bit both about computer operation and musical aesthetics. There are also numerous references throughout the book to instructive websites and further reading/listening.

This book is in three sections:

Section 1 covers electroacoustic music composition practice. Chapter 1 asks the question 'what is sound?' and suggests ways we can describe and understand it in order to manipulate it musically. Chapter 2 refers to two pieces of software in which, over the years, the staff and students of the University of Sheffield Sound Studios have developed a number of tools that enable the manipulation of sound. Whilst the software itself is complex, we have made front-ends, mini-interfaces if you will, that hide the bulk of the programming and let you quickly explore sound processing. Chapter 3 tries to tie our understanding of a sound's properties to the processes we might use to develop them, arguing that we tend to choose a process that helps us react against what we hear most strongly. Chapter 4 begins to investigate composition beyond stereo. Chapter 5 contextualises some 50 works, examining sound processing where appropriate but thinking mainly about the composers' working methods.

Section 2 picks up where Chapters 1 and 3 left off, covering aspects of space, time (Chapter 6) and broader philosophical concepts (Chapter 7).

Section 3 comes back down to earth by documenting the presentation of electroacoustic music. Chapter 8 looks at the performance of electroacoustic music over multichannel sound diffusion systems. Chapter 9 suggests ways to present electroacoustic music for examination at college, submission to conferences or competitions and for general public consumption or (heaven forbid!) public sale.

A number of appendices document the installation of software and toolkits, present useful tips and advice from colleagues around the world (something that I hope will be greatly enhanced online in the future) and provide a very basic introduction to programming.

The vast majority of this book is written in a rather impersonal third person, but switches to first person for certain sections, in particular Chapter 5 where I reflect personally upon a number of pieces. Thanks go to my colleague Dave Moore for his technical expertise, Martin Curtis-Powell for his careful and attentive reading of the initial text,

Alex Gowan-Webster for his repackaging of ussstools, Stephen Pearse for his advice and guidance, and all the composers that have contributed personal recollections over their extensive careers. Thanks also to the University of Sheffield Faculty of Arts for assisting me with this project.

Chapter 1

What is Sound?

Student: What sounds can I use in my composition?
Teacher: All sounds are available to you.
Student: Okay, so where do I start?
Teacher: Start with a sound that interests you.

1.1 Introduction

1.1.1 Jumping in at the deep end

This book is about composing with sounds. Composition can, but does not have to, start with sound; sound is all around us, and quite often we may wish to have more control over it than it has over us. The prevalence of recording technology means that we can capture sound quite easily and store it on the computer. But what do we do with it then? Trevor Wishart opens his book *Audible Design* (Wishart, 1994) by making three assumptions:

1. Any sound whatsoever may be the starting material for a musical composition.
2. The ways in which this sound may be transformed are limited only by the imagination of the composer.
3. Musical structure depends on establishing audible relationships amongst sound materials.

Each assumption opens up a wealth of opportunities. This book hopes to tie down some of the possibilities, block off some of the dead ends of sound manipulation and suggest a number of meaningful methodologies for selecting, developing and mixing sound so that, as a composer, you can make something *musical*. Wishart mentions musical composition, but for many the experience of shaping sounds will have little to do with the pitches and rhythms of Western classical or popular music. That is not to say that the music we all listen to will not have an effect upon us and will not influence how we work with sound in the raw; it is just that if we try to make a 'musical composition' of pitches and rhythms with raw recorded sounds, the chances are it will sound terrible.

So let us throw 'music' out of the window but bear in mind 'musical'; something with phrases, starts, ends, middles, highs, lows, louds, softs, breaths, pace, shape, form, emotion and energy. Think about working with sound like a potter works with clay. Take a sound and mould it to the shape you want. On some occasions that may be a fixed shape; at other times, we may end up with something completely random and fluid. What is it then? Clay, yes, but how do we describe the shape? As soon as we start describing things in terms of abstract details (thin, curved, round) and making references to other objects and emotions that have personal relationships with us (lively, frightening) the sooner we get a grip on how we can develop a structure.

As this book progresses we will look at how we might define a sound. It is unfortunate that in a book we have to define sounds with words, but the flip side here is that the process is quite liberating as it forces analysis.[1] We will listen to sounds and consider developing them over time. Time plays a huge role in the structure of any piece of sonic art. When we come to mixing sounds (one after the other, one on top of the other) we are shaping sound in time: sound is not just heard as A to B, but felt over a duration.

Having thought about describing sound, we will look at techniques to develop sound, techniques that work well with the salient properties that are contained within our sounds. We will look at a number of different software packages and concrete, usable examples will be given. All the software used will be open source and therefore free to install and run on almost any computer.

Finally, we will think about how we might tie sounds and techniques together and how we can build up a fluid set of skills that enable us to quickly hear the acousmatic-potential of a sound and develop it into something new. We suggest that it might be possible to work 'against' the sound, reacting for the most part in a negative fashion, always being resistive to what a sound wants to do. For example, if a sound is noisy, the chances are that over time it might want to become less noisy. (It is certainly easier for it to become less noisy than more noisy, though there are no hard and fast rules here). So we will outline a principle of defining sounds across poles (light/dark, soft/hard, high/low, fast/slow) and suggest, for example, that if a sound is slow, you may want to consider techniques that speed it up.

So if you want to get cracking and really jump in at the deep end, Chapter 2 might be a good place to start. If you want to see how techniques and sounds interact, Chapter 3 will help. This book is meant to be both a user guide and a textbook. What it is not is a piece of scholarly literature philosophising on the nature of sonic art. It is vital to note that if you do jump in at the deep end, the life preservers and water-wings are the texts and compositions of the past. Listening to music and reading supplementary literature will help make your journey as a composer faster, more exciting and infinitely more pleasurable.

1.1.2 Context of the book

Given the number of composers manipulating sound to all sorts of ends, and given the huge array of software tools on offer, it is hardly surprising that many have put some of their thoughts on paper. However, the vast majority of these publications are heavily academic. For readings concerning the relationship between theory and practice, John Young (Young, 2007) sums up very effectively the quite personal relationship a composer has with his/her sounds. And he mentions a small number of composers we consider to be highly influential in sonic art theory and practice, composers that have taken the time to write about what they do: Trevor Wishart (1986; 1994; 1996), Denis Smalley (1986; 1996; 1997; 2007), Simon Emmerson (1986; 2007), Jonty Harrison (1998; 1999) and Leigh Landy (1991; 1994; 2007; 2012). It may also be useful to reflect on recent publications that deal with sound design (Farnell, 2010). You may find quite a lot of terminology drawn from Denis Smalley's academic writings (words such as gesture, texture, utterance, energy, motion, space, environment), not because this book needs to be bound in academic terminology but simply because they are the right words for the job at hand.

Additionally, we can see numerous books that deal directly (or in passing) with the techniques of sound manipulation, synthesis and sound design. Miller Puckette's (2007) software Pure Data (Pd) is one of the key resources we have used to make toolkits for sound manipulation. A more focused introduction to this software can be found in Johannes Kriedler's book on the same software (2009). Having access to a book is great: fortunately, both the above texts are available as free downloadable pdf documents. We have constructed a number of toolkits that you can use and develop. Our toolkits exist in Pure Data and Csound, using an excellent interface designed by Stephen Yi called Blue (Yi, 2008). Links for downloads of all software are available from the University of Sheffield Sound Studios web pages www.shef.ac.uk/usss. Intimate knowledge of software tools over the years allows you to be flexible when designing sound manipulations. However, this book only assumes a 'working' knowledge of the computer (how to get sound in and out, how to edit a stereo file, and perhaps how to mix two files together). The computer is your instrument and it is important to practise its scales and arpeggios in order to gain proficiency. A very recent primer in Pure Data comes in the form of Andy Farnell's excellent book *Designing Sound* (Farnell, 2010), and his code examples are available from the MIT Press website. My book draws upon all the texts mentioned above but tries to keep technique and language grounded in practical 'what does it sound like to you?' terminology. Chapter 2 should enable you to investigate any recorded sound and try basic manipulations such as speed changes, filters and delays, thinking about the results in terms of 'bigger, smaller, louder, softer' and other polar opposites. Hopefully this book becomes something that you can dip into from time to time, as well as read wholesale should you so wish.

It is important to say a word about right and wrong in sonic art composition. Although the composer is in control, unless you want to play your music only to yourself, you should consider your audience. It is important to listen to your music as others might hear it otherwise you tend towards self-affirmation (you know what is about to happen so when it does, you are satisfied). Play your music to others during the course of your composition and be prepared for frank comments. Normally what feels right *is* right, but most importantly you need to know why it is right. It may well be easier to start off working out what is wrong with the music that you are listening to. (Medical discovery works in this way for the most part – reaction (to illness) rather than anticipation and precaution.) This book arises from countless handouts and wiki pages supporting courses in electroacoustic music composition at the University of Sheffield. Students start 'messing around with sound' in the first year with only their previous school studies to support them. Whether they can identify the right and wrong by the end of year three is irrelevant. Their final-year pieces are living proof that something has changed, decisions have been taken, understandings made. We hope to speed this process further still by suggesting some interesting 'recipes' for sound manipulation. To back up our suggestions we will provide a number of 'reasonings' based upon the author's experience. Like any good cookbook, eventually you won't need to use it but knowing where you can lay your hands on it may well be reassuring.

1.2 Composition and Recording

Acousmatic composition begins with source material that is processed and reflected upon. The acousmatic stance asks that you listen to your sound in terms of raw qualities of energy, direction, colour, density and texture (amongst other attributes). We need to come up with a simple, easy to use language to help 'tag' our sounds (or portions of them). Although identification of the sound in terms of more personal qualities or emotions, or indeed the identification of a real-world sound, may be ideal, try to dissect the sound in front of you into component parts.

If composition begins with sound, we need to record that sound. It may be recorded with its environment fully intact (a passing car, voices in the street, an airport tannoy) or it may be an object taken from its environment and recorded in the silence of the studio. When this happens you can normally get the microphones quite close to the source and use them like a microscope on a visual object, examining from multiple angles. At this early stage it is vital to get the recording you want at the highest quality possible. Bad sound in equals bad sound out, no matter how good your composition process might be.

1.2.1 Recording

We normally record in stereo and if we were outside we would aim for a good stereo field, to enable us to capture a wide variety of sources from left to right. In the studio our left and right need not be close together emulating the head. If we were recording some marbles in a bowl (and were moving the bowl around) we might place one microphone at the very left edge of the play space and the other at the very right.

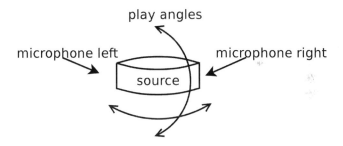

Figure 1.1 Microphone play space

As the marbles spin/swirl from the left to the right as we gently rotate and undulate the bowl, the resulting sound will move from the left ear/speaker to the right ear/speaker. Already we have made a major, non-real-world transformation and potentially created a texture with a rolling feel and a sense of acceleration from left to right. During a playful recording process it is clear that a number of compositional decisions are already being made.

Other important factors to remember when recording:

• Dynamic range. Sounds that are just too quiet are never going to be much use. Sounds that vary from loud to soft give you plenty of room to select. When recording, ensure that you get a good signal level on the recording device otherwise any future amplification will just bring up the level of the background noise. This is called signal to noise ratio.

- Texture/Gesture. You may well want to record sustained sounds and discrete sounds. Take the previous example. Whilst having lots of marbles swirling around is an excellent texture, one marble moving once from left to right might be an example of a simple 'swipe' gesture.
- Focus. Bringing a sound close to the microphones gives a sense of intimacy and normally aids in increasing the dynamic range. Moving the sound away from the microphones narrows the stereo image.

So already, during the recording process we have identified a number of spatial dimensions within which to play.

- Left/Right. Perhaps the most obvious. The source may move (marbles), but if it does not (your voice) perhaps you should change your focus and sing towards one microphone then the other. It is often more natural to move in accordance with your vocal utterance (though it does not look that graceful in the studio) than panning a mono signal in a digital audio workstation or DAW later on.
- Near/Far. You may not notice this at first but this movement changes the spectral characteristics of the sound. Normally, as you move further away the high frequencies drop off and you hear less of the source and more of the room.
- Up/Down. This is not easy to make happen in the studio but is almost always suggested by the sound recorded. You will find that pitch inflections (glissandi) tend to suggest motion upwards/downwards and that the spectral characteristics of a sound will suggest height. Light whispers – indeed, let us use the word 'whispers' as an audio example – suggest fleeting motion and a sense of height. Birdsong also suggests a certain lightness. Drums and other 'heavier' sounds are normally rooted to the floor. This 'small is light will fly' vs 'large is heavy will lie' is not a hard and fast rule. Exceptions could include the sound of a helicopter, for example. We know it is in the sky but its sound is often quite full-on. Trevor Wishart cites the sound of the rainforest including whalesong. Clearly a spatial contradiction but an easy possibility in the world of digital sound.

1.2.2 What sounds can I record?

As mentioned earlier, all sounds are open to you to record but some will simply never yield good results in the studio. Here is a list of source files that composers at the University of Sheffield Sound Studios (USSS) have used in the past.

- Coins, cowbells, crotales (sustains and chimes)
- Hung metals, percussion, pots and pans (harmonic and inharmonic)
- Parcel tape, Velcro, Styrofoam, (clicks and rhythms)
- Stones, other assorted objects in cardboard boxes, paper crunch and tear (gesture texture)
- Cars, street scenes, rain and thunder (environments)
- Human action, human voice, human situations
- Water pouring, objects in water, streams and rivers (inside outside)
- Wine bottles, wood blocks, Western classical instruments (pitch noise)

1.2.3 Where does composition begin again?

Composition often begins with an idea. That idea is not normally a concept but a sound or collection of sounds. It is better not to drive your compositions from conceptual ideas or stories as making sounds fit into these forms is often extremely difficult. Better to happen upon a sound, accumulate a collection of similar or contrasting sounds and see if an idea springs from your close listening to these sounds.

In the past, composers working at the University of Sheffield Sound Studios have used a number of Western classical instruments as sources (violin, french horn, piano, zither). These instruments are already familiar to us from radio and concert settings. Taken in isolation they can also create a full spectrum of colour and dynamics.

However, you may wish for an even more restricted range of source sounds. Alistair MacDonald's elegant work *Equivalence* (2007) is made from the sound of bricks being gently rubbed together. Jonty Harrison's *Klang* (1982) uses the sound of a casserole (lid and body). Adrian Moore's work *Study in Ink* (2000) uses almost exclusively the sound of a whiteboard marker on a board (ouch!)

And the process is then quite simple. (Simple to state, difficult to implement, and often quite time-consuming to complete.)

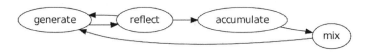

Figure 1.2 The work – reflect process

1.2.4 Reflect

Imagine the situation. The sound on your hi-fi is too loud. You need to make a qualitative adjustment, reach for the volume control and make the necessary change. You recognised a problem and reacted against it using tools specifically designed for the purpose. This is how the creative aspects of this book will develop. Taken to its extreme, you want to compose so you need to make sound; without sound you will have nothing. By contrast, if your piece/section is coming to an end you need to stop sound. Either way, we are always reacting against what we perceive in any particular situation.

Although this book is not probing the physics of the ear and the psychoacoustics of listening, it is important to briefly mention how sound affects us physically and psychologically. Most fit and able adults have a hearing range from 20 Hz to 20,000 Hz (1 Hz is one cycle per second). Sub-audio is more often felt and seen (earthquakes shaking buildings, etc.). Supra-audio is there but we just can't perceive it; other animals can and do, however. Our hearing is 'tuned' to perceive the frequencies most associated with our speech patterns. It will become immediately obvious once you start working with sounds that have strong frequencies in different parts of the spectrum that you will need to amplify some frequencies more than others. The most obvious will be the need to amplify low frequency sounds more than high frequency sounds (partly because you have to move more air for a low frequency sound – hence the reason why bass bins are so big and heavy!).

It is important to differentiate between intensity/amplitude and loudness, and between frequency and pitch. Intensity/amplitude is a measurable property; loudness is our perception of it. Similarly, frequency is definite; pitch is a rough approximation. When frequencies are tied together in harmonic (and sometimes inharmonic) ratios, we tend to perceive the sound as pitched. It is the structure and intensity of these frequencies (often called partials) that define the timbre of instruments. Our recognition of a source is often determined very quickly and is often related to the attack portion of the sound (where most energy is exerted). However, the sustained portion of a sound is also important in determining the size and shape of an instrument.

Many instruments – natural and synthetic – follow an ADSR shape (attack, decay, sustain, release), as in Figure 1.3. Moreover, when you come to make sound objects (small sounds with strong identity, often composites of a number of related sounds), you may find these objects being influenced by this profile.

Farnell (2010) provides a quick yet comprehensive guide to the science behind our perception of sound.

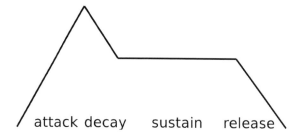

Figure 1.3 ADSR envelope. Attack: time taken to rise to peak energy. Decay: time taken to decay to a steady state. Sustain: time remaining at steady state. Release: time taken to decay to the closure of the sound.

And once sound has passed our inner ear and been converted to electrical signals, the brain takes over in ways that we still do not fully understand. We naturally process sounds quickly for similarity, difference, warning, survival, attack, defence, surprise, location, identification and discrimination.

We rely upon an innate understanding of (or at least a gut reaction to) the physics of the world to help us understand and break down sound as it happens. And in our musical world we are quite content to hear a phrase on the flute played by a human; content too (almost) with a never-ending, humanly impossible passage played by a Sibelius-created MIDI file. However, ambiguous sounds such as those created by noise-making machines and electroacoustic synthesis patches may be so unfamiliar and sound so unnatural that we have enormous difficulty accepting them into our repertoire of living sound. On the one hand, as listeners we should remind ourselves that the physics of the world should not need to work in our imagination; on the other, as composers we should consider that listeners may well expect to be led by the hand towards the complete unknown, lest they dismiss your work before it has even begun!

1.2.5 Listening

As I write this, I am listening to beat-based music that simply keeps my mindset focused upon the job at hand. In fact, I am not really listening at all; this music is simply blocking out the knocks on the door, birdsong outside, the telephone ringing downstairs. In fact, many people use i-devices for similar reasons. (Though it is often baffling to see people with earphones in while driving.) Clearly we can direct our listening, focus our memory and alter our attention consciously as we search through sound in time (especially when listening to music). Writers including Schaeffer (1977), Chion (1990) and Farnell (2010), amongst many others, have come up with a concoction of terms for different listening 'states'.

Schaeffer's (1977) modes of listening are as follows:

- Écouter: An analytical listening mode where we are detecting the event behind the sound.
- Ouïr: A passive listening mode where we just receive sound unwillingly.
- Entendre: An active listening mode where we tune in to certain aspects or qualities of a sound.
- Comprendre: A more global mode where we perhaps begin to understand some form of communication in a musical language.

Farnell (2010) adds to these the following:

- Reflexive: Startle response, defence reflex to loud sounds.
- Connotative: Often associated with a fight/flight response. Base understanding without the listener having to think.
- Causal: Listening with an ear towards the physicality of materials and events (the rise in pitch as you fill a container with water being linked with how much empty space is left).
- Empathetic: Listening that is focused towards the emotional state of a being.
- Functional: Listening to understand the function of the sound (sonar and other sonification methods are functional).
- Semantic: Listening for the meaning behind the sound (a telephone bell, for example).
- Signal listening: Being prepared for a forthcoming sound.

Additionally, Farnell mentions reduced listening, analytic listening and engaged listening. These are the methods by which we begin to appreciate the music behind the sound constructions in sonic art. Reduced listening is the acousmatic approach: listening not to source or cause but to the sound itself, its energy and flow. One cannot do this without being analytic and engaged. Engagement is up to the listener (and as a composer it is well worth thinking about just how you help your listener remain engaged). Engagement helps listeners become more, or less, analytic in their listening. It is important to remember, however, that you are a listener too. There are going to be times when you decide that you can dial down your analytical listening and just absorb the sound. Then there will be times when you need to become more engaged in order to remain interested. How you feel at any point in time, how much work you have to give to listening and how much reward you feel you are getting from listening equals value.

There is of course a huge difference between the value of a listening experience and value judgements made upon your own sounds as you work with them. When you listen to sounds you tend to relate quantity (how much) to quality (how good/bad). Like any training, as you listen to more sound, make more sound and think about sound/sound shapes, your hearing will become attuned to the acousmatic-potential of a sound. Throughout this text you will be learning a number of creative processes to develop sounds (Chapter 2). These processes have a habit of producing quite specific qualities in sounds, qualities which, once recognised, need to be controlled. This is why the working method in this book is reactionary. For sure, there will be times when you perceive a quality and say 'I need more of this', but with fundamental structures such as spectral shape, duration, texture and gesture, you will often find that the quality that is most apparent is the one that needs 'taming'. As you develop sounds away from their original characteristics you may well find yourself working in loops. For example: as your long, continuous sound becomes increasingly shorter and discrete you find that you are now working with *short* and *discrete* and therefore require methods to create *long* and *continuous*.

Trust us, you will not end up going back to your original sound! Instead you will be in a place that is *similar but different*. Working out these similarities and differences, how you got there and with what processes is *composition*. This book will suggest a multitude of pathways and recipes for a sound's development and link composition theory, analysis and practice with technological skill acquisition.

If you are recording sound, you will want to spend some time tidying up your session and editing down your source files. There are no hard and fast guidelines as to how to edit down a session. However, we would suggest that you create files that have single sounds in them, files with similar sounds, files with gestures and files with textures. Naming files according to the source used (water1.wav, water2.wav) does not really describe what you have. Consider using onomatopoeia from the outset (waterbubble.wav, watertrickle.wav) and remember it is wise to keep filenames relatively short to begin with and make sure there are no uppercase, spaces and odd characters like %$^&*!. To extend filenames it is best to use only hyphens and underscores.

It is worth having a number of files that are very short (good for testing, but these might also be the basic elements of your material) and a number of files that contain all manner of sounds (as we will introduce a number of techniques to 'shuffle' these files later on).

1.2.6 Analysis

Whether composing or listening, learning new tools or reading books like this one, the assimilation of knowledge so that you can draw upon it later is the basis of analysis. You will find throughout this book numerous representations of electroacoustic music: the waveform, the sonogram, the code snippet and the drawn graphic interpretation. All are clues to a greater understanding of what we/you hear. The majority are translations involving huge data loss (therefore presenting what is best presented according to the graphics available). Referring to the potential of the drawn graphic to render meaningful attributes, John Young writes:

> From the electroacoustic composer's perspective, two fundamental questions are frequently asked during the creative process: what do I hear in these sounds, and how can the shaping and presentation of the materials I create convey something of my explorations on to the malleability of sound? If a completed work is a reduction and embodiment of the composer's listening and manufacturing methods, analysis of that work is similarly not just located in the graphics or symbols that might be used to represent analogies, proportions or to sketch trajectories of development, but in their ability to embody something of the musical and compositional space that is articulated. Without that, the dark at the end of the metaphorical tunnel will remain for as long as we wish to continue. (Young, 2004, 8)

The vast majority of this book is about translation: translation from code to sound, translation from sound to words and translation from sound to image. There is every reason to assume that you will see shapes when making your music and indeed the visual analogies suggested later are all analogous to what you might expect to hear. Analysing one's own work (especially while in the process of making it) is rare, though it might be an interesting process: composers need to keep more notes on intermediate steps if they think the preservation of their work is important (and especially if they want to repeat a successful procedure or recompose a work later in life). The detailed analysis of the works of others is part of the contextualisation of your own work and is of course vital.

1.3 Descriptors

We have mentioned before that Denis Smalley's *'spectromorphology'* has aided many composers when analysing sounds. Some have indeed considered how the reverse may be true, that Smalley's terminology be used as a generative syntax (Blackburn, 2011). Manuella Blackburn's vocabulary and diagrams are indeed most helpful in considering shape, trajectory and density, but they are for the most part procedural and her elegant diagrams for starts, middles and ends suggest all manner of variety, a variety which is not described in words. We need a multidimensional space to describe our sounds that ties in specific qualities *and* 'gut feelings'. Stemming from two simple words defining a very expressive continuum, we start to home in on a number of descriptors based on metaphor:

- texture (metaphor using our sense of touch)
- gesture (metaphor using the body)

1.3.1 Metaphor

So we come to metaphor itself. Professor Bernard Hibbits gives us a very detailed description of how visual metaphor is used in American legal practice and how it is assumed to be stronger than any aural metaphor (Hibbitts, 1994). He does, however, cite many instances where aural metaphor is used, such as 'speaking out, really listening, let the material tell you what to do'.

And here we have our *abstracted syntax* drawn from Simon Emmerson's grid (Emmerson, 1986).

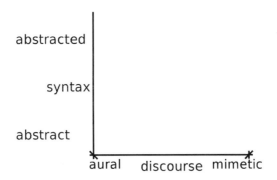

Figure 1.4 The relation of language to materials

This simple graph describes how we work with material and what we try to say with it. In most cases when working with recorded sound, we are going to let the material 'tell us what to do with it' (the syntax, or method of composition is abstracted or taken from the sound itself). The nice thing about the sounds we are using (whether recorded in the studio or sampled from nature) is that we can shift quite easily between an aural and mimetic discourse. Due to the difficulties of being truly acousmatic, focusing solely upon the sound itself, we may play with the recognisability of the sounds we have recorded. The problem here will be that a work which traverses the aural–mimetic discourse axis fairly erratically is likely to be lacking in formal coherence. Your position on the aural–mimetic discourse axis may well be different from others.

The really interesting thing about metaphor (and Scruton (1997) gives us a solid grounding here if you want to tackle some fairly heavy philosophical thinking) is that it provides a creative link with the composer/listener and tells us as much about the subject (us) as about the object (the sound). Two music psychologists, Roger Watt and Roisin Ash, considered how our description of musical excerpts might give away clues about the listener as well as the music (Watt and Ash, 1998). They presented their ideas of *disclosure meaning* in music. Part of their experimental process was to force listeners into either/or categorisations of music. Their thesis was that music can lead to similar reactions to those we experience when encountering another person: that music can have specific traits and states. This research had a profound effect upon my own music.

We are now going to present a number of categories that you might find useful in describing sound. Note now that they are all A/B pairs. It will often be the case that you are likely to have something that not only exists between A and B but that actively moves from A to B! We need to start simply, so let us think more theoretically to begin. Not all of the following descriptors will be useful (some never!), but they are there as a guide. The idea behind this book is that as you use some of this terminology to describe sounds *and* techniques you begin to associate a sound's characteristics with useful techniques that may help develop those characteristics.

1.3.2 Descriptors in real-world situations

Clearly, no particular sound is going to say to you 'I'm a lady, summer, hot and urban'. Some of these descriptors are going to be far more use than others, in fact some you may never use! And this is by no means an exhaustive list. However, by linking a number of these descriptors to your sounds, and to processes, you might be able to marry acousmatic-potential and manipulation-effect more quickly.

Take the sound of wine bottles, for example. Banging them together produces an attack with very little delay, generating short sounds. Rubbing the bottoms of the two bottles together gives a rough continuous sound. Letting the bottles bounce against each other gives an attack – release profile. The sound (where not an attack) is predominantly pitched but inharmonic. Because the material is glass, the sound is likely to be felt as harsh and bright.

Table 1.1 Table of opposites

sex	season	reality	size	colour
		Table of polar opposites		
adult	summer	artificial	big	black
child	autumn	natural	little	white
boy	winter	real	broad	dark
girl	spring	unreal	narrow	bright
male		life	thick	dawn
female		death	thin	dusk
gentleman			heavy	day
lady			light	night
woman			large	evening
man			small	morning
			long	sun
			short	moon
			abundance	urban
			lack	rural
			empty	red
			full	orange
			huge	yellow
			tiny	green
				blue
				indigo
				violet

So looking down our list, here are some explanations of how these terms might be applied to sounds.

Sex

You will find relatively little use for these descriptors, but you may wish to think about adult/child when thinking about developing form. Imagine phrases and sub-phrases that inherit from their parents. What characteristics do they inherit, and how is the child version different from the adult version?

Season

Vivaldi's *Four Seasons* springs to mind, but again you might wish to use these descriptors to hint at formal design, with spring suggesting growth, winter suggesting death. To some these descriptors might arise from an overriding suggestion from a piece. They are less likely to be attributed to individual sounds (although you can tell a great deal about a season simply by listening to the severity of the wind).

Reality

Artificial/natural could be used to highlight the differences between a mechanically designed sound and more free-form material. Linear directions and static sounds often sound artificial. Sounds that move or change exponentially or logarithmically tend to sound more natural. You will find that volume curves in DAWs that are like the natural shapes shown in Figure 1.5 tend to sound more realistic than straight lines.

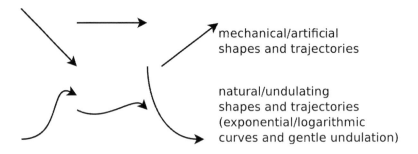

mechanical/artificial shapes and trajectories

natural/undulating shapes and trajectories (exponential/logarithmic curves and gentle undulation)

Figure 1.5 Artificial and natural shape design

Real/unreal: you identify a real sound. A subtle transformation still keeping some semblance of the original may lead to this sound becoming unreal. Remember Trevor Wishart's mix of whalesong against the backdrop of a rainforest? Jonty Harrison includes the term 'surreal', and perhaps the above example is as surreal as it is unreal. If one considers Salvador Dali's melting telephones or human cellos, there is every possibility to create what is seemingly a real situation out of unreal objects. This real/unreal/surreal intersection has been used by many composers as a means of transporting listeners between worlds, whilst providing 'something to hold on to' (Landy, 1994).[2]

Size

- Big/little/large/small. These are very inaccurate metaphoric descriptors for volume or spectral power. One tends to describe small sounds as sounds with very little power, sounds that often lie in the high frequency portion of the spectrum. Small sounds tend to gather together (agglomerations) and fly apart (dissipate) without significant quantities of additional energy being provided.

- Broad/narrow. Technically, these terms are normally applied to frequency bands (bandpass filters might be broad or narrow) only allowing a certain range of frequencies to pass.

- Thick/thin. This may be applied to the perceived weight of the sound. If the spectrum is weighted towards the lower end, the sound may be thick. This may also mean that details are hard to distinguish. (Imagine trying to draw fine details with a thick 6B pencil.) Equally, thin normally refers to perceptual content, especially a texture that does not have enough power to motivate itself forwards.

- Heavy/light. When applied to movement a heavy sound will be resistant to movement. Lighter sounds will probably want to be panned or spatialised in some way. Heavy/light tie in with large/small but are not quite the same.

- Long/short. Normally applied to duration of sounds, phrases, delay times and reverberation times. A description of length.

- Abundance/lack. Terms used to focus upon density. When you have heard or not heard something that you were expecting (within one sound or within a section containing a flock of different sounds) you might note an abundance or lack.

- Empty/full. The perception of space or texture. This involves not only the definition of a space, but the location of occupants within the space. Moreover, it is the occupants which tend to define the space.

- Huge/tiny. The perception of space, normally reverberation size. An exaggeration of large/small.

Colour

The condition where one sense triggers another is known as synaesthesia. In music, sounds tend to trigger colours. Most people do not have a direct association between sound and colour. However, frequency spectrum placement has some attachment to colour. High equates to bright, low to dark. Blue is often associated with cold and red with hot. Blue is also associated with water, green with pastoral scenes. Day/night alludes to a sense of space and our perception of objects within that space. Urban/rural can be associated with machines/nature/darkness or green/brown/yellow hues. The mind always wants to use the eye, therefore it will often be hard for you not to conjure images, landscapes or worlds, whether they be real, unreal or surreal. If your landscape is sparse and large, the chances are it is dark and therefore individual colours will not make themselves known. A brighter world will highlight many more specific colours. To a certain degree, noise is known by colour depending upon the amplitudes of its component frequencies. We call all frequencies at equal amplitudes white noise. As high frequencies decrease in amplitude we find pink and brown noise. As low frequencies decrease in amplitude we find blue and violet noise. Finally, if frequencies drop in the middle we hear grey noise.

Appearance

- Clean/dirty. Often used to describe signal to noise ratio. A clean sound may well have been synthesised and be completely without background interference. Dirty sounds (since the rise of glitch-based sonic art) are rough around the edges and often appear to be untameable. They signify a cultural outcast, something that breaks the rules or does not conform to norms.
- Complicated/simple. Normally associated with a perceived measure of textural density or sound object activity.
- Dry/wet. Normally applied to technical issues regarding the ratio of original sound to manipulated output and most often seen in reverberation processes. A wet space affords multiple delays and reflections. A dry space leaves you only with your input sound and very few reflections.
- Hard/soft. Normally associated with the perception of high frequency content in particular on attack portions of a sound. Figure 1.6 shows the well-known mapping of consonant–vowel word shapes to image (an effect attributed to psychologist Wolfgang Köhler). Can you tell which shape is 'kiki' and which is 'bouba'?

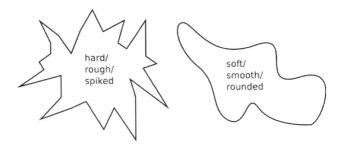

hard/
rough/
spiked

soft/
smooth/
rounded

Figure 1.6 Graphical analogy of the 'kiki, bouba' effect

- Loud/quiet. The perception of amplitude.
- Rough/smooth. There are potentially many areas where these terms may be used. Rough/smooth may be taken to differentiate the sound

of stones versus the sound of a bowed glass (used as a metaphor for texture). They may be related to spectral variation. Equally, they may be applied to something as similar as a violin note played by a beginner without vibrato and one played by a professional, perhaps with vibrato. The vibrato in this instance would be applied evenly, so contributing to the perception of a smooth tone.

- Gritty/smooth. Again used to talk about textures. Note that both words are highly onomatopoeic.
- Pointed/rounded. Can be applied to both attacks (like soft/hard) or phrases, sections or statements. Again, these are highly ono-matopoeic words.

Character

This section is all about higher-level functions within your sonic art, especially the emotional response that a sound or sounds may trigger. They are all very 'human' characteristics and might suggest very formal approaches to listening.

Perhaps most obvious for use are the following:

- Exciting/boring. Possibly pertaining to the perceived speed of a section.
- Funny/serious. Sound choice and juxtaposition can often generate humour.
- Gentle/violent/powerful/weak. We use these terms to describe the power of the wind. A similar degree of turbulence in audio is entirely possible.
- Happy/sad. More obvious in tonal music where happy equates with major mode and sad with minor mode music. However, in electroacoustic music pitch inflection can often indicate this state with a downward slide tending towards emotions of sadness.
- Public/private. This may well correspond to a near/far spatial position indicating a degree of intimacy. Filtered voices often tend to sound closer and therefore more personal and private to the listener. Small sounds may well be private. These terms therefore tend towards descriptors of form rather than content.
- Safe/dangerous. Composers may well have experienced feedback gradually moving out of control. It is possible to formulate a nervous textural or gestural energy that is suspect and dangerous. In glitch-based music, the drone that sounds like a jack plug halfway out is also particularly 'dangerous'. So too the 'sound' of electricity arcing.

Scene

This section has far more literal consequences for the description of materials.

- Background/foreground. Concerning sound in space, this clearly is important for changes in perspective possibly involving reverberation or high frequency content. This could well be a structural definition where both background and foreground exist at the same time and together define the space.
- Near/far. Slightly more poetic and subjective view of background/-foreground, perhaps more to do with motion.
- Beginning/end. Pertaining to shape not just in terms of a piece but phrase and sound-object. Beginnings may well be full-on downbeats or have an upbeat or anacrusis immediately prior.
- Bottom/top/floor/ceiling. Normally referring to position in the frequency spectrum. Using these terms it is possible to consider canopied or rooted settings (pedal points, etc.) where low/high drones support material within the space.
- Front/rear. Normally used in performance where sound is projected in a 3D space.
- High/low. Frequency content or pitch. Perhaps the most obvious 'positional' element.
- Deep/shallow. Rarely used, probably because of their analogy with water.
- Horizontal/vertical. Possible descriptor of shapes in time, relating to frequency more than any other parameter.
- Left/right. Panning and spatialisation.
- Rising/sinking. Descriptors for pitch glissandi.
- Up/down. More aggressive descriptor for frequency spectrum movement.
- Together/apart. Structural placement in time. Formal perception of structural divergence/convergence.
- Under/over. Relationship of one set of materials to another (often associated with canopied/rooted settings where A is rooted under B, for example).

Energy

This section is again more subjective but is based upon a number of common features of sound in time and space.

- Unstable/stable/excited/calm. Normally the perception of textural content but equally can be applied to a sequence of gestures.

- Cold/hot. Perception of frequency content and subjective assessment of landscape.
- Fast/slow. Perception of speed in terms of texture or gesture.
- Harmonic/inharmonic/focused/unfocused. Perception of pitch whether singular or streamed.
- Gesture/texture. Perception of structure in time.
- Discrete/continuous. Perception of time often related to our ability to 'chunk' data.

Growth

Perhaps the most important (and therefore potentially incomplete) section, growth leads us to think about structure.

- Accumulate/dissipate. The addition/subtraction of materials and energy.
- Departing/arriving/open/closed. Structural devices that are the result of material leading up to or moving away from either a beginning or an end.
- Ascending/descending. A slightly more objective view of pitch glissandi and better terminology than up/down.
- Forward/backward. Pertaining to the basic perception of time. (Remember that reverse envelopes are rarely used except for situations such as pre-reverberated sounds.) Possibly also as a structural descriptor where sections may move forward and backward in time (ABCBA).
- Emerge/disappear. Perception of amplitude but more subtle than start/stop.
- Attack/release. Perception of energy profile, normally in sound objects.

1.4 The Sound Object

The sound object is commonly understood to be a composite object made up of a number of smaller sounds, often with a global ADSR shape and, as Manuella Blackburn (2011) points out, emergence, transition, release envelopes or upbeat, statement, disappearance envelopes. However, the sound object is considerably more complicated than these two or three archetypes.

At a basic level we can define sounds emerging from the distance and moving towards a closure:

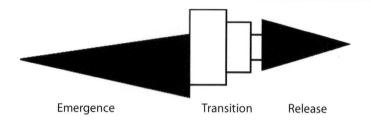

Emergence   Transition   Release

Figure 1.7 Emerge–release profile

For sounds with more potency, marking their space more dramatically by seeming fused together – a sense of purposefulness as one sound transfers its energy to the next:

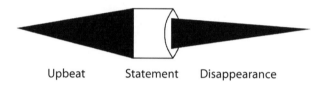

Upbeat   Statement   Disappearance

Figure 1.8 Upbeat profile

Gradually we realise that the composite can be in both the X and Y directions:

Downbeat, short
continuation to
upbeat closure

Figure 1.9 Downbeat profile

Leading towards a complex object:

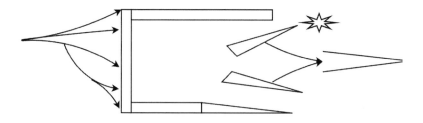

Figure 1.10 Complex object profile

Additionally, each block of sound may well be an object in itself. If the sound is not a composite then it may simply be shaped by an amplitude envelope or a change in one particular spectral parameter.

Always remember a 'similar but different' policy when working with sounds and remind yourself that unless you are working very mechanically, nothing ever stays still (even silence has a direction).

For example, take the following drone-based sound:

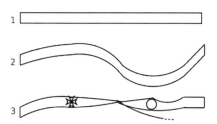

Figure 1.11 Similar but different profile

Example 1 in Figure 1.11 is rather boring and mechanical with no loss or injection of energy. Potentially usable but quite difficult to lead into and get out of. We might consider adding some undulation to the drone. Example 2 has turned into something completely different and the up–down rollercoaster ride we are taking has the same degree of redundancy (potential insignificance) as the static drone. Example 3, however, stays with the overall shape of the original drone but adds in a couple of small gestural elements and gently sways the drone with musical expansion and contraction. Imagine curtains blowing in the wind from an open window.

Sound objects can then become the thematic motivators for your sonic art. Their onsets are powerful enough to trigger continuant sounds, from which you can conclude a sound object or move into something more textural.

Consider the following example:

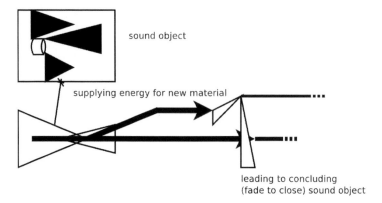

Figure 1.12 Sound object as trigger

Here the opening object supplies sufficient energy for a steady-state drone or texture to emerge and for a rising glissandi to reach a steady state in parallel with the original drone. From this comes another sound object that saps the energy of the drone, killing it off, leaving each drone portion to fade naturally into the distance.

Sound objects need not always be of high intensity or contain a large dynamic range. One particular trick to help foster the generation of a multitude of small sound objects is to take the undulating motion of one soundfile (possibly a texture or drone) and use the points of articulation as a trigger for a particular sound object (a continuation object). Denis Smalley calls this kind of material 'texture carried' because the texture literally carries the gestures that lie thematically above it. But because these gestures appear (or should appear) to spring from the texture, they almost become de facto sound objects.

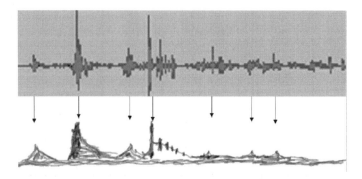

Figure 1.13 Sound object texture carried

In this example the continuous waveform has a number of large and small perturbations which could supply sufficient energy to allow for the addition of other material that maps with the attack, decay, sustain, release profile of the texture. The idea here is that at each point we feel that the drone is being articulated by the gesture/sound objects and not the other way around! Where this fails and you hear a distinct separation between the texture and the objects, the working method is no longer continuous but discrete with the texture being A, and the individual objects, B, C, D, E, and so on. If this does not feel natural then this will not be a good experience for the listener.

In a similar way, gestures may frame particular moments in time. As gestures get smaller and/or become more dense, the boundary between clear identification of something gesture-framed or texture-set may become blurred. Denis Smalley surmises thus:

> Both *gesture-framing* and *texture-setting* are cases of an equilibrium capable of being tipped in either direction by the ear. They indicate yet again areas of border tolerances, ambiguities open to double interpretation and perceptual cross-fadings depending on listening attitude. On the whole, gestural activity is more easily apprehended and remembered because of the compactness of its coherence. Textural appreciation requires a more active aural scanning and is therefore a more elusive aural art. (Smalley, 1986, 84)

1.5 Gesture

Our discussion of sound objects has naturally taken in the idea of gesture, as gesture is at the heart of the sound object. It is the perceived intention of your sound object or, at a lower level, the action of a (normally) human agent to generate a sound by striking, hitting, rubbing, or by shouting, whistling or breathing. Denis Smalley talks about the degrees of removal from the *human-ness* of the gesture (first, second and remote surrogacy; Smalley, 1996, 85), but in the studio there are a number of key gestures that you should consider trying to create:

- Attack with quick release. This is often delivered by a synthetic patch that has a very tight envelope or by recording attack-based sounds: drum hits, plucked strings, vocal exclamations. In many circumstances you are going to get some sort of decay attached to your attack. Don't chop this off; it adds to the natural feel of the gesture.
- Attack with multiple contiguous starts and 'torn flag' ending. Here, the attack is comprised of multiple soundfiles that are similar enough to sound as one unit. Constituent sounds decay at different times

giving a timbral decrescendo. Imagine a piano chord where each finger is lifted over time, leaving only one note. This could also be achieved spectrally using filters to gradually chisel out portions of a complex (noisy) initial sound, leaving something very sinusoidal at the end. Sometimes this approach is just too subtle to be audibly significant.

Figure 1.14 Attack with 'torn flag' ending

• Swipes. A swipe has a logarithmic shape that starts slowly and gets increasingly faster. A more onomatopoeic interpretation might be *swish*. A swipe or swish at the start of an object normally falls over into an attack. A swipe or swish at the end of an object normally acts as a full termination (perhaps with reverberation).

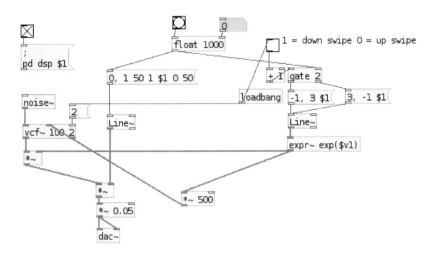

Figure 1.15 A Pd patch to generate a quick filter swish or swipe with frequency and amplitude shapes

• Acceleration/deceleration methods. Similar motion to the swipe/ swish but with discrete components rather than continuous sounds. Often heard in electroacoustic music created with MIDI synthesisers and samplers in the 1980s and 1990s.[3] Now easily created with `usss.dynamicdelay`, a delay-based tool, not dissimilar to the GRMTools Delay plugin (see Figures 1.15–1.17 for examples).

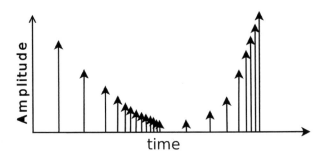

Figure 1.16 Bouncing ball motif, accelerate to gesture

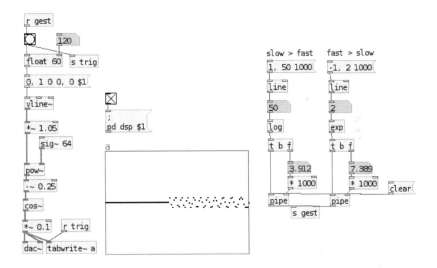

Figure 1.17 A chirp based on Farnell (2010) with acceleration and deceleration motions

If gestures are considered as the potential 'motifs' of our work, we may well create gestures with different durations of attack and resonance, different component parts, multiplying or adding to our original. This may help create structure in a larger phrase.

Because each gesture has a different energy and speed, we may create a 'melody' of gesture, stringing gestures together one after the other (or with slight overlap). We really do need to be in careful control of the ebb and flow of energy here else our phrase becomes nothing but a series of attack/resonances. It is increasingly rare in electroacoustic music today to hear bold gesture in a solo/dry environment. Gesture is more often used to articulate and define textures.

1.6 Texture

When talking about texture, we can refer to Table 1.1 and the following extension to it.

Textures tend to arise from mixing streams of material. This material has often been manipulated in a granular fashion in that portions of an original have been selected and repeated (with modification) many, many times. Granular synthesis[4] allows you to select a small portion of sound and extract it like 'audio DNA'. In most granular synthesisers you can select a grain's size, pitch, location from the original, rate of repetition and placement in the final mix.

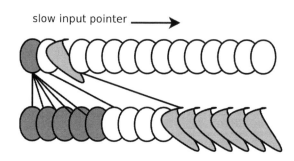

Figure 1.18 An illustration of granular synthesis to create a time stretch texture

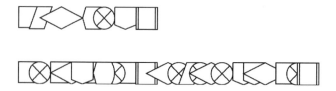

Figure 1.19 Randomised input pointer delivering hyper-mixed resultant

Table 1.2 Table of opposites continued

		Table of polar opposites continued		
appearance	*character*	*scene (position)*	*energy*	*growth*
clean	angel	background	unstable	accumulate
dirty	devil	foreground	stable	dissipate
clear	good	beginning	cold	changeable
cloudy	bad	end	hot	constant
complicated	brave	bottom	warm	closed
simple	cowardly	top	cool	open
dry	enemy	floor	excited	departing
wet	friend	ceiling	calm	arriving
hard	exciting	front	extreme	ascending
soft	boring	rear	moderate	descending
healthy	sweet	high	fast	forward
ill	bitter	low	slow	backward
liquid	fear	deep	harmonic	freeze
solid	courage	shallow	inharmonic	melt
gas	funny	near	focused	emerge
loud	serious	far	unfocused	disappear
quiet	gentle	horizontal	pitched	attack
mess	violent	vertical	noisy	release
order	happy	left	gesture	upbeat
young	sad	right	texture	downbeat
old	active	rising	continuous	
pretty	lazy	sinking	discrete	
ugly	noisy	up		
rough	silent	down		
smooth	polite	together		
sweet	rude	apart		
sour	powerful	under		
soft	weak	over		
hard	public			
fat	private			
thin	safe			
gritty	dangerous			
smooth				
pointed				
rounded				

Remember that each time a grain selection is made, the output grain may be changed in pitch. Depending upon the size of the grain, the resulting texture might bear a strong similarity to the original or it may sound as though the spectrum of the original has been captured. Large grain sizes of greater than 250 milliseconds tend towards a technique more commonly known as brassage (or micromontage) where the sounds taken are still recognizable. As the grain size decreases, we move towards more drone-like textures that are potentially smoother (depending upon the pitch variation of the output grain). In most programs that allow granular synthesis, parameters can be varied or randomised. Some settings will be better than others for the sounds you have. Vocal sounds are particularly good with granular synthesis. Remember also that if your input sound has silence in it, chances are your output sound might have silence too. This is a great way to create randomized 'splatterings' of sound.

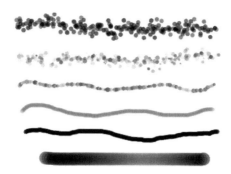

Figure 1.20 Granulation as a sonic airbrush

As Figure 1.20 suggests, granulation can create textures that are solid or more 'bubbly' in nature. The analogy with an airbrush works quite well. The brush can vary in density, vary in distribution, vary in volume and consequently create a texture that is (from top to bottom) dense pointillist, airy pointillist, string-of-pearls, continuous undulating, same but louder, continuous steady-state. As stated previously, at no point do any of these diagrams sit absolutely still; even the bottom line has a variation in density. Absolute repetition is just so difficult to get out of. If you allow for the possibility of change, you give yourself an exit strategy.

Granular synthesis is enormous fun as you can create huge quantities of sound from very small sources. The acoustic DNA extraction allows you to play your source and continue a drone-based texture alongside it with ease.

1.7 Landscape

When we listen to individual sounds, whether in a reduced listening[5] mode or not, we are looking for some reason for a sound to be 'there'. The best reason (musically speaking) is its relation to sounds that have gone before or that are coming after. Consequently we are well suited to creating a landscape within which we place our sonic 'inhabitants'. As

Figure 1.21 Acoustic DNA being snapshot and continued; a great way of contextualising sounds within a landscape

we walk out of the door in the morning, we immediately get a grip of the sonic landscape in terms of perspective (our next-door neighbour's car versus the cat across the street, versus the milk float down the road, set in the mid-20s heat of a summer morning). It is this final characteristic that is most interesting. The perception of heat and the feeling of an 'open, almost relaxed' environment sets the size of your environment (very few players, large space). Trevor Wishart (1996, 140) breaks down the perception of landscape into three components.

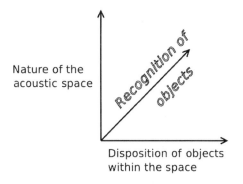

Figure 1.22 Wishart's three components of landscape perception

Whilst we can use time and frequency cues to assess the shape and size of any real or created space, we are most interested in what that space then *suggests* to us from a programmatic or, dare we say it, romantic point of view. This is where, for some, as composers and listeners, we can for example move quite quickly from a relatively objective description of size ('large, spacious') to a subjective appreciation of 'barren'. Barren immediately suggests a colour; there's not much light here, and compositionally a number of potential techniques suggest themselves. Sounds can come out of the darkness, make themselves present and fade back into the mist. Like twinkling stars in space or mysterious figures moving around a misty graveyard in the middle of the night, our perception is hazy and therefore our sounds need not be in focus at all. We, as composers, can hint and suggest and save the real personal introduction for when the scene changes.

Consider too the bustling city landscape. Noise. Not just literally but metaphorically. All manner of colours, all manner of shapes and sizes rushing past us at speed, not just loud but multiple changes in volume. Now consider the photographer's trick of zooming out so that sounds that were around you in three dimensions now appear as though on a two-dimensional canvas.

Landscape comes out of texture and gesture, but texture in particular plays a key role in defining the world in which we are listening. Wishart, Harrison and others talk about the real, unreal and surreal in their landscapes (or environments – perhaps heard as a more cohesive filled landscape), especially when playing with our ability to recognise and formulate a sense of place and our understanding of scale. Landscape as seen here is much more to do with a painter's vision, not a narrative, and is much more to do with background than foreground. In many respects it is a few trees gently swaying in the wind, placed on the brown forest floor, set against the rocky mountains, behind which the sun gently sets against an azure sky. Or it is a heat haze obscuring the simple oasis set against the rolling sand dunes of the desert. Or, consider the countless apocalyptic scenes from every TV movie you have ever seen. Skeletal structures, set against a backdrop of decay. As one final, comedic example, consider space. The vast emptiness as we contrast a near-focus earth with a distant moon. Or a moonscape with spacecraft fly-by. Where is the camera, where are the lights? Deep in the vacuum of space (potentially at absolute zero, not to mention with absolutely no sound whatsoever), it seems we can suspend disbelief quite easily. We should therefore question why we have difficulty using our visual imagination when presented solely with audio.

1.8 Environments

This is perhaps what Wishart refers to as landscape; the scene with background, foreground, major players, walk-ons, cameos, props, lights, camera, action! However, we should try not to consider the real world at all as, chances are, we have recorded some water, some drums, some wine glasses and we are working in a very abstract domain.

Environments such as the above can be honed down to something very abstract too. Foreground, background, big, small, near, far, up, down, left, right, light, dark. An environment in electroacoustic music needs to be plausible. And in many respects this implies the existence of some concept of nature. Perhaps more than this, it might be possible to draw upon the concepts of object-oriented programming to shed light upon our process of constructing sounds, sound objects, gestures, textures, landscapes and environments.

1.8.1 Object-oriented concepts

This is not a proposal for a composition system. This whole book is about fusing sounds, composers and tools together and seeing what happens. However, you have already seen from the description of sound objects, gestures and textures that 'anything goes' is just not acceptable. In a plausible environment we may well have sound objects that are related (in any music you will expect to be able to 'chunk' data and 'relate' it to other 'chunks' during the course of a work, and electroacoustic music is no exception). They will relate to each other, adapt or sit well in the landscape and have a sense of growth or decay. Energy will arrive or drain from the system. The sun will rise and then it will fall.

Object-oriented concepts include:

- Object/class. A class may be trees; an object one individual tree. Methods are procedures that act on objects and may include growth patterns, number of branches, etc. Functions are more to do with how objects work within the environment (in this instance, how the branches sway in the wind).
- Inheritance. Consider a class of cars. The class of trucks may inherit from cars and bring their own additional functions and methods.
- Polymorphism. The ability for an object comprising many sub-objects to react in different ways depending upon how they are called.

1.8.2 Naturalness and plausibility

Although not hugely constructive, the natural focus of object-oriented design is a helpful metaphor to consider plausible environments. Our related sound objects fit neatly within a class structure. Our textures or drones (created out of sonic DNA drawn from objects) are inheriting certain genes and turning into completely different (but related) creatures. Our sounds (as we will see in Chapter 3) will respond differently to different processes (from 'very well' to 'not at all') depending upon their sonic content (as described in this chapter).

Landscape and environment are particularly energising when heard in full surround sound (or multi-channel works). However, it is just as useful to consider the stereo space as even here it is possible to create a fully immersive environment. In addition to setting the scene, laying out a number of characters and injecting energy into the system, composition becomes an animation process, attributing behaviours to sounds so that they react in potentially fruitful and musical ways with each other and with their landscape.

Our discussions on landscape (Section 1.7) and environments (Section 1.8) will figure more in later discussions concerning structure (Section 3.3) and form (Section 3.4).

1.9 The Continuum

In previous examples we mentioned how gestures might gradually accumulate into a texture and textures might dissipate into gestures. When considering the list of poles used to describe sounds earlier, our sounds are rarely going to be at the extremes of the continuum. Instead they will be somewhere towards one or the other pole or traversing the continuum in a multidimensional space. It is for us to find the acousmatic-potential of a sound that suggests further transformation or take a brute-force method of applying a process to shift one sound out of its dimension of least resistance into another realm. An example here is taking a noisy texture and creating a very smooth pitched sound by using resonant filters. Such is the wrench away from noise that a subtle crossfade between original noise and pitched effect often appears very noticeable.

1.9.1 Morphology

Seamless morphologies in the continuum between chalk and cheese are practically impossible. A morphology between 'sssss' and 'zzzzz' is, however, distinctly plausible. Unfortunately the wow factor compared to well-known visual morphs is nowhere near as potent. The continuum, like any attribute, is well worth exploring and manipulating to the point where the listener recognises its use.

1.9.2 Composition

Composition therefore is magic: twisting sound to your design, leaving a plausible trail for the listener to follow. You need to show enough to draw the listener in but not too much that they know precisely what is coming next. The *frustration of expectation* is a very useful axiom in this instance. Again, frustrate the listener for too long and your labours will be in vain; give the game away too soon and the direction of your work is weakened. Composition itself rests uneasily within a multidimensional continuum.

1.9.3 Performance

Of course, once your piece has been completed you may present it in performance and this may involve thinking about sound diffusion. Although this book is about composition, the final presentation of your work will influence the composition of the work from day one. Sound diffusion is well documented by composers such as Jonty Harrison (1998) who have spent considerable amounts of time and money creating loudspeaker orchestras that enable composers to diffuse (or project) their sound into a space, giving audiences an accurate and exciting listening experience by rendering imagined textures, landscapes and environments initially encapsulated within a two-dimensional stereo listening space into a real three-dimensional space with loudspeakers positioned all around the audience. You may find that some sounds that feel 'high, fast and fleeting' and which you perceive as being 'in the sky' when listening over headphones can actually be placed in loudspeakers well above the audience so giving them an extra sense of life. Part of Chapter 3 reflects upon the relationship between a sound's descriptors, its potential development, its potential place in a mix and consequently its place in performance (loud, soft, high, low, fast, slow, front, rear, static, moving and so forth). Chapter 8 defines the sound diffusion performance process more completely.

Notes

1. Similar too is the process of making a graphic score of an existing piece: it focuses our listening as we move from sound to graphic.
2. Landy's project inspired further research of great importance to understanding practical listening experiences. Interested readers should track down Robert Weale's excellent thesis on the role of intention versus reception in electroacoustic music (Weale, 2005).
3. The interested listener should listen to the early works of Alejandro Viñao such as *Son Entero* which opens directly with such motifs.
4. For a more comprehensive discussion of granular synthesis, see *Microsound* by Curtis Roads (Roads, 2004).
5. Reduced listening is the technique that allows us to adopt the acousmatic stance, listening to sound without reference to source or cause. The repetition of a sound or passage often tends towards the acousmatic as we are led to shift our attention from surface or superficial details to the interior qualities of the sound.

References

Blackburn, M. (2011). The visual sound-shapes of spectromorphology: an illustrative guide to composition. *Organised Sound*, 16(01):5–13.

Chion, M. (1990). *Audio-Vision: Sound on Screen*. New York: Columbia University Press.

Emmerson, S. (1986). The relation of language to materials. In Emmerson, S., ed., *The Language of Electroacousic Music*, pages 17–39. London: Macmillan.

Emmerson, S. (2007). *Living Electronic Music*. Aldershot: Ashgate.

Farnell, A. (2010). *Designing Sound*. Cambridge, MA: The MIT Press.

Harrison, J. (1982). *Klang*. Évidence matérielle IMED 0052 pub. 2000.

Harrison, J. (1998). Sound, space, sculpture: some thoughts on the 'what', 'how' and 'why' of sound diffusion. *Organised Sound*, 3(02):117–127.

Harrison, J. (1999). Imaginary space: Spaces in the imagination. Australasian Computer Music Conference Keynote Address. http://cec.concordia.ca/econ tact/ACMA/ACMConference.htm, [Online; accessed November 2009].

Hibbitts, B. J. (1994). Making sense of metaphors: visuality, aurality, and the reconfiguration of American legal discourse. http://law.pitt.edu/archive/hibbitts /meta_int.htm [Online; accessed November 2015].

Kreidler, J. (2009). *Loadbang: Programming Electronic Music in Pure Data*. Hofheim am Taunus: Wolke Verlags.

Landy, L. (1991). *What's the Matter with Today's Experimental Music? Organized Sound Too Rarely Heard*. Chur: Harwood Academic Publishers.

Landy, L. (1994). The 'something to hold on to factor' in timbral composition. *Contemporary Music Review*, 10(2):49–60.

Landy, L. (2007). *Understanding the Art of Sound Organization*. London: MIT Press.

Landy, L. (2012). *Making Music with Sounds*. London: Routledge.

MacDonald, A. (2007). *Equivalence*. Personal issue.

Moore, A. (2000). *Study in Ink*. Traces IMED 0053 pub. 2000.

Puckette, M. (2007). *The Theory and Technique of Electronic Music*. Singapore: World Scientific.

Roads, C. (2004). *Microsound*. Cambridge, MA: The MIT Press.

Schaeffer, P. (1977). *Traité des object musicaux: essai interdisciplines*. Paris: Seuil, second edition. Originally published in 1966.

Scruton, R. (1997). *The Aesthetics of Music*. Oxford: Oxford University Press.

Smalley, D. (1986). Spectro-morphology and structuring processes. In Emmerson, S., ed., *The Language of Electroacoustic Music*, pages 61–93. London: Macmillan.

Smalley, D. (1996). The listening imagination: listening in the electroacoustic era. *Contemporary Music Review*, 13(2):77–107.

Smalley, D. (1997). Spectromorphology: explaining sound-shapes. *Organised Sound*, 2(02):107–26.

Smalley, D. (2007). Space-form and the acousmatic image. *Organised Sound*, 12(01):35–58.

Watt, R. and Ash, R. (1998). A psychological investigation of meaning in music. *Musicae Scientiae*, 2:33–53.

Weale, R. (2005). *The intention/reception project: Investigating the relationship between composer intention and listener response in electroacoustic compositions*. PhD thesis, De Montfort University.

Wishart, T. (1986). The relation of language to materials. In Emmerson, S., ed., *The Language of Electroacoustic Music*, pages 41–60. London: Macmillan.

Wishart, T. (1994). *Audible Design*. York: Orpheus the Pantomime Ltd.

Wishart, T. (1996). *On Sonic Art*. Amsterdam: Harwood Academic Publishers.

Yi, S. (2008). Blue software environment. http://www.csounds.com/stevenyi/blue/ [Online; accessed October 2009].

Young, J. (2004). Sound morphology and the articulation of structure in electroacoustic music. *Organised Sound*, 9(1):7–14.

Young, J. (2007). Reflections on sound image design in electroacoustic music. *Organised Sound*, 12(01):25–33.

Chapter 2

What Does all this Software Do?

Student: What does all this software do?
Teacher: Ah, anything you want.

2.1 Introduction

2.1.1 The flip side of anything is nothing at all

Having some idea about what a sound may be saying to you, you might now want to come back at it and force some change. And to do this you need to use some form of sound manipulation software. We are primarily using a graphical programming language called Pure Data (or Pd). If you are completely new to the software mentioned in this book, you might like to have a look at Appendix D or follow some of the tutorials within the Pd distribution. The *Loadbang* book (Kreidler, 2009) is also an excellent start and is a free download from www.pd-tutorial.com. So too is the FLOSS manuals website http://en.flossmanuals.net and their own guide to Pd, http://en.flossmanuals.net/pure-data/.

We would suggest trying Pd before experimenting with the other software used in this book. Pd is a graphical programming language where you link boxes together and the flow of information is very clear. Csound is text based, older and, as consequence, huge. Despite a number of graphical interfaces in a front-end called Blue to enable quick access, you will require a certain confidence with sound processing software to entertain the challenge of Csound. Pd will give you this confidence. You have to start somewhere and if we can make jumping in at the deep end as safe as possible, we think you'll enjoy the experience more.

We have made the manipulation of sound in the first instance quite easy by making a number of ready-made objects that perform specific functions. Once you become more familiar with the tools on offer, you can open up our patches and adapt them to your needs. You will actually find that many of our tools emulate the techniques and processes found in the Pd help files as this, not surprisingly, is where we began too. We start with one process at a time, but remember that not only can processes be joined together in series (one after the other) or in parallel (one alongside another), but a sound can be processed many times through multiple processes. But before you think you will end up processing yourself into oblivion, hopefully you will hear a finite end to a sound's potential or that sound A just does not work with process X. Some processes are so 'invasive' that they identify themselves quite clearly. Be wary of this as it could lead to clichès (which is not necessarily a bad thing either!)

2.2 The USSS Pd Toolkit

2.2.1 Plug and play

With very little Pd experience you should be able to get sounds into and out of the USSS toolkit. Open a new file (File:New) and save it immediately somewhere useful. Having downloaded the files that go with this book, including the USSS toolkit,[1] make sure that you point Pd in the direction of the ussstools folder. Normally this can be done as a relative directory path, 'go from where I am, out of my folder and into the USSSTOOLS folder' (as shown in Figure 2.1). Make an object box (ctrl+1 on a PC, ⌘+1 on a Mac) and type the following:

```
declare -path ../ussstools
```

Figure 2.1 Relative declare path

You may have to go out of folders (. . /) a number of times to find the ussstools folder and you will have to save your file and reload it for the path to be found. If you want a direct path to your ussstools you might type:

```
declare -path /mydrive/myhome/mypdfolder/ussstools
```

Figure 2.2 Direct declare path (Linux and Mac)

And of course a direct path on Windows might be

```
declare -path C:/USSSTOOLSKIT/ussstools
```

Figure 2.3 Direct declare path (Windows)

If you have downloaded ussstools.zip, extracted the contents, entered USSSTOOLSKIT and the Puredata_Examples-Open Me First folder to explore the examples and Blank_Canvas then you will need to jump up *one* level to find the ussstools folder. If you have proceeded to Chapter_2_Pd_Examples then you will need to jump up *two* levels. If Pd is not finding your objects (boxes have the name in but are just a red outline), then you will need to experiment with the path. This is troublesome but once you are used to it, you should have no problems and you can always cut and paste from existing example files that work (and 'Save As' into the same folder).

The folder ussstools when opened should contain all the Pd patches and help files. Once you have set the correct path, an object box looking like the following should build the necessary ready-made patch. Note that usss.sfplay is the name of the object we have made; mysfplay1 is the name of this 'instance' of the object. You can have multiple players but they must have different names.

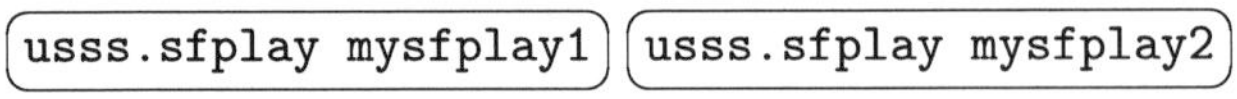

$$\boxed{\texttt{usss.sfplay mysfplay1}}\ \boxed{\texttt{usss.sfplay mysfplay2}}$$

Figure 2.4 Calling a ussstools object box

Whilst you can work through the examples in the book, if you type usss into an object box, right-click and select help, you see all the objects we have made. Right-clicking and selecting help in each of these objects should bring up a working help file.

$$\boxed{\texttt{usss}}$$

Figure 2.5 A patch containing all the tools

2.2.2 Input, output

The input module normally takes the sound from your microphone. Connecting interfaces and working with sound drivers is never quite as simple as plug and play. The sfplay object requires you to load a sound (selectfile) and then check 1 for play, 0 for stop. Note too that the names mysfplay.play can be placed in send and receive boxes so that playback can be automated.

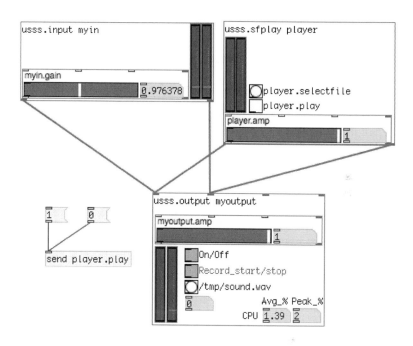

Figure 2.6 ussstools input, output and `sfplay`

2.2.3 Envelopes

The envelope tool requires you to draw in a simple envelope. For this to start you need to place the mouse at the bottom left-hand corner of the drawing area (as marked by a cross in Figure 2.7). You also need to specify a duration for the envelope to run its course (`total_time`). Finally, make sure you trigger the envelope with a `bang`. More creative use is made of the envelope tool in Figure 2.35. This is quite a powerful tool when the `bang` is automated by, say, a metronome or the amplitude of another soundfile passing over a threshold.

2.2.4 Filters

usss.bandpass

Please use the `help files` to figure out what each parameter does. The bandpass filter can really 'squeeze' a sound's profile. The old-fashioned

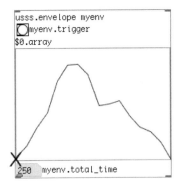

Figure 2.7 usss.envelope **tool**

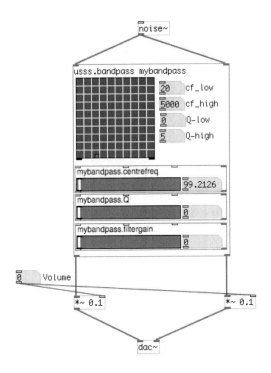

Figure 2.8 usss.bandpass

telephone generates the best-known bandpass filter sound. Because the phone's loudspeakers are so small and inefficient, the spoken voice ends up sounding considerably weaker through the phone. It can therefore be used as a means of spectrally fading sounds out (by sweeping one side of the spectrum towards the other) or as a means of creating 'waves' of sound by sweeping the centre frequency with a constant bandwidth. Once you have a thinner, filtered version of a sound, you may well consider mixing this with other sounds, creating strata.

usss.combfilt

The comb filter is a very basic tool that is normally used to colour a noise-based sound on or around a resonant frequency. Often you find comb filters stacked in parallel so that you can create chords. The well-known GRMTools Comb filters allow you to stack five filters in parallel. You can vary the pitch (expressed as a MIDI note) and the intensity of the filter in this patch. If you want to make multiple instances, this is possible. A sequence of numbers can be unpacked to the farthest right inlet of each instance to create chords.

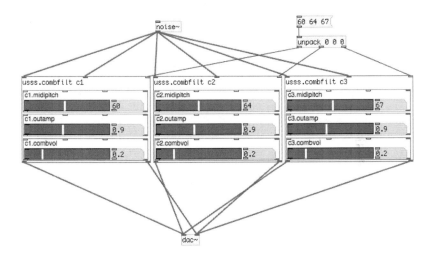

Figure 2.9 usss.combfilt making a C major chord

usss.combplayer

The combplayer combines all the features of a standard comb filter as per usss.combfilt but adds ten-note polyphony. Once your keyboard of choice is connected to the computer and you are receiving MIDI notes, this should allow you to colour your sounds by playing chords on the keyboard. cvolume is the overall volume of the filters, coutamp is the 'ringing-ness' of the filters. Anything above 1.0 and the filters ring for a long time.

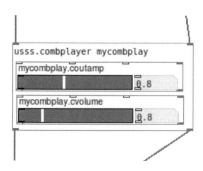

Figure 2.10 `usss.combplayer` allowing chords to be played on the keyboard

usss.fftfilter

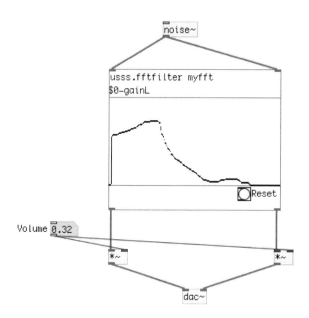

Figure 2.11 `usss.fftfilter`

The FFT filter is more like the bandpass filter than the combfilter in that you draw the shape of the area under which you want the frequencies to *pass*. However, in your drawing you are not only selecting frequencies (very broadly) but also adjusting the amplitude of those frequencies. This is because the patch uses an FFT which splits the input sound into component frequencies and amplitudes. As with the envelope function, you need to place the mouse on the baseline (in the far left-hand corner) so that the mouse icon turns 90 degrees clockwise before drawing. However, you can write algorithmically to the graph; see the functions below which make interesting frequency selections.

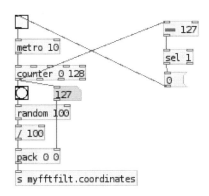

Figure 2.12 Random filters

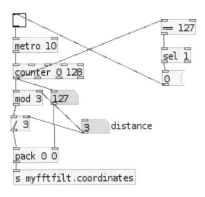

Figure 2.13 Spaced filters

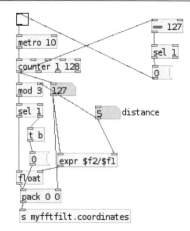

Figure 2.14 Spaced filters decreasing amplitudes

usss.filtersweep

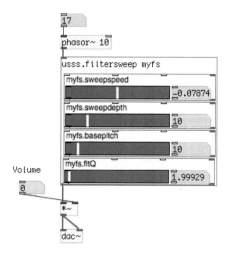

Figure 2.15 `usss.filtersweep`

Figure 2.15 with the values approximately as shown in this patch puts a sawtooth wave at sub-audio rate through a swept rising filter. The phasor~ becomes a series of clicks with each click containing all frequencies so activating our filter effectively. The filter's *Q* or quality is high so the filter only lets a very small frequency range pass. Although the patch in Figure 2.15 is mono, `usss.filtersweepst` caters for stereo.

usss.reson

The resonant filters here are not dissimilar in output to the comb filter.

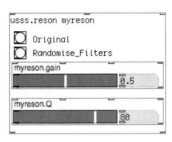

Figure 2.16 `usss.reson`

There are 16 filters in total. You can send a harmonic series as a list (100 200 300 ...) in the right-most inlet or randomise the frequencies. Once you are familiar with Pd you may want to adapt this patch so that you can specify the number of filters (although this is quite difficult to do). However, this patch clearly places a 'sheen' of pitch colour on any sound with moderate to full spectrum activity.

Remember that the filters above are quite 'invasive' and are clearly different in style from traditional equalisation or EQ. Included in the toolkit are standard high-pass and low-pass filters that you see in traditional DAWs. EQ is often used to subtly adjust particular frequency areas of your sound. It is a tool that can be used anywhere in the processing stage: alongside the editing process or towards the mixing stage. Alistair MacDonald recommends that all sounds should receive some EQ, even just to 'hear' more clearly the spectral content of the sound (see Appendix B.4).

usss.dynamicreson

The dynamic resonant filter patch assigns filters between start and end frequencies and proceeds to make the filters 'on the fly'. They, like the dynamic delay patch, may be arranged linearly (generating noticeable harmonic pitched sounds), logarithmically or exponentially (generating inharmonic sounds / diminished chords) using the *direction* checkbox. You can vary the number of filters but not tune them with any great accuracy. All the filters are given equal amplitudes. This patch emulates in part the GRMTools plugin, Reson. As this was a relatively new patch to the collection, it contains a volume slider to add the original sound back in. From a compositional point of view, it is more often the case that a 'trace' of the original is required to stabilise the transformation.

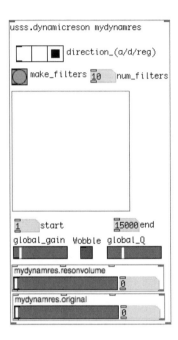

Figure 2.17 usss.dynamicreson

Advanced users may well wish to automate or change a number of internal parameters: see Section 2.4.

2.2.5 Granulation

usss.granular

Granulation is cited periodically during this text as being one of the easiest and most efficient ways of generating material. Granulation was always with us as a technique as it is essentially repetition but on a small scale, often with small or gradual change.

Figure 2.18 shows a granular patch. You can load in a sound directly into memory or record live. Position is the position in your soundfile from zero (start) to one (end). This you can randomise. The grainsize is the small 'grain' of sound shown in Figures 1.18 and 1.19 that is repeated. This grain can be altered in pitch and this pitch can be randomised. The graingain is normally put to 1 as without this you will have no volume. Finally, the grainpan moves from 0 (mono) to 256 (grains placed randomly in the stereo field). This is normally the default setting as it is rare that you would want a mono output. In

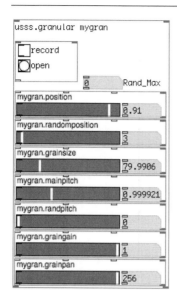
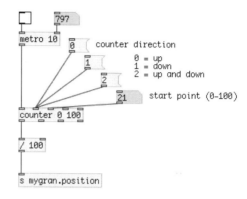

Figure 2.18 `usss.granular`

this figure you also see a metronome that scrolls at your speed through the position. This emulates a very basic time stretch if you slow the speed right down (and this means increasing the number going to the metronome which 'ticks' every X milliseconds). If your input sound is 10 seconds (10,000 milliseconds), to create an 'at pitch' playback you would need to create a 'tick' every 100 milliseconds. Granulation across multichannels (more than two) allows you to explode your timbre in the space, a truly fascinating concept. You will note that most of our tools are for stereo soundfile creation. They can all be adapted to suit multichannel output but within the patch this is probably something advanced users might contemplate. Composers at Birmingham University associated with BEAST (Birmingham ElectroAcoustic Sound Theatre) have made a toolkit for multichannel soundfile development in MaxMSP (BEASTTools).

If working in 5.0 or surround sound of some type, you might consider using multiple instances of the granular patch, each with *the same* sound but *slightly different* parameters. With one granular instance going to the left (L) and right (R), another to the Ls and Rs, and even a mono output from a third instance going to the centre (C) speaker, you could create textures that perturbate through the surround space.

usss.granularX

The granular object has been made more dynamic. As shown in Figure 2.19, it is instantiated by `usss.granularX <name>`.

The number of channels represents the number of speaker pairs. As can be seen from the outputs of this object, this number can be 1, 2, 3 or 4, giving stereo to eight-channel output. You can then connect any number of outlets to the multichannel output modules for recording. In order to experiment with number of channels and number of grains, uncheck the toggle boxes and hit bang to `makegrains`.

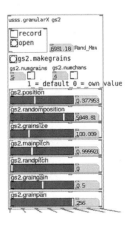

Figure 2.19 `usss.granularX`

usss.samplehold

A slightly simpler version of the granular patch involves a cyclic 'sample and hold' that works in a very similar way to the pitch-shifting example.

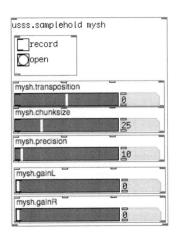

Figure 2.20 `usss.samplehold`

Small chunks of sound are repeated, depending upon the precision. The chunksize is variable and this affects the resulting pitch that develops in the sound as you stretch it out (make the precision smaller and smaller). At the same time the sound can be transposed upwards or downwards. Idiosyncratically, this patch has individual left and right channel output gain controls.

2.2.6 Pitch and frequency shifting

usss.varispeed

Varispeed emulates the old-fashioned 'tape machine' where as you speed the tape up, the sound gets higher in pitch and as you slow it down, the sound gets lower. As with all music, there is a very close link with mathematics. You know that the A-natural the orchestra tunes to is 440 Hz. The A, an octave above is 880 Hz, a factor of two.

440 hz 880 hz

Figure 2.21 Musical notes and frequencies

Not surprisingly then, as your tape speed doubles, all frequencies increase by one octave; as it halves, the pitch drops by one octave. If you are not dealing with pitched sound, all you need worry about is the maths. Consider the sound in terms of frequencies (100 Hz, 700 Hz, 1500 Hz). As the speed increases to 1.2, you will expect to hear frequencies of 120 Hz, 840 Hz and 1800 Hz.

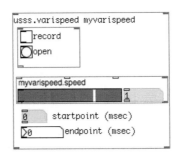

Figure 2.22 usss.varispeed

usss.pitchshift

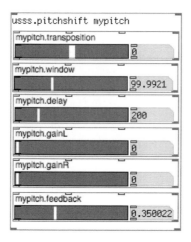

Figure 2.23 `usss.pitchshift`

Pitch shift will transpose your sound without changing the speed. This is done in the time-domain, so as your transposition reaches extreme levels, distortions will appear (however, they are often interesting and beguiling, though perhaps quite well used by composers). Remember to lift the `gainL` and `gainR` faders. The window function can be seen as a grain. As the window exceeds 100 milliseconds, you hear explicit repetitions of sound. As it falls below 40 milliseconds, the timbre of the input sound will change dramatically. However, for 'quick and dirty' transposition without changing speed this patch works extremely well. The feedback control allows you to create rising or falling glissandi based around manipulation of the window and delay times. Once you are familiar with Pd, open this one up and try to figure out how it manages to shift the pitch using delay lines. The Doppler shift taken to extremes!

2.2.7 Spatialisation, delay-based effects

Spatialisation is rolled up in your very first recording so it is hard to consider it as an independent effect. Placement of sound can be defined at grain, sound and sound object level and may be fixed or moving. At a structural level (sound, sound object), placement and motion deliver momentum and create landscape and environment. Be wary of placing long mono (or spatially thin) sounds in very specific, non-central areas in the stereo space as, especially when wearing headphones, this effect can become tiresome. However, whenever you are working with streams of sound, panning is a very useful structuring device that works well with a variety of metaphorical descriptors. Short impulses of sound often suggest one particular 'place' in the stereo field. Their careful positioning will allow you to play more impulses faster and give a sense of structure and meaning to the space.

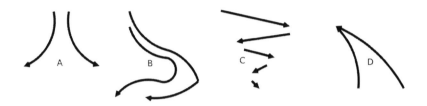

Figure 2.24 Four panning profiles

In Figure 2.24 A we see a `closed->open` metaphor as material (either sounds with a stereo image or individually panned particles) moves from constrained to free (or focused to dispersed). The opposite also works well and can be seen in Figure 2.24 D with an 'exit stage right' profile.[2] Figure 2.24 B represents a meandering but focused image while Figure 2.24 C suggests `far->near` or an approach to importance. Your sounds, particularly in this last case (C), need to be able to define the space within which they move quite well. They will need to be identifiable and will probably have a well-defined spectral shape (in short, be a little bit noisy, possibly comprising discrete, repeated sounds) so that you can pick out the movement. Try panning a 100 Hz sine wave compared to a 100 Hz pulse wave to realise just how much the ear needs some (high) frequency content to articulate spatial movement.

usss.reverb

There is very little to say about reverberation here as it is quite a well-understood phenomenon. Some reverbs ask you for a reverb time, others talk about damping. If there is very little damping, you are likely to have a larger reverb time. `Roomsize`, `damping` and `width` all affect the quality of your reverb. You can then adjust the balance of 'real' with 'reverberated' or 'wet' signal. Finally, as an added bonus, the `freeze` provides a very accurate acoustic snapshot (not dissimilar to sitting on one small grain in `usss.granular`). This patch is built around the highly popular freeverb object by Jezar at Dreampoint.

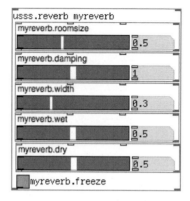

Figure 2.25 usss.reverb (based on freeverb)

usss.delay

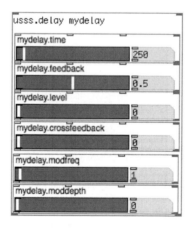

Figure 2.26 usss.delay

Delays are at the heart of reverbs on a small level, and on an even smaller scale, filters. They are also used to create chorus, phasing and flanging effects. As with other patches, the level needs lifting before you hear sound. Extreme effects can be heard as you move the modfreq and moddepth far from the left-hand side of the slider. Beware of feedback when using values greater than 0.5.

usss.dynamicdelay

The dynamic delay differs from `usss.delay` in that it creates a number of static delay 'taps' against one delay line. The sound trickles into the delay line and is sampled or repeated at numerous points. These delay taps may be spaced regularly, exponentially or logarithmically and may be densely packed or sparsely separated between a start and end delay time. This patch is particularly effective in achieving acceleration and deceleration patterns, as shown in Section 1.5. This patch emulates in part the GRMTools plugin, Delays.

Figure 2.27 `usss.dynamicdelay`

Advanced users may well wish to automate or change a number of internal parameters; see Section 2.4.

usss.panner1

This panning patch works on a mono signal. This patch is useful if you want to create specific patterns of sound movement. When working with a stereo signal you may wish to tilt and sway the balance of the image. This may be as simple as multiplying the left and right signals by different amounts.

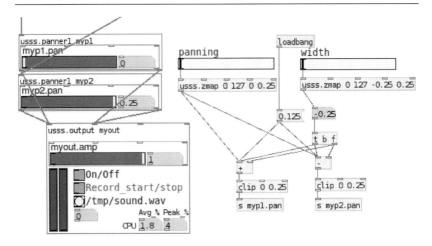

Figure 2.28 `usss.panner`

In Figure 2.28 both the left and the right signals of a stereo file are going to different panners. The sliders on the right allow you to set the width of the stereo and then pan that width, so enabling some of Figure 2.24. This kind of accurate panning is often better achieved with automation in your DAW, however.

2.2.8 Synthesis

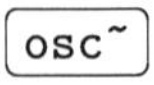

```
osc~
```

Figure 2.29 Sine wave oscillator

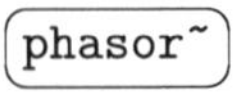

```
phasor~
```

Figure 2.30 Phasor

These and other waveform types are demonstrated in `usss.waves.pd` where a phasor going from 0 to 1 is transformed according to mathematical rules.

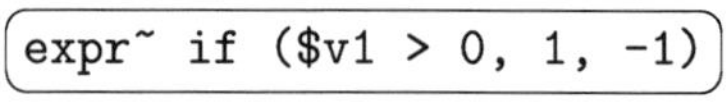

```
expr~ if ($v1 > 0, 1, -1)
```

Figure 2.31 Square wave

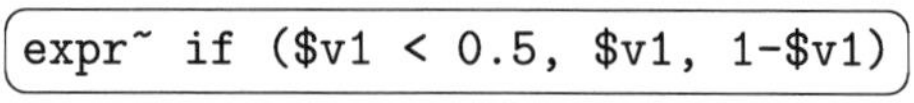

```
expr~ if ($v1 < 0.5, $v1, 1-$v1)
```

Figure 2.32 Triangle wave

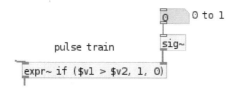

Figure 2.33 Pulse train where signal 2 controls the width of the pulse

Remember that these all output values from 0 to 1, so in order for them to become *symmetrical* audio about the X axis, you should multiply the output by 2 and take 1 away to get a correct result symmetrical about the X (time) axis.

2.2.9 Cross-synthesis

usss.shapee

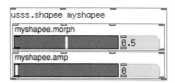

Figure 2.34 usss.shapee

Shapee affords cross-synthesis, a sharing of frequencies and amplitudes between two sounds (normally with one influencing the frequency and the other, the amplitude). The algorithm was devised by Christopher Penrose. Versions are available for the PC by Jez Wells[3] and as a plugin for Pd by Eric Lyon and Christopher Penrose under the collection

FFTease.[4] This kind of cross-synthesis is somewhat similar to vocoding, where the amplitude of one sound shapes a drone or noise depending upon the original's spectral content. From a compositional point of view this is an excellent technique as it forms a hybrid deep within the sound itself. It is not just 'A meets B', rather something more carnal. We expose a number of tools later in this chapter that perform similar functions (see Figures 2.38 and 2.53).

The Pure Data patch `sustains_shapee.pd` sets up conditions for loading files or granulating files into `shapee`.

2.3 Compound Tools

Having seen the individual tools in action and having listened to the effect they have on, say, the sound of a voice (a sound you know well, so something with which you can easily identify change), you are probably guessing that it is easier and quicker to plug multiple effects together in order to create a more flexible manipulation. This section looks at compound tools, where generative processes are given a second (or third) manipulation to effect a particular outcome. As disk space is cheap, you can keep most of your intermediary manipulations. As you become more proficient with these tools and develop vast quantities of sound, you may find yourself developing sounds to help you develop sounds (i.e. sounds that will never end up in the mix but which exist just to help you animate other sounds).

Let us consider the process of breaking down a sustained sound. The easiest way to break down a sustained sound is with some kind of amplitude modulation. Traditionally we have done this with envelope modulation.

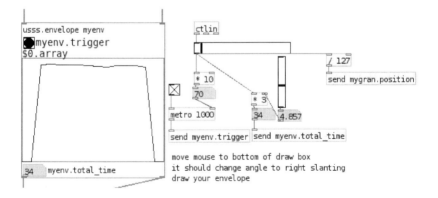

Figure 2.35 Envelope triggering to break down a sustained sound (`sustains_-envelope.pd`)

In this diagram the **usss.envelope** object sits in between any soundfile or granular object providing a sustained sound, and an output module. The metronome repeats a drawn envelope over a specific duration. The duration of the envelope may roughly equal the time between triggers or it can be substantially less (giving you more silence between chunks of sound).

Imagine mixing a sustained 'Ah' sound with a pulsed 'a' as in Figure 2.36. Here, not only do you add a forward momentum to the original sustain but you provide the opportunity to break out of the sustain by crossfading into the pulsed version which then splutters to an exit or accelerates to something new.

Figure 2.36 Mixing a sustained sound with a pulsed envelope

A similar result could be obtained by ring modulation in sub-audio frequencies. The Pure Data patch (`sustains_ringmod.pd`) allows experimentation with ring modulation.

In both of these instances, the resulting envelope tends to be non-random (and may often be repetitive). If you wanted to shape the envelope of the sustained sound with the envelope of another sound, Csound's 'balance' opcode could prove useful. Csound and the Java-based environment for Csound called Blue will be discussed in greater length in Section 2.5.

Figure 2.37 Envelope follower instrument in Blue

When loaded into Blue, the patch (ussssustains_balance.blue) affords envelope following. The Csound code is shown below. You can spot the stereo nature of this code as most commands are repeated for left and right channels.

```
afol1, afol2    diskin2  "<filefollow>", <speed1>,
    0, <loop1>
asig1, asig2    diskin2  "<fileimpose>", <speed2>,
    0, <loop2>
aenv1   follow afol1, .002
aenv2   follow afol2, .002
aenv1a  tone    aenv1, 100 ; smooth
aenv2a  tone    aenv2, 100
atemp1  = asig1*aenv1a
atemp2  = asig2*aenv2a
as1out  balance atemp1, aenv1a
as2out  balance atemp2, aenv2a
blueMixerOut    "<route>", as1out, as2out
```

However, in cases like this we need to potentially consider designing our enveloping sound. With a sustained sound in one channel and a dynamic soundfile in the other, spectral shaping may be an option. Spectral shaping has the added bonus of not only modulating the amplitude of the source but influencing it by the frequencies shared by both soundfiles. If both sounds have strong spectral content (the sustained sound with lots of harmonically related partials and the dynamic sound being at times pitched and at other times dynamic and noisy) the shapee tool may work well.

In the Pure Data example patch (sustains_shapee.pd), the output of **usss.shapee** goes to a delay in order to slightly spread the stereo image.

Additionally, the Vocoder instrument in Blue may work well. This instrument is also quite easy to use. You do not need to worry about many of the variables as they start at reasonably default values.

This instrument takes the frequency components of one file and the amplitude components of another and fuses them together. *Tip*: This is a great way of getting amplitude-shaped materials from pitched sounds, and because of the filtering effects that take place at the same time, we get additional levels of subtlety. It is always useful to have some sounds that are used only to articulate others (we use recordings of balloons and stones being heavily 'played'). These are often granulated with lots of random 'action'. From a compositional point of view it is good to begin thinking about files that might be good *for your piece* and files that might

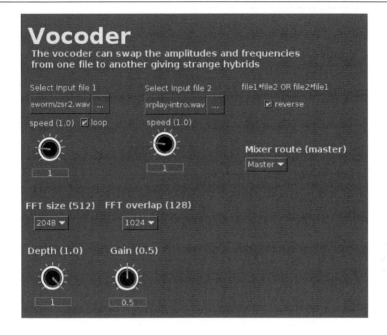

Figure 2.38 Vocoder instrument in Blue

be good *manipulators*. If you make sounds that you know will never feature in a work, it is not necessarily wise to trash them immediately!

Returning to our initial Pure Data patch for enveloping, you might consider randomising more parameters such as envelope time and granular position, as in Figure 2.39.

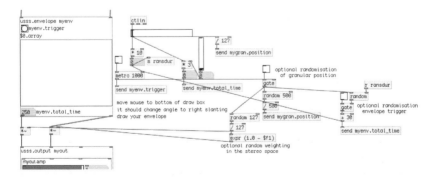

Figure 2.39 Further randomisation of enveloping parameters

The advantage of processing using multiple effects chains compared to multiple single processes (saving the file each time) is clearly a saving in time and a complexity of *effect*. Moreover, you begin to create the idea of an *instrument* in software. You may need to become familiar with sub-patching in Pure Data and conditional exits in Csound (if add_chorus=1 then goto addc) so that you can create usable interfaces (and do make use of comments so you remember what you did previously when you return to a patch after a break away!)

2.4 For Advanced Users

Clearly, in order to use the USSS tools you need some familiarity with Pure Data and you need to understand computers, files types (Pd, text, sound-binary programs) and data flow. Hopefully, you can follow the ready-made files above and have tried the help files for each of the tools (right-click within the tool frame and scroll to 'help'). If you are ready for advanced work, you will most certainly want to automate parameters. You may have noticed that when you make an object box (ctrl+1) and type usss.sfplay mysfp (name of tool, space, instance name), the instance name is copied to all sliders and toggles giving you mysfp.selectfile, mysfp.play and mysfp.amp in the slider. These names can be referred to outside of the tool itself using send objects.

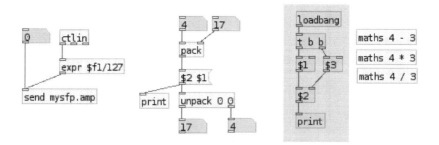

Figure 2.40 Sends and the dollar sign

In Figure 2.40 you can see a send to mysfp.amp. This mini patch also demonstrates the different uses of the $ sign which are increasingly important for the dynamic patches. On the left, the expression object (expr) takes a variable (signified by $f1) from a controller (normally 0–127 with the 'f' indicating a floating point number) and divides by 127, giving a number between 0 and 1. The example in the middle packs two numbers (and in Pd, the pack will not send anything out until the left-hand number has been sent). This list then goes wholesale to the message box which is expecting two numbers ($1 and $2) but outputs them in reverse order. They are then unpacked and displayed. Finally, the shaded Pd code beginning with the {loadbang} object is an abstraction (code that has been saved in a separate file called {maths}). Inside this patch are three object boxes with $ signs in them. When you make an instance of this object, you will need to supply three variables (as shown on the far right-hand side). $1 and $3 should be two numbers; $2 will be the mathematical symbol you want to use (see the three examples at the far right).

When you want to automate variables that are **not** shown in the tool frame you right click in the frame (in white space) and select 'open'. WARNING: be careful, you are now inside that ready-made object. You should not, unless you are very experienced, make any changes to the patch. But you can see the programming that has taken place. And in the patch {usss.dynamicdelay} you'll see all the variables begin something like $1.initdel. The $1 takes your instance name, so when you type mydelay.initdel and give it a pair of numbers you set the start and end delay times. You might also wish to randomise the organisation of delays (metro into random 3 into $1.initdirection) as shown in Figure 2.41.

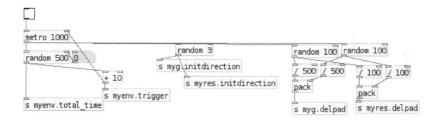

Figure 2.41 Sending variables to the dynamic delay and reson objects

Rather clumsy code, but made 'on the fly' to give more than one thing at a time from the mouse. Left-hand side: metronome that triggers randomly, changing an envelope time that carves out sound from a constant source (giving a 'blip'). Middle: randomised (log, exp, lin) clustering of delays and filters. Right: randomised(ish) taps on the two trackpads for delays and filters. Denser and lighter textures can then be created by changing the size of the random number employed in the {metro} object.

The Pd USSS tools are there for you to explore, adapt and make your own. But hopefully, as you become accustomed to making compound tools, working with sends, creating multiple instances of the same tool, you will find yourself making sounds you did not realise could come from your initial source.

2.4.1 Multichannel playback, recording and development in Pd

As has been mentioned, it is possible to use multiple instances of these tools to manipulate multichannel files. However, for this to happen you either need to read from or write to multichannel files. If working from a stereo file but developing towards multichannel (multiple variants of the granular object, for example) you will need to construct a way of listening to and recording multiple channels. This will mean swapping out usss.output for the following:

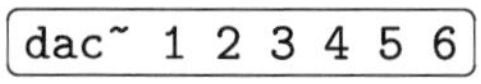

```
dac~ 1 2 3 4 5 6
```

Figure 2.42 DAC with multiple outputs

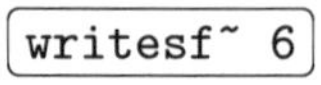

```
writesf~ 6
```

Figure 2.43 Pd: multichannel write to file

Or you may now wish to adapt usss.output to be four, six, eight or more channels. Or, as a challenge, you may realise that in theory you should need only one my.output X patch that *dynamically* creates its inputs and assigns them to an X-channel dac~ and an X-channel writesf~. A lot of this groundwork has been completed and is documented in Chapter 4.

2.5 Csound and Blue

Where Pure Data (Pd) allows for real-time interaction and, with the USSS toolkit, the chance to record all your 'play' for future selection/deletion, Blue and Csound are a little more explicit in what they require from you. Nonetheless, we have supplied a number of quite easy-to-use tools that take the pain away from learning Csound.

2.5.1 Csound

Csound is a text-based computer programming language that has a long and chequered history. Csound began as an offshoot of one of the MUSIC languages pioneered by composer/programmers Max Mathews (1926–2011) and Barry Vercoe (b.1937). With over 25 years of development, this software resource has turned into a 'real monster' with hundreds of 'opcodes' (mini-programs). As with Pure Data, lots of tutorials exist and we hope that together with our code snippets and working examples you can begin to understand the real processing power of this program.

2.5.2 Blue

Blue is a music composition environment for Csound written in Java by Stephen Yi (2008). It allows for a whole host of graphical interfaces to be incorporated into the Csound environment and brings other programming options closer to the music maker.

2.5.3 Blue examples: A soundfile player (usssblue_playback.blue)

We begin simply by making a soundfile player based upon the {diskin2} opcode. The interface shown below is found by clicking on the instrument name (sfplay) in the Orchestra tab under Interface.

Figure 2.44 Simple playback instrument

The code for this instrument is as follows. It is shown in the Orchestra tab under Code:

```
;usssblue_playback
;simple playback instrument where user selects file,
;speed, skiptime and loop.
iflen filelen "<filein>"
istart = <skptime>*iflen
asig1, asig2   diskin2 "<filein>", <speed>, istart,
<loop> blueMixerOut "<route>", asig1*<volume>,
asig2*<volume>
```

Here the skip time (where you start in the file) is given by 0–1 and is then multiplied by the length of the file. Select an audiofile and push play. If Blue is configured correctly then you should hear your soundfile. There is no 'one setup fits all' to do this: as with Pure Data, if the software is not communicating with the computer's soundcard, there is some 'under the hood' work to be done.

Where Blue gets interesting at this level is in the Score tab.

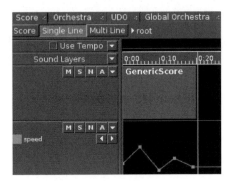

Figure 2.45 Adjusting playback speed

Here we see a *Generic Score* representing a one-time triggering of our instrument playing back our soundfile. Underneath is a separate layer controlling the variable <speed>. What this allows is a more constructed approach to soundfile creation and a more controlled shaping of transformation parameters. File>Render to Disk when ready to save to your hard drive.

2.5.4 Blue examples: A brassage filter machine (usssblue bandpass.blue)

We now jump to a different level of complexity in this example. At the outset, in the Orchestra tab we get a soundfile loader like before.

If you load up a file and then switch to the Score tab you can define how long your instrument will play by adjusting the white PythonObject block. Make sure you also have green start lines at zero (left-click at start on the timeline) and yellow end lines after the end of your object (right-click on the timeline).

If you do not see a new interface you need to select Window::SoundObject Editor and look for the interface tab. You should then see the following:

Filter Sweeper

This instrument looks at a portion of the file plays it back applying a series of randomised filter parameters

filename

ack/speech.wav [...] ☑ usefilter

Figure 2.46 Another soundfile loader

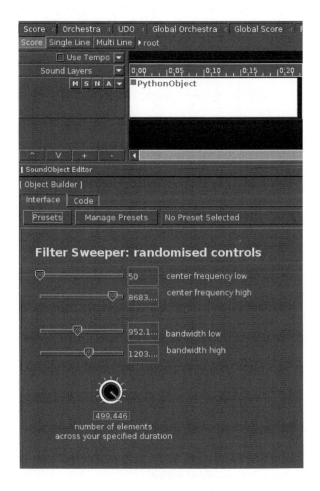

Figure 2.47 Bandpass filter score Python object builder

This patch samples from the full range of your source file taking a small segment of sound (almost like a grain but a little larger, here called an element). To this element it applies a filter sweeping randomly with randomly varying bandwidth change. The number of elements taken is specified at the bottom of your randomised controls. This is almost like a granular synthesiser except that different processes are happening to each element. As the sound is filtered quite heavily you may need to bump up the gain of the output file by normalising to −3 dB after rendering to disk.

2.5.5 Blue examples: A more complicated Python example – multiple soundfile brassage

Taking this one step further, the (usssbluesfmangler.blue) contains three Python functions which work on a complete folder of files. Pitch and duration are experimental. Density is the number of snippets of sound you want over the duration of your object.

Figure 2.48 SF mangler front-end. Brassage over all soundfiles in a folder

For advanced users, sometimes it is worth having a look at the code. The myscore function is a relatively normal mixer, articulate applies an acceleration or deceleration to the elements and regulator spaces elements evenly. To enable this to work effectively you will need to have a solid understanding of the Python code and know where to find your folder of files. As the examples used in this Blue patch are from a Linux machine, the soundfile directories are of the form /home/myfolder/anotherfolder/. File paths will be structured and named differently on your computer. You might have some luck just adjusting parameters from the sample code provided.

For the soundfile mangler, we have produced a simple front-end that allows you to create a folder of soundfiles of any duration and randomly select portions of these files, as though one had taken four decks of cards and shuffled them.

2.5.6 Blue examples: A simple granulator

Granulators exist in all our toolkits and Blue is no exception. Performing a function very similar to the sample and hold patch in Pd (see Section 2.2.5) is Csound's Diskgrain object encapsulated in the (usssbluediskgranulator.blue) patch.

Figure 2.49 Simple granular synthesiser in Blue

This object can vary pitch and speed independently and, with Blue's time-varying graphs in the score window, you can quite easily go from the real to the unreal as you stretch a sound towards a drone.

2.5.7 Blue examples: A special granulator

(usssbluepartikkel.blue) uses the Csound partikkel opcode. This opcode was written to explore the full range of granulation described by Roads in *Microsound* (Roads, 2004). We have covered up many of the variables, leaving only an essential selection in the interface.

If you read Adrian Moore's composer recollections (Appendix B.5) you will see that there is something rather interesting about this granulation. The controls function pretty much as the granular synthesiser in Pure Data.

- *speed*: speed at which you traverse through the input file.

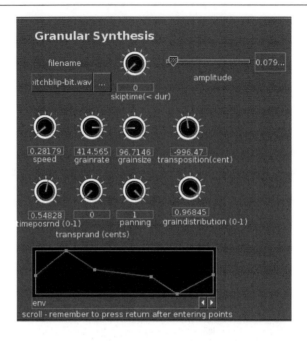

Figure 2.50 Granular synthesiser in Blue

- *grainrate*: number of grains used to create output file (giving an overall level of density of output).
- *grainsize*: length of each grain (normally between 50 and 150 ms).
- *transposition: (cents)*. Transposition of resulting output file. There are 100 cents in a semitone so there is the potential for some large positive and negative numbers here.
- *timeposrnd (0–1)*: A degree of jitter applied to the input pointer (where in the input file a grain is taken).
- *transprand (cents)*: randomisation of output grain transposition (0: steady state, anything else: pitch jitter).
- *panning*: 1 for stereo panning.
- *graindistribution (0–1)*: where each grain should be placed randomly in the stereo space (this should normally verge towards 1 to give a good stereo spread).

Finally, there is an envelope that you can draw to say exactly where in the input file the granulation takes place. This is dubiously related to *speed* and *timeposrnd* so may deliver unexpected results. Some people like these unexpected results more than others. Compare and contrast this granulation with `usss.granular` in Pure Data. We hope you will find noticeable differences.

2.5.8 Blue examples: Comb filters

(`usssbluecombs.blue`) uses the Csound `vcomb` opcode in addition to a host of other functions.

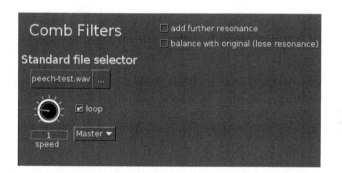

Figure 2.51 The Comb orchestra interface

The orchestra interface is simple, with a file selector and check boxes to experiment with additional filtering and envelope balancing with the original soundfile (which, as it states, will lose any resonance you have acquired along the way – but an interesting modification none the less).

Subsequent to selecting a soundfile, you need to proceed to the Score and SoundObject Editor. The Python code that is most important here is:

```
direction = random.uniform(1.0, 1.0)
//
//and
//
score = combit([50, 100, 200, 300, 400, 500, 800,
     1000, 2000, 5000, 8000, 10000],
1.0, 0.5, 20.0)
```

Changing the direction randomisation will give you glissandi in frequency. (0.5, 1.5) will create upward and downward glissandi. The score line is the main performance line. As you add more comb filters (specified by frequencies between the square brackets) be wary to adjust the amplitude at the end of that line. The start and end reverb times provide a nice way of moving from dry to wet.

If you like this kind of filtering then (ussscombobjbuild.blue) adds a neat front end to the comb filter patch giving you control over resonance, filter frequency fundamental and number of filters (see Figure 2.52).

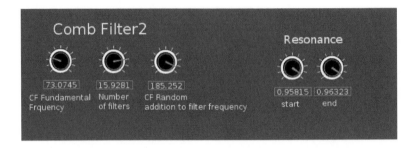

Figure 2.52 The CombFilter PythonObject interface

2.5.9 Blue examples: Convolution – a different kind of cross synthesis

Convolution in Csound is very different to the cross synthesis you have seen in Pure Data.

(usssblueconvolve.blue) uses the Csound convolve opcode.

Figure 2.53 A convolution instrument

In the commercial world convolution is used for reverberation. An acoustic snapshot is taken from a venue (a very short recording, called an impulse response) and used to colour all input sounds. The impulse

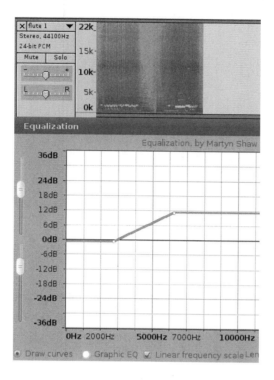

Figure 2.54 A filter of some 12 dB on a convolution file to maintain high frequency output after convolution

response is the response of the building to every frequency. Therefore as you filter your input sound through this impulse response, every frequency that is in your input sound is affected by the degree to which that particular frequency was affected in the space when the impulse response was recorded. So when a noise burst is fired in the Sydney Opera House, some frequencies will decay quicker than others. It is this decay multiplication that gives you the reverb profile of the hall and therefore allows you to theoretically place your dry input sound in the Sydney Opera House (at a considerably reduced cost compared with flying to Australia).

You can create reverberation profiles of your favourite spaces by popping a balloon, hitting a snare drum, firing something legal or potentially clapping your hands. Take off the original sound and you have a profile. It is not that clinical but you could then convolve your profile with your dry input recording and add reverberation. However, this profile need not be an impulse response. In fact it could be any small strand of sound (more acoustic DNA profiling).

Figure 2.55 A phase vocoding time stretch instrument

The Blue convolver takes a playfile and a convolution file. You select from where in the convolution file you wish to sample (and this is trial and error as the start point is 0–1 representing the total duration of whatever file you load). The slice is normally less than one second. The smaller the slice the more you continue to hear any articulation in your playfile.

A word of warning: it is very easy to lose high frequencies with convolution so it might be worth considering artificially increasing the high frequency content of your convolution file (often to a ridiculous level). Remember we are using this process for compositional purposes and if you get a resultant soundfile with frequencies between 20 Hz and 2000 Hz, not only have you got one dull sound, but there's nothing really left to process in the future. There are times when you want this loss of quality but they are rare. So consider ramping up the higher frequencies of your convolution file (and remember to 'save as' because you are probably creating a file that will not feature in your composition) (see Figure 2.54).

2.5.10 Blue examples: The phase vocoder – time stretching

The phase vocoder is a particular kind of synthesiser that works by analysing the spectral content of your sound through tiny windows. We are now working in the frequency-domain as opposed to the time-domain which was used for the majority of the previous patches, especially those in Pure Data. The time stretch unit allows you to change pitch without changing speed (compare to usss.varispeed which emulated an old analogue tape machine – slow became low, half speed equalled an octave drop in pitch, fast became high, double speed equalled an octave rise in

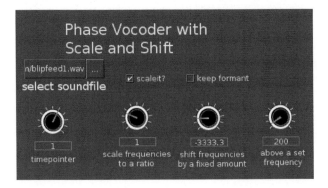

Figure 2.56 A frequency scaler and shifter

pitch) or change speed without changing pitch. When changing speed without changing pitch, you will use the time pointer (probably within the score window so you can make time-varying adjustments). With the time pointer at zero you are just sitting at the current input file read point.

The phase vocoder windows can be of various sizes and we normally use 128, 256, 512, 1024, 2048, 4096, 8192. As the FFT size increases the pitch analysis of the input file is increased. However, rhythmic definition is decreased as the distance between 'slices' has grown. This tradeoff is useful and audibly very noticeable. If you want to slightly blur a file with strong articulation you might consider using a higher FFT size. If you want to keep the articulation intact, make sure the FFT size is 512 or less.

2.5.11 Blue examples: The Phase Vocoder and frequency shifting/stretching/blurring

(usssbluestretchblur.blue) affords time stretching and *blurring*. The blur function acts as an averaging device on both frequency and amplitude. It has a very particular output sound so should be used sparingly.

(usssbluescaleshift.blue) affords *frequency shifting and scaling*. Here the amplitudes of component frequencies remain the same but the frequency placeholders are changed. A frequency spectrum of 100, 200, 400, 800 Hz scaled by a factor of two will change to 200, 400, 800, 1600 Hz. Depending upon at what starting frequency scaling begins, when the scale function is a fraction, harmonic input sounds can become inharmonic on output; this is certainly the case when harmonic frequencies are simply shifted by a number of hertz. Additionally, the scale and shift functions can change over time in Blue (see the Score tab). The shift function literally shifts a block of frequencies from place X to place Y. This can be good for shifting a cluster of frequencies from one region to another.

2.5.12 Blue examples: Spectral warping

(usssbluewarp.blue) affords experimentation with *spectral warping*.

The warp tool is like a more refined spectral scaler. The graph maps input frequency content to output frequency content.

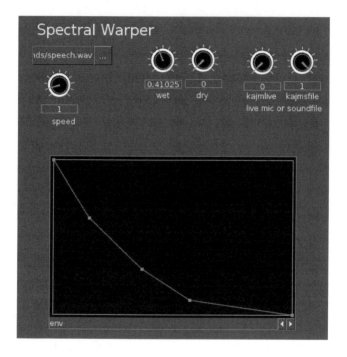

Figure 2.57 A spectral warper

(usssbluewarp.blue) was ported into Blue after researching Pieman Koshravi's experiments porting the GRMTools spectral warper to Csound and Max/MSP (Khosravi, 2009, 2011). Csound examples can be found at http://Csounds.com/. This version is not as sophisticated as the GRMTools version. Imagine the line drawn from top left to bottom right. A straight line implies input frequency equals output frequency (for each partial in the spectrum). As the gradient increases or decreases, so the output frequencies become either 'scrunched' together or shifted further apart.

(ussspbluewarp2.blue) affords warping between position A and
position B over the duration of the soundfile.

2.5.13 Some final thoughts on Csound

Csound is perhaps the most versatile (and well-documented) language
available for computer music. Whilst we have produced many examples
shrouded by a Blue interface, there are countless other toolkits available.
Composers at Sheffield continue to use the set developed by composer
Iain McCurdy.[5] These tools perform a number of classic and novel
manipulations on sound and use the FLTK interface built from within
Csound (so all you need is the latest version of Csound to get going).
Iain has given us a number of very useful implementations of granulation
which continue to provide useful results.

2.6 Computer Music Software

The difference between Csound and Pd is clear. One uses text; the other
graphics. There are similarities in function codes (for example, for filters,
reverberation, delays, mathematical and logical operations). Csound has
numerous 'front-ends', graphical wrappers that allow you to interface
more adroitly with the software. Our Pd toolkit allows similar 'ease of
use' in that it hides all but the most essential sliders and dials.

Csound and Pd are but the tip of the iceberg that is audio synthesis
environments. Readers are encouraged to look at the Wikipedia entry[6]
listing a number of environments that do similar things to Csound and
Pd but often using different syntax. They are compared according to:

- Usability. All are difficult to use and it is for this reason that we –
  amongst many others – have made toolkits that enable beginners to
  make interesting sounds quickly.
- Learnability. All are difficult to learn and we have tutorials that
  guide students through the process from the ground up. It tends
  to be the case that software that has been around for a while has a
  solid set of tutorials closely associated with it.
- Sound 'quality'. This is a red herring. There should be very little
  discernible difference between a digital to analogue conversion in Pd
  and one in any other environment. It is also better to worry about
  your microphones and loudspeakers first, and then see if a sine wave
  in environment A is more pure than one in environment B!
- Creative flow. This is particularly interesting from a composer's
  point of view. One might assume that software is creatively
  'transparent', that it is the user that sculpts the software to their
  needs. However, some software (in particular third party tools with

very closed interfaces) will only allow you to do what the software engineer has decided can be done. Fortunately this is not the case with either Pd or Csound. Both environments are completely open ended. What this does mean is that the beginner will need something like a toolkit which will (by necessity) do 'less than everything'.

Ultimately you may find that each piece of software has its own beauty, style, use and community. You are very likely to find one piece of software that suits you and most of your needs. However, as you probe each tool, not only will you find the similarities quite reassuring but you will realise that there are aspects of each which will speed your workflow and potentially bring order and structure into your transformation operations. You will also find the communities for most software environments to be very welcoming and, if you have made an effort to understand something and present your problem clearly (especially to email lists), other composers and programmers will help you find a solution.

2.7 SoX

Finally for this chapter on toolkits, it is worth mentioning a very useful set of tools that sit alongside other more involved text-based environments. SoX[7] is cross-platform and works as a quick and effective tool for editing and processing. From the command line try the following:

- Removing silence:
  ```
  sox infile.wav outfile.wav silence 1 0.1 1%
  -1 0.1 1%
  ```
- Changing file type:
  ```
  sox infile.au outfile.wav
  ```
- Normalise:
  ```
  sox infile.wav outfile.wav gain -3
  ```
- Filtering bandpass:
  ```
  sox infile.wav outfile.wav bandpass 100 10
  ```
- Filtering high-pass:
  ```
  sox infile.wav outfile.wav highpass 100
  ```
- Filtering low-pass:
  ```
  sox infile.wav outfile.wav lowpass 100
  ```
- Filtering band reject:
  ```
  sox infile.wav outfile.wav bandreject 100 10
  ```
- Pitch bending:
  ```
  sox infile.wav outfile.wav bend -o32 0,1000,2
  ```
- Pitch shifting:
  ```
  sox infile.wav outfile.wav pitch 1200
  ```

- Pitch speed change:
```
sox speech.wav speechspeed.wav speed 2
```
- Chorus:
```
sox infile.wav outfile.wav chorus 0.6 0.9 55 0.4
0.25 2 -s
```
- Companding:
```
sox infile.wav outfile.wav compand 0.3,0.8 6:-70,
-60,-20 -5
```
- Delay:
```
sox infile.wav outfile.wav delay 0 0.2
```
- Echo:
```
sox infile.wav outfile.wav echo 0.8 0.8 60 0.4
```
- Amplitude fade:
```
sox infile.wav outfile.wav fade 1.0 0.0
```
- Flanger:
```
sox infile.wav outfile.wav flanger 0 2 90 71 0.2
sin 25 quad
```
- Phaser:
```
sox out.wav outphasor.wav phaser 0.8 0.8 3 0.4
 0.5 -t
```
- Pad with silence:
```
sox infile.wav outfilepad.wav pad 0 2
```
- Multiple:
```
sox infile.wav outfile.wav trim 0 2 pad 0 2
 reverb
```
- Time stretch:
```
sox infile.wav outfile.wav stretch 2
```

2.8 Reverberation

We have left reverberation almost until the end (though it was briefly discussed in Section 2.2.7) as for the most part it is the final transformation that you will make (and quite often you will incorporate reverberation into your mixing environment as a real-time addition). Reverberation is a natural phenomenon so correct use should sound 'natural', though it is often used as an extreme sustain effect. In electroacoustic music, as we want to play with dry/wet, near/far concepts, reverberation is never usually applied wholesale to a sound but is often applied over time to make it appear like a sound is drifting into the distance. When it comes to mixing, you will not have to worry about the volume of a reverb channel as a sound will be injected into it and the resulting reverb will end when it ends. You just need to worry how to make the right wet/dry transition/balance.

2.9 Mixing

2.9.1 Introduction

Having recorded numerous sounds and developed them through many of the Pd examples above, you may wish to start to further edit sounds and place them one after the other, or one on top of the other. Sounds simple? Mixing is perhaps the most challenging and exciting part of electroacoustic music composition. Most electroacoustic composers will use a DAW to mix their work. Whilst mixing environments such as Audacity are free to download, many are not. However, they all run in much the same way: time moves from left to right and sounds slot into lanes or channels. These sounds can then be shifted left or right and edited. This is not a hard edit but rather just a frame around the original sound which is read in real time from the disk. This is called non-destructive editing. In many of the examples above it has been possible to say 'use a dynamic sound' or 'filter this noisy sound' because the effect is primed to do a specific task. A mixer mixes. That really is all, so it is impossible to predict or suggest what you might want to start mixing first. However, you will find below that mixing enables you to build anything from complex polyphonies (many sounds of different types) to complex monophonies (many sounds fusing to make an enigmatic 'composite'). Mixers of course allow you to do this, and more: mix, edit, repeat, transform (creating new files), transform (in real time), automate (volume, panning, effects), group, organise and structure your work. This section will not be a guide to using a DAW. Rather, it will demonstrate *an* art of mixing and prove that there are no hard and fast rules – only to *listen carefully*.

2.9.2 Setting up the reverberation channel

As was mentioned in Section 2.8 it is often wise to leave adding reverberation to sounds until the very last minute, i.e. within the DAW. To set up a reverberation channel in any DAW is relatively simple. You need to add an effects channel with a reverb plug-in on it that can receive sound from what is called a pre-fade send, (the opposite of which is called post-fade send, by the way). See Figure 2.58, an example from Steinberg's Nuendo,[8] showing the necessary steps required.

Once a sound is placed in a lane, this lane can be expanded to show a volume curve and, if a send is set up, the level of sound that should be sent to the send. The volume track in this example fades out (dry) as, irrespective of that volume fader, *pre-fade* – the sound is sent to the reverberation effects channel (whose volume remains at 0.0 dB as the reverb will die away naturally).

Figure 2.58 Creating a pre-fade send for use with reverberation

2.9.3 Mixing techniques

Mixing electroacoustic music is about as different from mixing popular music as it possibly can be. Tracks will carry multiple sounds and will not be dedicated to a microphone/instrument mapping (like 'kick', 'snare', 'guitars', etc.) Volume curves will vary dramatically and most tracks will have a number of pre-fade sends attached to them. See the full mix of *Click* by Adrian Moore in Figure 2.59.

One of the key things to remember when making manipulations prior to mixing electroacoustic music is that your sounds *need not* sound like they should exist on their own in a mix. Therefore you might make a sound that is very dark and bass heavy, or one that is very fragile, light and high-frequency. These two files might, when mixed, form the perfect canopied and rooted settings for material to be placed within the spectral space. Drones that you hear from composers like Andrew Lewis or Monty Adkins are more than likely to be composites of many smaller drones. It is quite often the case that composers seek a full-bodied sound (sometimes dubiously labelled 'phat') directly from all their manipulations. Try to imagine the potential of a sound to exist as part of a composite at mix time.

2.9.4 When to start mixing

There are many different answers to the question 'when should mixing begin?'. Some may start a mix file right at the start of the composition process. Others will tend towards creating a solid bank of sources and manipulations before considering mixing. Either way, you will never

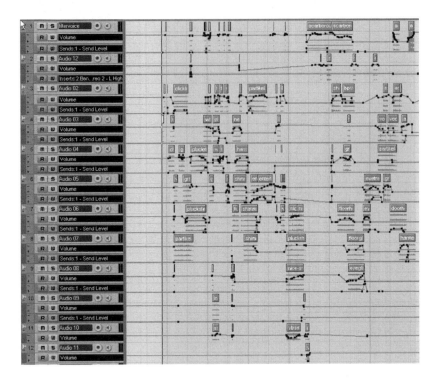

Figure 2.59 Mix page for *Click* by Adrian Moore

have all the sounds you need prior to a mix. The generate, reflect, accumulate, mix diagram (Figure 1.2) suggests that you will, at some point, find gaps in your mixing where the creation of a *specific* soundfile is required. It is at points like this where a really solid understanding of technique and an intimate knowledge of the sounds you have to hand are vital.

2.9.5 Where to start mixing

On a practical note, *never* start mixing at 0:00:00 in your DAW. Chances are you are not actually starting at the beginning of your piece so to then shift a whole bunch of sounds and effects in order to insert a new sound will give rise to errors. Start at an arbitrary time, well into your DAW's timeline.

Consider the mix in stages or, indeed, in phrases. Bear in mind, too, that phrases may eventually need to be split (DAW folders help enormously here). For an example, see Figure 2.60.

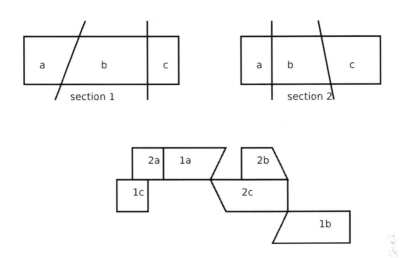

Figure 2.60 Two phrases subsequently remixed

Remixed phrases may need some additional 'glue' to make transitions seamless or to cover up changes in density. Critics of this style of composition have called this bricolage, as properties shared between 'blocks' of sound are not easily identified. The process requires some 'fiddling' (*bricoler* in French means to tinker) but as composers such as Jonty Harrison have argued, the concrete link between you and what you hear directly from the loudspeakers as you juxtapose two blocks of sound has just as much validity as two related sequences of notes on manuscript. Unfortunately, despite a vast array of powerful processing tools, when it comes to mixing we almost always appropriate the rock-and-roll oriented DAW where time moves from left to right and tracks are normally meant to contain one particular instrument. Frustrating moments arise when you drag in a two-minute granulation file and use five seconds of it in a mix. What do you do with the remaining sound? It would be wonderful to see, when you click back on that sound in the pool, where in the mix that sound was used and what portion of it was used. There is a nagging feeling in the back of your mind as you drag in another file from a pool of two gigabytes worth of sound that perhaps this is not the sound you were meant to be using. The only way around this is to have a very solid understanding of all your soundfiles and to mix, mix and mix again. As you become more confident at mixing, consider not bothering about making sure each phrase has a start and an end; sort those out later.

Juxtaposition (with or without slight overlap) of submixes or phrases as in Figure 2.60 is very different to juxtaposition of sounds to create sound objects, as mentioned in Section 1.4, as the timescales are so different. You are now working more at a 'scene by scene' level: time is moving slower. That is not to say that you cannot cut away or insert dramatic changes in sound. It is that these cuts or insertions are going to form key moments in the formal design of your piece. They work best in the following two scenarios:

- Sudden dramatic insertion of attack-led phrase.

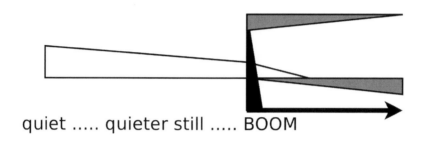

quiet ..... quieter still ..... BOOM

Figure 2.61 Surprise attack

Clearly, tension is easing and as this texture or drone section carries on, we are less and less sure of what to expect next. There is an air of suspense. Small sounds could appear but in this instance we have a sudden explosion of sound that should come as a complete shock. That shock is sufficient justification for it to be there: memories are yanked completely into the present as we assess the barrage of sound around us. It is only later that we can reflect upon what has just happened. This technique (someone/something approaching from behind) can be seen in films and we suspect that the first, second, maybe third time round, it is not going to be the foe approaching but a friend (a false alarm). This is harder to achieve in sound, unfortunately, and this process quickly loses its potency if repeated often.

- Sudden cut away to steady state.

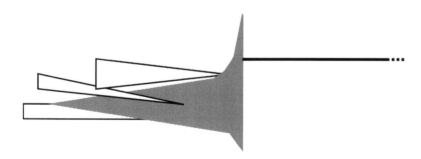

Figure 2.62 Mix cut away

The cut away is perhaps even more effective than the surprise attack. When sound suddenly appears we require justification for it to happen (where has that energy come from?). The sudden cut away is like someone turning off the lights. We accept far more easily the sudden loss of energy. There is an easy justification for whatever remains as a remnant or echo of the previous energy-filled activity. We are still moving along at a hundred miles an hour so as we slow down we are happy to pick up on the small, inconsequential sounds left behind. The best example of this cut away is in Bernard Parmegiani's work *Dedans Dehors* (1977) in the third movement, 'Retour de la forêt', as shown in the sonogram in Figure 2.63.

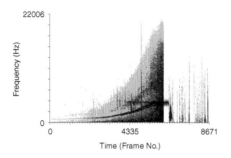

Figure 2.63 'Retour de la forêt' from *Dedans Dehors*

For over two minutes Parmegiani sustains a crescendo of epic proportions, including the surreptitious mixing of a rising synthetic drone within an otherwise natural environment and a sustained tone that anchors the listener, when the rest of the environment is torn away. The relief felt when another sound breaks this virtual silence is palpable.

Finally, remember overlaps? In a great deal of classical music, you often hear a phrase-end overlap the start of a new phrase. The same often applies in electroacoustic music, especially if reverberation is used as a termination feature. Where phrases start and end, however, is precisely up to you. As a phrase ends, breathe and conduct where you want the next sound to start. Then make sure you place that sound at that point in your DAW mix page. Silence is used less and less in electroacoustic music as attention spans immediately dwindle, but if you need............silence............between......phrases, use it carefully.

We are verging on a discussion of structure and form tentatively worked through in Chapter 3. However, from the above you can see that structure is organic: you only have to be invasive when structure starts to go wrong. Form can be both organic (intrinsic to the sounds/objects/gestures/textures you are working with) and artificial (extrinsic, the most obvious being movement form). Where structure ends and form starts is a nebulous boundary in many cases.

2.9.6 A more complex example

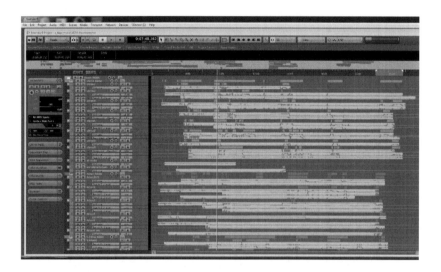

Figure 2.64 Mix page for *The Battle* by Adrian Moore

Figure 2.64 represents one of the final 'master' mixes from my work *The Battle*. It looks a bit of a mess, but is explained below

- The original working title was *A Day's Truce*. *The Battle* began a series of works related to war.
- Channel list: some 40 individual tracks.

  1. audio: nine stereo channels.
  2. audio: six four-channel files (front-left and right, side-left and right).
  3. audio: four six-channel files (including centre and sub).
  4. audio: six 'spot' channels (one for each loudspeaker).
  5. fx: three or more reverbs with numerous pre-fade sends on stereo and multichannel tracks – if you can't afford a surround reverb

(and I cannot), just use two or more stereos and pan to different configurations of loudspeakers then send in different proportions to front/back. Bear in mind different reverb times for front/back.

6. fx: at least two reverbs as *continuants*. A good 20 seconds of reverb time with one reverb unit keeping only highs (Bang – ssssssssssssssssssss) and one keeping only lows (Bang – rumblerumblerumble).

7. fx: effects that you want to control in real time.

8. MIDI: one or more synths. Even if you deign to use a preset, a synthesised tone can help support other materials depending upon how 'obtrusive' you want your synths to be. In my normal practice I want listeners to never know I have used a synthesised sound (unless it is obvious I have synthesised it myself).

9. MIDI: samplers. I do use a sampler, mainly with one sample (usually short attack sounds) assigned to each key on a keyboard. A great way to repeat short sounds and create rhythmic patterns.

• A lot of layering and reinforcement of four/six channel files derived from Pure Data/Csound manipulations by stereo soundfiles which are panned using the default stereo to six channel panner.

• Composition clearly in phrases building outwards left and right from a central 'shot in the dark'.

There is a transition in *The Battle* where a crescendo leads to a cut away before a solid downbeat attack triggers a section of pulsed activity. The cut away was originally pure digital silence (for about a half-second). Following my own advice in Appendix B I played this section to my colleague Adam Stansbie. He quite firmly recommended no digital silence. As a consequence a small residue was left dying away. Adam had a number of other comments. All were constructive: 90% I agreed with and I made a number of small changes.

In a number of composition classes we work through the idea of initiating, extending and terminating. One simple example of this is attack, sustain, release (but not like an ADSR envelope). Over the course of thirty seconds or so, an attack would initiate a sustained granulation which would gradually 'dissolve' to blips, the last of which would 'disappear' with reverberation. This kind of phrase is typical. Beginnings and endings (tapered or strongly articulated) are then interchanged to see how this might affect the main material. As has been mentioned many times, the flow and transformation of energy from attack to sustain to release is what ultimately drives most phrases.

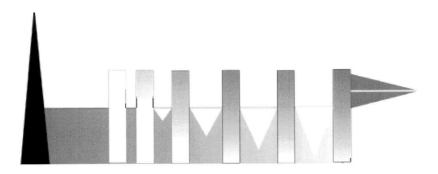

Figure 2.65 From attack through granular sustain to dissolve and gentle reverberation release

2.9.7 It is rarely one effect at a time

Many sounds may exist as preprocessed materials made outside of the main mixing environment. How much real-time processing is done within the mix will vary from composer to composer. Real-time transformations have advantages and disadvantages. They are easily changed as nothing is set in stone; it is all done through automation. However, processes are often linear and when the virtualised output from one effect is sent into another, given EQ and finally output, it is difficult to visualise what is going on, especially as your time-varying automation lines are not necessarily overlaid upon a graphic of the sound.

That being said, aside from reverberation and EQ, it is rare to see single (first-order) transformations either through processing or in the mix. The case above where a sound finally melts away may well require an additional panning profile as shown in Figure 2.24. This sound may also need to 'rise' either through EQ (high-pass) and/or pitch shifting. If pitch shift is used, as the sound fades, so the feedback may need to be increased to 'smooth' and the final tail further 'synthesised'. Thus, for around five to ten seconds of sound we may have four or five different effects, each with multiple varying parameters. Our DAWs are easily capable of doing this but it is time consuming and the interface of automation lines is not practical. One word of warning. If you move the block of sound you are working on and automation (hidden way down on another track) *is not* attached or related to said block, you may undo many hours of finesse and subtlety. One possible compromise here is to work in submixes where you encapsulate sections which are clearly 'complete' mini-mixes. I have sadly never had sufficient time to be able to fully explore the automation power of my DAW. However, since purchasing an excellent software sampler, more of my processing, mixing and montaging is taking place within the DAW.

2.9.8 Multichannel vs. multi-channel

There have always been multichannel pieces ever since John Cage played two records at the same time. The DAW examples above have been multichannel mixes that are mostly rendered down to two (still multi) channels. However, there is a huge difference between a scene where a drone rests on one plane and an attack appears in two loudspeakers then miraculously disperses into smaller files, each one flying in three-dimensional space, and the same in stereo where sounds separate only because of their frequency components, some judicious sound diffusion and some imagination on behalf of the listener. Electroacoustic composition rendered to multichannel is becoming increasingly common, though I continue to believe that stereo plus imagination is effective. Multichannel mixes afford maximum agility of sounds, a polyphony of scenes and a greater perception of space. It may not require much in the way of sound diffusion (see Chapter 8) but it will require at least the number of loudspeakers as rendered channels, if not more. And a 24-channel work will normally lose a great deal of its finesse when rendered to stereo for broadcast. Given the ability to move one sound extremely accurately between say 8 to 16 loudspeakers whilst setting a scene on an additional set of loudspeakers it is equally possible to use combinations of loudspeakers to play *completely different* material that would otherwise never go together in stereo. Again, the stereo downmix would be next to useless unless the density of sound were lightened. The electroacoustic community is loathe to explore this avenue as it begins to avoid the use of loudspeakers for spatial purposes. However, it goes to highlight one of the main problems of electroacoustic music: the difference between polyphony of sounds that are self-contained but which can be unravelled by the listener, and an audible polyphony of vastly different materials. The question 'when two sounds are mixed together, do they sound like one new sound or two sounds?' remains at the heart of the mixing process and mix subtlety is often something that can set a composer apart from their peers.

2.9.9 Repetition

And if the mixing question were the 'vertical' axis of our grid, so repetition is our 'horizontal' axis. I often thought the axiom *similar but different* was the way to approach repetition of anything larger than a grain of sound. However, the mechanical repetition of sound *can* drive a musical process and overcome structural stagnation just as powerfully as any accelerating or decelerating gesture. There are a number of clear questions that must be posed when repeating something *exactly*.

- The repetition creates a hierarchy. The repeated sound must therefore be *important*. Is it a good enough sound to be repeated?
- Once you repeat something once, should you repeat it again?
- Once you have something repeating over and over, how do you stop it?

As a teacher I hear repetition too often as a result of a lack of transformation. It is certainly my experience that repetition is a lot easier when one has plenty of closely related material to chose from.

2.9.10 Cataloguing soundfiles

And here you might find yourself coming full circle because if you need to catalogue soundfiles for a mix, you need to be able to 'chunk' files into *at the very least* folders of some type or other. These folders may exist on your local drive or exist in your DAW profile. Similarly, soundfiles will need meaningful names. Research into data management (Eaglestone et al., 2007; Collins, 2001; Dahan et al., 2003) continues to highlight the gap between a quick and successful means of grasping the most pertinent qualities of a soundfile short of playing the sound and its incorporation into a mix. Machine profiling and learning has developed a great deal since researchers such as Michael Casey helped develop the MPEG-7 media content description standard (Casey, 2001), but automatic listeners embedded in your DAW are still some way off (though some specific programs such as Soundfisher[9] have been around for some time). Whilst a number of useful taxonomies of sound exist, the link between sound source (if recognised), any surrogate spectromorphological trace (any broad ranging descriptor of a sound), the meaning of the sound (often, by this time quite personal though not necessarily wholly subjective) and *the necessary tool to develop it* continues, for the most part, to rely upon the experience of the individual composer. This book helps (hopefully) to fast-track experience in a creative direction.

2.10 A Few Words about Kit

'A few words' was another joke that, like the original title of the book, went over numerous heads as this book developed. This is not a book about kit. Owning something like a tablet computer, MIDI controller, graphics tablet or keyboard will enable you to design experimental interfaces to work with your experimental patches and enable real-time control. If you do not have these you will probably be using random functions and line signals to simulate turning dials and pushing sliders. A word of warning: do not get heavily into making a perfect interface.

Use the flexibility of Pure Data or your processing software to quickly make sound happen. It is far too tempting to spend all day programming and no time composing. Regrettable as it may be to design control interfaces each time you make a series of manipulations, such are the changing circumstances of compositions that it keeps your programming swift and effective. The USSS toolkit can quickly map 0–127 to any other pair of numbers with usss.zmap and pipe it to any parameter in Pure Data with a 'send' command. The vigilant will also have noticed that the properties on number boxes and sliders (right-click) in Pure Data can also send and receive (in fact they can be given commands to change what they send and receive to) and the sliders can also scale their outputs.

2.11 But If You Are Going to Buy Something

Microphones Consider whether you want something for the studio (condenser mics), something for location (stereo with windshield and pistol grip), or less obtrusive (in-ear).

Recording devices If you are not necessarily using external microphones you can use the internal microphones from a portable recording device. Think about the quality of recording. Think also about the ability to plug in additional microphones (XLR inputs).

Computers The main difference here remains between a laptop and a desktop. One is portable; one is not.

Soundcards Most computers do not have good internal sound input and output so a USB soundcard or similar is essential.

Speakers Depending on your situation, listening over speakers is always preferable to listening over headphones.

Headphones The main difference here remains between open-back and closed.

And of course, all of this depends on budget. Additionally, such is the rapid change in technology, making any recommendation in a book like this would be futile.

Notes

1. www.shef.ac.uk/usss.
2. Remember that actors – and the same is true for sounds – never walk off 'stage centre'. Also, 'stage right' is from the point of view of the actor not the audience.

3. http://jezwells.org/Computer_music_tools.html.
4. http://puredata.info/downloads/fftease.
5. http://iainmccurdy.org/csound.html.
6. http://en.wikipedia.org/wiki/Comparison_of_audio_synthesis_environments lists some 12 different systems. At the University of Sheffield, we tend to move between Csound and Pd fairly seamlessly. Many students also use Supercollider (another text-based environment that affords huge synthesis power for very few lines of code) and MaxMSP, a graphical environment very closely related to Pd but with strong commercial backing and a very wide user base.
7. http://sox.sourceforge.net/.
8. Although Steinberg's Nuendo is a commercial piece of software, open source alternatives exist and include Ardour. Unfortunately setting up pre and post sends is quite difficult to implement in Ardour.
9. www.soundfisher.com/.

References

Casey, M. (2001). General sound classification and similarity in MPEG-7. *Organised Sound*, 6(02):153–64.
Collins, D. (2001). *Investigating computer-based compositional processes: a case-study approach*. PhD thesis, University of Sheffield.
Dahan, K., Brown, G. and Eaglestone, B. (2003). New strategies for computer-assisted composition software: a perspective. In *Proceedings of the ICMC 2003 Conference, Singapore: ICMA*.
Eaglestone, B., Ford, N., Brown, G. and Moore, A. (2007). Information systems and creativity: an empirical study. *Journal of Documentation*, 63(4):443–64.
Khosravi, P. (2009). Implementing frequency warping. www.csounds.com/journal/issue12 [Online; accessed July 2011].
Khosravi, P. (2011). Circumspectral sound diffusion with Csound. www.csounds.com/journal/issue15 [Online; accessed July 2011].
Kreidler, J. (2009). *Loadbang: Programming Electronic Music in Pure Data*. Hofheim am Taunus: Wolke Verlag.
Parmegiani, B. (1977). *Dedans Dehors*. InaGRM, also from www.electrocd.com.
Roads, C. (2004). *Microsound*. Cambridge, MA: The MIT Press.
Yi, S. (2008). Blue software environment. www.csounds.com/stevenyi/blue, [Online; accessed October 2009].

Chapter 3

The Theory of Opposites

Student: Are there *any* rules here?
Teacher: Yes, the trick is to know which rules you can bend and which rules you can break.

3.1 Introduction

3.1.1 Questioning, opposing, arguing

In Chapter 1 you were given a whole set of descriptors that went some way to making a sound personally useful and meaningful to you, making it possible for you to describe potential development strategies and place the sound within a mix. As you begin to work with particular techniques you may find they associate themselves strongly with particular sound families. You may well be able to predict (imagine) the resulting sound's manipulation. You may also think that something might work but have to try a 'what if' approach. There is absolutely nothing wrong with this as it either generates positive or negative results, both of which are a useful addition to your experience.

A sound may suggest to you its acousmatic-potential by being strongly focused towards one or more particular descriptor. It tends to be the case that this potential is audible because of an abundance of said quality, not because of a lack. Therefore it would be reasonable to assume that you might want to lessen said quantity rather than amplify it when it comes to processing. This simple theory, and it should be taken as but one of a limitless number of theories that you will no doubt formulate throughout your composition career, considers that we *choose transformations based upon a reaction against a sound's most potent descriptor.*

In Chapter 2 we introduced a variety of tools that perform quite specific functions. In describing the processes and in listening to the results of said processes on a number of test files (and we have mentioned before that quite often the best test file is some recorded speech[1]), it should have become clear that these processes *also* tend towards very specific results. Processes least likely to have such a polarised effect are EQ and mixing. However, both EQ and mixing may be used to extremes should you so wish.

It is evident too that our processes produce their *best* results when given the right sort of soundfile. The results of a high-pass filter or resonant/comb filter on a simple flute note, for example, would be negligible. Anyone familiar with what a filter does will tell you that essentially it is subtractive and therefore if it does not have anything to work on (noise-based or dynamically and spectrally active material), results will be inconclusive. Similarly, pitch shifting where no recognisable pitch is present produces a result that is far less convincing than if, say, the above flute note were used. Time stretching a sound with lots of silence is futile. (Time compression, on the other hand, may work). However, you might well consider editing out the silence before compression or stretching, either manually or with SoX (see Section 2.7).

Let us consider a very simple series of examples:

Table 3.1 Working against single sound descriptors

Descriptor	Process (per sound)
Gritty (implies broad spectrum)	Filter (lessen), reverberation (dissipation)
Dull spectrum	Stretch spectrum
High pitch	Make low through pitch transposition or mix as strata
Low pitch	Make high through pitch transposition or mix as strata
Short	Make longer (reverberation, granulation, time stretching)
Discrete	Make continuous through repetition and granulation
Continuous	Make discrete through envelope shaping
Static (Mono)	Add motion either through panning or granulation
Spatially very dynamic	Make mono

It is very difficult to produce concrete examples of sounds that have undergone such processes, but let us consider a simple text phrase. Here is a passage from Goethe's *Faust*. It is a simple line of text that I recorded and is used all too frequently at Sheffield (see Note 1) 'To please the good old public I've elected, who live, and let live, them I'd recreate'. Out of context this sentence is meaningless so we should perhaps consider our first process to be to destroy any sense of word recognition. However,

Table 3.2 Working against sound descriptors with multiple files

Descriptor	Process (per multiple sounds)
Sound A works with sound B	Mix (vertical) or montage (horizontal)
Sound A is rich dynamic, sound B is pitched	Hybridise through convolution
Sound A is rich dynamic, sound B is pitched	Hybridise through filters (resonance or comb)
Sound A is sustained, sound B is pulsed or angular	Envelope follow

Table 3.3 Articulating spatialisation

Descriptor	Process (spatialisation)
Low bass	Static position in the sub woofer
High frequency, wispy material	Quick motion, above our heads
Thematic material	Generally front and centre

we will probably want to keep the sense of 'voice' as this is something tangible for the listener to work with.

Our options are:

- Granulate individual syllables giving us relatively smooth 'ooooo', 'eeeee' and other noise-based sustains.
- Edit the file taking out first vowels, then plosives, fricatives and other vocal stops (either shortening the file or inserting silence). Granulate this file to give a slightly longer variety-pack of vowel-based material or percussive/noise-based sounds.
- Working against the static pitch nature of the 'oooo' drone, create a number of undulations or glissandi either in a phase vocoder instrument in Blue or a simple pitch shifter (Blue or usss.varispeed).
- Working against the mid-range content of the percussive material, or perhaps more obviously, breaking the rules and assuming that you want something percussive but *lighter*, high-pass filter the percussive sounds leaving quite a weak, wispy version that can fly around in the space (and consider adding randomised panning at this point).

> An effective tool for this purpose would be `sustains_ envelope_panned.pd` (see Figure 2.39 and consider adding a bandpass filter or `hp~` object just prior to output.)

- We are mainly working in a pitch-free zone. Try some delicate comb or resonant filters (see Figure 2.51) to add some pitch to our percussive sounds.
- Work against the continuous pitched files by first amplifying high frequency content then spectrally shaping against some of the percussive files. This could be done more simply by using amplitude modulation (Csound's `balance` opcode) for example.
- Generate some short acceleration and deceleration motifs using single plosives and the `usss.dynamicdelay` tool. Play the file through an envelope generator that goes into the delay unit so as to give you space between input 't' and output 't....t...t..t.ttt'.

You will notice that we have come full circle from creation of sustained vowel sounds and creation of percussive textures drawn from hard consonants to amplitude or amp/spectra modification of sustains by percussive sounds, giving rise to a hybrid of (probably) softer percussive sounds. All these new sounds are not only ripe for mixing against the original versions but are more than likely fit for further development.

Tables 3.1, 3.2 and 3.3 are just three snapshots of possible activity. As you begin to describe your sounds more accurately (perhaps beginning to feel them rather than catalogue them), and understand the potential ramifications of processing tools, so you will, for the most part, continue a process of:

- sound+manipulation = sound
- +manipulation = sound
- +manipulation = sound
- and so forth.

3.2 Effects and Descriptors

In very broad terms it is worth specifying the effects from Chapter 2 against the more obvious poles to which they may process your sound.

Clearly it is never a certainty that the effect matching the opposite of sound A's descriptors will deliver good results. You may well have to take your sound and physically move it towards one pole (or many) by using a process quite aggressively, so that sound A actually gets 'into the system' – a 'what if' approach. Although this sounds like cheating, you will have recognised the acousmatic-potential of a sound. Remember, a sound that sounds like the process that made it has lost a significant amount of its own acousmatic-potential but has taken on a completely new life.

Table 3.4 Subtractive effects

Subtractive tools (filters)	Descriptors
Bandpass	Requires signal with full frequency content
Comb	As bandpass. Colouring filter. Rough becomes smooth as resonance increases
Reson	As comb filter
FFTfilter	As bandpass. Noisy can become sinusoidal
Filtersweep	As bandpass. Spectral (time-domain) glissandi added. Flat becomes undulating
FFTBlur	Rough becomes smooth
FFT window size	Discrete becomes continuous (as fft size moves from 128 to 8192) see Section 2.5.10

Table 3.5 Pitch-based effects

Pitch and frequency shifting	Descriptors
Varispeed	Low and slow frequencies and gestures tend towards high and fast, and vice versa
Pitch shift (Pd)	Speed remains the same, however low to high or high to low
Phase vocoder pitch shift	As Pd pitch shift
Phase vocoder spectral stretch and shift	As Pd pitch shift, though harmonic becomes inharmonic and, in extreme cases, centered (together) becomes split as a clear divide can be made either side of a certain frequency, giving a root and canopy
Spectral warp	Stretch and compress, harmonic to inharmonic

Listeners well versed in electroacoustic music seem happy to accept EQ, mixing and granulation alongside quite a few spectral manipulations as part of the everyday toolkit. Comb and resonant filters still remain somewhat clichéd, however. You will note too that only a very few of the descriptors from Tables 1.1 and 1.2 are used in the examples in Tables 3.4 through 3.8. Clearly the effects used can be nuanced to a much greater degree as you become more familiar with their operation.

Table 3.6 Granulation and brassage

Granulation and brassage	Descriptors
Granular	See Figure 1.20. Granular normally tends towards the continuous but can be scattered or cohesive, dense or sparse, flat or undulating
Brassage (Blue filter sweeper)	Scattered and undulating with focus upon repetition (but not at granular level)

Table 3.7 Spatialisation and delay-based effects

Spatialisation and delay-based effects	Descriptors
Reverberation	Discrete becomes continuous. Near becomes far (or if wet and dry are mixed, you can get a full depth of field with frontal image and distant reverberation) Dry becomes wet. Strong becomes weak
Delays (del time > 0.5s)	Single becomes multiple
Delays (del time < 0.5s)	Discrete becomes continuous (as delay and original merge)
Delays with feedback	Discrete becomes continuous as object receives 'delay tail' as feedback dissipates
Panning	Focused becomes spread. Cohesive becomes scattered. See Figure 2.24

Table 3.8 Cross-synthesis effects

Cross-synthesis	Descriptors
Shapee and Blue vocoder	Continuous becomes discrete as you normally cross-synthesise a drone with articulated material
Convolution	Discrete becomes continuous the longer the convolution 'slice'. Rough becomes smooth as convolution is like a reverb or colour filter

So-called 'technological listening' is only a problem when it detracts the attention of the listener from the flow of the music. Easy to say; impossible not to fall into this trap. Hopefully, the technology-spotter listener, if they are enjoying your music, will soon regain control of their acute aural skills and re-enter your musical dialogue.

3.2.1 The theory of opposites

It may be useful to think about a sound's descriptors and about what processes work well against those descriptors. From a compositional point of view, as we tend to think less about the sound itself, less too about the process and more about abstract concepts or personal emotions, theory and technical manipulation become secondary tools, serving the needs of our composition. It is a lofty aspiration but it ties neatly in with our desire to move away from 'chunking' sounds/phrases (in any music) towards a holistic acousmatic and subjective understanding of the structure, form and meaning of a work.

3.3 Structure

3.3.1 Smalley's use of structure

And it is here that the theory of opposites ends (though find me a work where 'fast' has not eventually been offset by 'slow') and we enter a much more natural world of pace and design at a much larger scale than the sound or sound object. In this book the actual concept of *structure* begins at the mix despite the fact that you are bound to be thinking about structure while making sound. Do not be confused by authors talking about a sound's structure. This is but a minute analytical rendition of a sound's shape. We suggest in this book that structure is organic; that it results from the growth of sounds through objects, gestures, textures, landscapes and environments. Denis Smalley's brief discussion of structural relationships in 'Spectro-morphology and structuring processes' (Smalley, 1986, 88–89) is dealt with in a vastly different manner in the revision in 1997, 'Spectromorphology: explaining sound-shapes' (Smalley, 1997, 114). In 1986, his diagram of structural relationships seems to suggest time units larger than that of sound or sound object. Additionally, there is a noticeable use of polar opposites such as vicissitude versus displacement.[2] In the 1997 reworking, terminology from the development of the object (see Section 1.4) is explained at larger time levels. The key terms are *onsets continuants* and *terminations*.

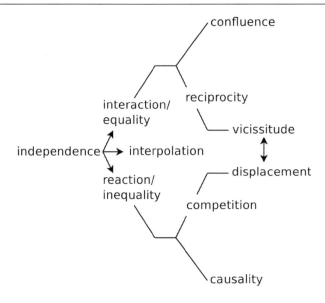

Figure 3.1 Denis Smalley's diagram of structural relationships (Smalley, 1986, 88)

Table 3.9 Structural functions (Smalley, 1997, 115)

Onsets	Continuants	Terminations
departure	passage	arrival
emergence	transition	disappearance
anacrusis	prolongation	closure
attack	maintenance	release
upbeat	statement	resolution
downbeat		plane

Again, we see the continuum fully in action from pole to middle ground to pole. And these structural functions may operate at the sound, sound object, phrase, section and completed work level.

3.3.2 Other structure(s)

It may also be useful to think about the *structure* of other large-scale objects such as buildings. Components here for all manner of shapes and sizes of building include foundations, walls, bricks, mortar, windows, roofs. It is a simple analogy to the above but you may well, at some point in your composition, find yourself with two phrases which need to go together but which require a transition, a kind of 'glue' if you like. You could also see the foundation and roof as floors and canopies with bricks, windows being grains or larger objects. The point here is that a multitude of parts are stuck together to complete the whole and one would not work effectively without the other. Whilst we have not mentioned the word 'time', it pervades everything we do. What is perhaps most interesting about the way you and others comprehend your work is that, during the piece, comprehension is bound by the time frame of the work but during it, before it and after it, we may also assess the work outside of this framework.

3.3.3 Beginning, middle, end

Although the techniques in Chapter 2 can be applied to all manner of creative outputs like interactive pieces, installation art, audio visual works and the like, this book's aesthetic is directed towards the completion of a self-standing work that starts at the beginning and ends at the end, going somewhere via the middle. Get this recipe right and you are 90 per cent there. However, we must continually question this linear trajectory and embellish it to allow us to further define our methodology outside of the aural experience.

3.4 Form

Eventually, after listening to a complete work you may come away with an understanding of how the whole thing works. This may be your gut reaction that you loved it, hated it, or that it requires further attention. It may also be a representation in your mind of a very high-level abstraction of the work. The easiest examples (and we are using very simple renditions here) are Andrew Lewis' *Scherzo* (1993) and Alistair MacDonald's *Equivalence* (2007).

- *Scherzo*. Dense gestural 'clutter' clearing to technical mastery of vocal manipulations with a very specific narrative, diffusing to seashore sound recording.
- *Equivalence*. Bricks and granulation. Increasingly dense towards the middle. A difficult piece to listen to but if you are familiar with granulation, you'll relish the attention to detail and the almost impenetrable levels of mixing and EQ.

Both viewpoints are naïve in the extreme and should be far more detailed. However, the point about a form in electroacoustic music is that you can rush through the piece successfully at fast-forward speeds and get a sense of the work. It is not just that Jonty Harrison's *Klang*

(1982) is 'an earthenware casserole piece' but that its introductions, developments and recapitulation (start, middle, end) are of scales that are manageable. The start is gentle, the developments become quite forceful and the consequent relaxation is precisely what we hoped for.

Some forms are quite obvious. *Dedans Dehors* (Parmegiani, 1977) was in five movements over some 25 minutes. If the work is short, it may have but one kind of pacing and style. However, after a certain duration (and this remains one of those 'undefined' numbers) your piece probably will have sections. After periods of intense activity it is often the case that there are moments of tranquillity and vice versa. The coherent placement and timing of fast and slow is *structure*; the perception of different pace over a space of time in a certain proportion is *form*. Form is perceptual not conceptual ('form first' will normally lead to disaster). Structure is constructional and compositional and can be perceptual too, but where structure has worked when listening we often find ourselves moving forwards in a piece. We might unpick the structure later on but we are almost working with the form at that point.

3.4.1 Does this matter?

Given that everything in this chapter is sound driven:

- Great sounds, great manipulations, dynamic sound objects, fluid phrases, tight structure, tangible form. Excellent.
- Poorly recorded sounds, very little transformation, no sound objects, some phrases, loose structure, clear ABA form based upon a direct repetition of sound. Terrible.

Student: Is this always the case?

Teacher: No, but my experience tends increasingly towards this conclusion.

3.5 Originality

A number of electroacoustic composers have used water sounds in their pieces (indeed water, or the idea of water, is heard across quite a few compositions detailed in Chapter 5). We have a strong affinity with water as it tends to be either exhilarating (rapids, waterfalls) or intensely peaceful (streams, brooks, seashore). There is a beautiful spectral 'slurp' in closely recorded water, exquisite 'twinkling' pitches and strong metaphors through the ebb and flow of the tides and the tension and release of waves. There is no reason not to use water in a work. But how to make your work original? There is one very easy justification: record your own water sounds. They are immediately personal to you, and your playback of these sounds comes with the guarantee that 'you were there'. It is immediately easier, too, to be able to retrigger the emotions felt as you recorded the water and amplify, extend or modify these by processing and mixing a work. You may think that your recordings of water are not dissimilar to those from any sound download site. Luckily, not all water sounds sound the same and many recordings for download are of very poor quality. Your personal audio recording work will normally be evident.

As mentioned in Alistair MacDonald's composer recollections (see Appendix B.4), make sure you play your work to other people. You need to be there in the room too. That way you suddenly start to listen in the third person (as though you were the other person). Do not assume your piece works. Make something then deliberately break it up and see if you cannot glue it back together in a different order. Finally, you must listen to music by other composers. It is extremely easy to find music on the internet (SoundCloud, Myspace, sonus.ca are three places to start) and many works are available on compact disc and DVD-A (Empreintes DIGITALes, www.electrocd.com/, is a good place to start and clips of most recordings are available). The words electroacoustic and acousmatic have been used freely throughout this book. Look them up in Wikipedia and peruse the history of the genre. Whilst acousmatic music and more rhythmically driven music have merged since the start of the 21st Century, adapting to the changing nature of performance and dissemination of sound art, please consider rhythmically driven music a subset (and a highly focused subset too) of free sound art. As mentioned in Section 1.8.2, we have a strong affinity to 'naturalness' in sound. Pitch, therefore, the harmonic structuring of partials, is clearly something we can easily latch on to. Rhythm and pulse suggest machines (which, for the most part, we detest) but pulse in music is ubiquitous and alludes to the pulse of life and the dance.

Nobody is going to expect to get up and dance to your experimental water-based sonic art (you never know!), but even streams, rivers and dripping taps have a natural pulse. Breaking into and out of full-on pulse is as hard as leaving a solid steady-state drone. Given that a standard electroacoustic piece can vary in duration from three to thirty minutes, pitch and rhythm focus may well be devices that carve out the form of your work. It is very easy to create a pulse-based lattice and not have regular repetitions. You maintain drive without suggesting a clinical structure. With quasi-pulsed granulation it is possible to obtain a sense of pulse whilst changing many other parameters. In my own work, *Dreaming of the Dawn* (Moore, 2004), there is a passage that, in the programme notes for the work, is likened to 'the interplay of clutch, accelerator, gear shift: we are propelled forwards but there is a constant acceleration, deceleration as we move up and down the gears'.

What have I been trying to say here? Imagine the student instrumental composer desperate to write something in the film-score vein but with a limited harmonic language. As their music tends towards a sub-Mozartian chamber sound, not only do you question what they are trying to say but you wonder if they have ever listened to any Mozart or looked at his scores! The same applies to music technology and so-called popular beat-based styles. This style of music is *very* hard to do! It is also extremely difficult to force electroacoustic music into this genre, but potentially easier to gradually hybridise the two and, in so doing, create something original.

3.6 Revisiting the Mix

The theory of opposites presents us with some broad-brush recipes linking perceived acousmatic-potential with one or more techniques for arresting that potential. In Section 2.9 we mentioned that sounds developed and stored would rarely act alone in a mix: they may form composite objects on a short timescale or may be layered to form textured material. It may sound bizarre to suggest that as composers we have an idea of a mix when we are producing our sounds but this *must* be the case if we are ever to hear a sound and retain it for the purposes of putting it somewhere in our composition (a kind of self-fulfilling prophecy)!

Therefore, it may be reasonable to assume that as we are developing sounds we are defining frameworks of articulation, often between polar boundaries, upon which we loosely hang our material in the mix. We hint at these through presentation of extremes (the most obvious being a loud opening gesture versus a fade to nothing at the end, examples that can be found in many works of electroacoustic music and across many other genres) and traverse along these paths using the time-varying nature of many processing functions available to us. Section 3.5 justified the originality of your work through the ownership of *your sounds*. Composition is a time-based experience; an experience of the finished product for the audience, but for you, during the process it is the experience of a multidimensional space, perhaps even the definition of a multidimensional space. Imagine walking into a room with only bare walls and the ability to decorate it to your own taste. You would paint, light, add objects to further define the space, making it liveable. Now what if you had to drop the walls into place? Here we return to our thoughts on environments (Section 1.8). The building analogy for mixing our composition is very similar to the object-oriented programming practice analogy. Both are a means of creating objects and structuring relationships between them. Both imply and require the setting of constraints. What are these constraints and how do we go about locating them, putting them in place and working within them? Constraints are partially defined by our exploration. It is a chicken and egg scenario: in order to find out how far to go to put the fence up, we have to go that far out (but this is why we experiment and reject material). Constraints are the boundaries of our expression – what we are trying to say to the listener and what lies in between are the subtleties. Mixing becomes a balancing act where we tip the scales in one or more directions then find ways to come back to equilibrium. And this is where it gets personal.

Our constraints are clearly the poles of our definitions. If we move from pole to pole within a piece we could quickly introduce a level of redundancy that effectively negates our understanding of these poles in the first place. Therefore, it is often a useful strategy to limit the number of dimensions (pole pairs) explored in depth within a piece. This simple strategy immediately poses problems because one of the grand scale pole pairs is *texture/gesture*: the division of time between long/sustained and short/discrete. Works where gestured material sits within or on top of textured or drone-based material can often sound unmatched despite the very natural concept of foreground and background. This is potentially a legacy hang-up from note-based music where chords and pedal points have set up a hierarchy of speed of change. It is, however, something that is frustratingly difficult to resolve in electroacoustic music, perhaps even more so as a work's duration increases. Composers that have managed to explore this particular boundary include François Bayle. In many of his larger-form pieces, the sheer timescales used require gesture to be subsumed into texture. Gestures, unless repeated heavily, are simply not sufficient to act as 'themes' once durations extend beyond certain limits (and these limits must vary depending upon the spectral content of the gestures and textures being worked on). Gesture after gesture after gesture leads to redundancy if not carefully managed, as does gesture–texture–gesture–texture. A work with highly defined sections of gesture and texture becomes obvious. You can no doubt see where we are going here. Suffice it to say, having some redundancy to create structure and hierarchy and to give the listener time to relax is good; having too much will be less good. Knowing where to draw this line is a matter of experience.

If you limit yourself too far you might find yourself slipping back into an unambitious, concept-driven world that whilst on the outside seems 'challenging' is, in fact rather lacklustre. Take, for example, the wonderful work by Alvin Lucier *I am Sitting in a Room* (1969). This piece takes a text and plays it into a room, rerecording it at the same time. This new tape is then played and rerecorded, and so on. ... (a bit like photocopying a photocopy, etc.) Interestingly, the prescriptive score leaves the interpreter with an opportunity to make a piece of short or long duration depending upon the choice of text. What happens is the acoustic properties of the room act like a resonant filter and after a number of iterations of the text, intelligibility is lost and one hears 'the room'. There is a reason why this piece (especially in its 45:21 original version) does not get played too often. Once the effect is known there really is no more to the piece than the process. However, analyses of inner details do exist (Broening, 2006), and as a concept piece (not an acousmatic piece of sound art) it is a masterstroke in the understanding of time and place.

3.7 A Very Obvious Conclusion

If you have some recorded sound, have taken some time to read but a fraction of this book and have experimented with any of the software mentioned in Chapter 2, unless you have given up, you might be enjoying your ability to shape sound (and time). Composition is an ongoing, lifelong process and, barring expensive microphones, sound recording devices, loudspeakers and computers, can be absolutely cost free. We hope you continue to enjoy composing and continue to develop your compositional style, and we ask that you make sure you communicate this pleasure, through pieces, performances, social networks, emails, books or conversation to any and all interested parties. If you want to start using the USSS tools now, please have fun! If you want to carry on reading, Chapters 4 and 5 investigate multichannel composition and probe some wonderful examples of electroacoustic music.

Notes

1. ftp://ftp.shef.ac.uk/pub/uni/projects/cmd/guit_and_voc/speech-test.wav.
2. Vicissitude is the continuous development of sound through morphology; displacement is a rougher transitional phase.

References

Broening, B. (2006). Alvin Lucier's *I am Sitting in a Room*. In Simoni, M., ed., *Analytical Methods of Electroacoustic Music*, pages 89–110. London: Routledge.

Harrison, J. (1982). *Klang*. Évidence matérielle IMED 0052 pub. 2000.

Lewis, A. (1992–93). *Scherzo*. SCD 28046 pub. 2002.

Lucier, A. (1969). *I am Sitting in a Room*. LCD1013 pub. 1990.

MacDonald, A. (2007). *Equivalence*. Personal issue.

Moore, A. (2004). *Dreaming of the Dawn*. Reve de l'aube IMED 0684 pub. 2006.

Parmegiani, B. (1977). *Dedans Dehors*. InaGRM, also from www.electrocd.com/.

Smalley, D. (1986). Spectro-morphology and structuring processes. In Emmerson, S., ed., *The Language of Electroacoustic Music*, pages 61–93. London: Macmillan.

Smalley, D. (1997). Spectromorphology: explaining sound-shapes. *Organised Sound*, 2(02):107–26.

Chapter 4

Multichannel Composition

Student: I'm in the 7.1 studio. Is the composition process any different to working in stereo?
Teacher: No, but it's at least twice the amount of effort and (in this case) four times the file size.

4.1 Composing in a Multichannel Studio

4.1.1 Just how different is it?

In many respects the teacher's comments here are apposite. The sound probably still dictates what needs to be done to it. In a multichannel studio this now becomes slightly more explicit. If we think about 'space', a sound may now live behind the front stereo pair (with reverberation and equalisation) but it may also now live physically behind us (in a pair of loudspeakers that surround us; the typical 5.1 or 7.1 surround speakers). We 'place' this sound depending upon a sense of 'distance', often in a relationship with sounds in front of us.

This chapter will consider how sound may be placed and moved through a fixed loudspeaker studio (it does not really matter what configuration of loudspeakers you have but you do need to consider the 'architecture' of the studio). It will also consider how you may develop sounds prior to mixing that enable you to take advantage of having many more channels of 'information' (independent sound tracks).

There are many different 'methods' of multichannel mixing and manipulation. From quadraphonic to Dolby Atmos to Ambisonics, it is possible to record in multichannel, manipulate 'N' channels and mix to a variety of output specifications. This chapter will work with those environments most commonly seen in electroacoustic studios: 5.1, 7.1 and 8.0. However, many of the manipulations are simply extensions of stereo techniques. The important question then becomes, 'what is the difference and is it worth the effort?'

4.2 Multichannel Sound Manipulation

From a technical point of view the opening quotation is correct. Historically an 8.0 studio setup would look something like Figure 4.1 without the centre (C) and bass (low frequency effects, or LFE) speakers. The speakers are Left (L), Right (R), Wide Left (Wl), Wide Right (Wr), Side Left (Sl), Side Right (Sr), Rear Left (Rl) and Rear Right (Rr). For a more traditional surround sound setup like 5.1 or 7.1, the Side Left and Side Right would become Surround Left and Surround Right for 5.1 and the Centre and LFE speakers would come into play. For 7.1 the Side Left and Side Right would remain and the Rear Left and Rear Right would become Surround Left and Surround Right (perhaps again with some movement).

The sub-woofer (LFE) speaker channel is fairly self-explanatory. Using this compositionally has significant implications for performance. You could use it as a means of 'crossing over' the remaining speakers, filtering bass from (in particular) front loudspeakers to the sub. Alternatively you could assume full range for most speakers and use the sub as a special

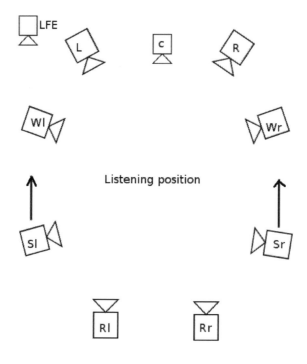

Figure 4.1 Traditional multichannel speaker studio

effect, adding bass when appropriate. Similarly the Centre speaker can be used as 'filler' between Front Left and Front Right, steadying a stereo image, or it can be used as a 'soloist'. In film, it is the dialogue speaker. It is clearly mono, with no opposite number. It can be extremely effective when a texture 'disappears' or 'sucks down' to just this speaker. However, in performance it is likely to be quite a small speaker so it may not balance well with others in the system (or studio).

Panning is clearly the most obvious manipulation. But pan what and why?

4.2.1 Surround sound to polyphony

If a monophonic soundfile was played from all the loudspeakers in a surround studio, localisation would vary depending upon the listening position and output volume for each channel. The listener is fortunate to have sound surrounding them in space. Indeed, the multichannel studio is a very small version of the basic performance system mentioned in Chapter 8. Sound power is increased by sheer quantity of loudspeakers. Vary the balance of each output channel and your sound moves. If the sound is that of a flute playing a tune, our spatial gestures may well seem inappropriate as we expect a flautist to be (probably) front and centre and (probably) static. If the flute is now played more like a shakuhachi, and melody ceases to exist, we focus upon sharp changes in timbre and gestured breathing. This motion of air could well be exaggerated into the space. If, for example, the sound changed to that of a wasp, we would *expect* this sound to be moving. We would expect not only to pan the sound through the space, but apply some Doppler effect as the sound approached and moved away from the central listening position.

Most sounds that move erratically in stereo space can move erratically in multichannel space, but again we must ask 'what is the difference between stereo plus imagination and multichannel?' The answer is that when used subtly, multichannel spaces can enhance the feeling of being in an environment. They can also allow the listener to take a more active role in the process, by freeing them to listen to different sounds from different speakers, clearly located.

Take, for example, a scene at the seaside. You are standing on the beach facing the sea. Ahead you can hear the water. Behind you are people, cars, habitation. There are clear divisions of sound image but yet the environment is totally plausible. Rotate 180 degrees and experience the opposite. In the electroacoustic studio sounds can be as disparate as water and street scenes but their cohabitation has to sound 'natural' in order for an environment to emerge. If this does not happen and the sounds do not fuse, a polyphony of materials begins. The listening situation has immediately become abstract with sound A from speaker 1 and sound B from speaker 5. Unless there is a strong binding narrative to a work using this structuring principle, sound becomes quantified to its position and its presence as *sound* is weakened.

We have moved a long way from Stockhausen's architectonic vision of spatiality as evidenced in works such as *Kontakte*.[1]

Denis Smalley has written extensively about the dimensions and confines of the spaces we might imagine, create and explore through listening (Smalley, 2007). Prior to this very important text, Paul Doornbusch and Peter McIlwain drew from Smalley's earlier work and extrapolated something which is hugely important in the understanding of the multichannel surround sound spatial experience, namely, *the concept of environment.* Their paper on integrating spatial parameters in composition practice (2003) neatly contextualises the practical with the theoretical but does not go into much technical detail.

Smalley (1996; 1997; 2007) articulates various spaces through polar opposites, both in terms of the behaviour of sounds (active/passive) and the spaces they permeate (open/closed) whilst at the same time recognising the confluence of the listening space with the composed space.

Ambrose Field in conversation with Larry Austin in 2001 talked about the links between environment and landscape when working with surround sound fields (Austin, 2001). We find ourselves returning to Trevor Wishart's writings on landscape to confirm how our presence within an ever-changing landscape influences our acousmatic listening experiences, particularly in multichannel. (We can hardly not bring this aspect of our existence to any listening event.)

Eric Clarke calls it as he hears it when listening to a recording of someone eating crisps from a packet. 'I perceive them as perfectly real, but I also perceive that these events are broadcast or recorded, and that the actual events are not happening here and now' (Clarke, 2005, 71). When the sounds are less obvious, Clarke cites Albert Bregman's extensive work on auditory scene analysis. Although this particular quotation is concerned with orchestral music, a real-world situation is described when Bregman differentiates between real and virtual sources in music.

> In a natural forest environment the individual sounds in a succession of frog croaks or footsteps are all treated as coming from the same source, and it is this idea of common sources that holds the succession together. Surely this must also be true for orchestral sounds, except that in the orchestral case the source is not a real one but a virtual one created by the acoustic relations in the music. It is the virtual source that is heard as having this or that quality, as

being high or low, soft or loud, shrill or dull, staccato or legato, rapid or slow-moving. Experiences of real sources and of virtual sources are both examples of auditory streams. They are different not in terms of their psychological properties, but in the reality of the things that they refer to in the world. Real sources tell a true story; virtual sources are fictional. (Bregman, 1994, 460)

In electroacoustic music, the success of the 'virtual' environment (and we know it is virtual as it is emanating from loudspeakers) is achieved through trying to be as 'real' as possible.

4.2.2 Environmental complexity

Furthermore, both spatial and spectral integration play a huge part in Bregman's untangling of the auditory scene. The auditory percepts of masking and fusion become compositional methodologies and the illusory nature of sound streams and conjunctions become the means by which electroacoustic music's diverse sounds can exist in time. All spectral and time-related aspects of sounds come in to play: onset time; frequency range and density; continuity; direction and momentum; and amplitude. Of course, in both Bregman's work and follow-up studies mentioned by Schnupp, Nelken and King in their book *Auditory Neuroscience: Making Sense of Sound* (2011), our perception of the auditory scene must be (and has been thus far) tested through quite rigorous science using scientific sounds (tone clusters, noises) and when venturing into the real world using only speech and Western classical music. It is surely time to broaden this research into our understanding of much more complex scenarios.

Peter Lennox covers enormous philosophical ground when expanding upon the nature of 3D sound and spatiality in music. He questions how *real* an environment can be even when we *know* that environment to be *artificial* (Lennox, 2004). We should bear in mind that this ambiguity is precisely what drives electroacoustic music; the assurance of a reality set against the knowledge of artificiality (in all its forms). Working in multichannel can help achieve this level of assurance more successfully than working in stereo. Lennox distinguishes between surround sound (an immersion more of quantity than quality) and spatial music (an environment where the listener has a significantly greater role). Key to the power of extended spatial formats is that, 'by satisfying *inattentive* processes so that attention is not involuntarily summoned for causal background items, realism could be increased' (Lennox, 2004, 29). Ironically, whilst sounds of perhaps lesser teleological importance may be relegated to the Surround Left and Right speakers, the Centre and LFE speakers can be used exclusively for their prominence and power.

As Lennox proceeds to discuss height information as part of the design of plausible 3D sound fields, we must consider advances in technology such as Ambisonics and proprietary systems such as Dolby Atmos.[2] However, our perceptual separation of events is rooted in reality. Our feather-light sound affords probable placement above the head and is conducive to movement whereas our bass drone has a weight that defies motion, and a sense of all-pervasiveness. As it happens, our perception of frequency in the lower ranges, especially if there is very little articulative content, means that if this sound emerges from the LFE alone, we are unlikely to be bothered about 'spotting' it.

It serves to point out again that humans are predisposed to engage with three-dimensionality in sound worlds from the outset. But equally, it is pointless to imagine that, though using our full real-world listening capabilities when listening to spatial music, we need to be able to identify content sufficiently to be engaged whilst being fully aware that our listening environment exhibits quasi-real-world causalities but is as unreal as can be.[3]

And thus Lennox begins to define the cartoonification of environments.[4]

This cartoonification both simplifies and engages. Imagine using the 'posterise' effect on your favourite picture editor: the outline is sufficient to express the key qualities of the picture. Many of the visual *effects* that are used to heighten an image – motion blur, for example – are not only the most noticeable but subsequently engage the viewer to search for the real object and, in so doing, heighten the meaning behind the image. They are also predominantly used to exaggerate. So here the rule of opposites does not apply, at least to begin with. Certainly, the active sound *must move*. But (applying the rule) it must eventually come to rest.

In untangling our *everyday listening* with our musical (or spectro-morphological) listening we tumble upon two hugely important texts by William W. Gaver (1993a; 1993b). Whilst both papers focus upon our perception and modelling of the real world, Gaver spotlights both the fascination with and conundrum of the acousmatic listening experience. As Harrison and Smalley have consistently pointed out, and indeed as Harrison uses to great effect in many of his works, our tendency to 'source' a sound, no matter what, is strong. Moreover, as Gaver attempts to synthesise the interaction of materials in order to better understand them, he uses the very same tools that model the real world and that electroacoustic composers have to hand: delays and filters, albeit used at a fundamental physical-modelling level. Again, we come full circle to the writings and simulations of Andy Farnell in *Designing Sound* (2010) and Pure Data's own physical modelling synthesis; tools that help us synthesise in order to analyse and in so doing explore beyond the real (by exploring; by switching that dial to 11).

So we might expect our best spatial audio to be something that starts mono and is subsequently manipulated. Garver's first example of 'everyday listening' is the car approaching in darkness. We not only hear the sound of the engine but our perception of direction and distance is aided by the sound's dispersal, reflection and refraction within an expanding cone of appreciation, focusing upon the listener's head and expanding out towards the most significant amplitudes and their surroundings. We are very sensitive to stereo information. The vast majority of speaker systems maintain a symmetry of loudspeakers down the sides of the concert hall. The already information-laden stereo recording is often well suited to expansion in the surround environment.

Peiman Khosravi focuses directly upon the spectral parameters of sound when considering space and many of his deliberations bear importance upon the way we consider the differences between 3D listening and composing spaces (Khosravi, 2012).[5]

Khosravi points to numerous scientific studies evidencing the nature of sound to embody inherent spatial characteristics, but it is when he focuses his attention on texture that his research becomes really interesting. He states that spectral texture can be defined as 'the manner in which spectromorphologies occupy and pattern the extent of spectral space' (Khosravi, 2012, 91). Khosravi evidences this patterning by examining a technique described by Gary Kendall in a paper entitled 'Spatial perception and cognition in multichannel audio for electroacoustic music' (Kendall, 2010). Kendall describes the process of decorrelation across channels through subtle frequency and amplitude modulations of the same sound to enable a more democratic audition of 'image dispersion' so enabling more than simply the person sitting in/near the middle of the room to experience movement. Khosravi implements this idea with the programming language Csound. A more rudimentary version of this spectral disperser is contained within the multichannel USSS toolkit using multiple FFT filters. It is true to say that dispersing partials of a sound relatively evenly around speakers neither breaks the sound up nor affords a spectral 'spread'. As with many effects, a noticeable change is only noticeable when it has perhaps already gone too far. For example, low frequencies to the front, mids in the middle and highs in the rear.

Whilst spectral decorrelation is a technical solution to an aesthetic problem using one sound, this principle can be taken to its extreme when using multiple sounds. With both multichannel composition and sound diffusion a democratisation of space and material should be taken into account. Perhaps the person sitting near the back left *should* have their moment and the person in the middle *should not* be privileged all of the time.

And thus a great deal of speculative and investigative work meets creative practice. The scene is currently one of turmoil but is of great interest to composers. The USSS toolkit now has a number of tools that enable you to work using multiple channels of output and ask similar questions.

4.3 Multichannel Additions to the USSS Toolkit

4.3.1 Multiple inputs, outputs and recorders

In addition to usss.output there are now usss.output4, usss.output6 and usss.output8. Similarly, in addition to usss.sfplay there is usss.sfplay4, usss.sfplay6 and usss.sfplay8, though you will find that usss.sfplay8 will play a file of any number of channels up to and including eight. Figure 4.2 shows the interface of the usss.multipan8 object to a usss.output8. Each output slider controls the gain to the output soundfile. The globalgain only controls the monitoring volume. Do not forget to gradually raise this value (hold the shift key whilst click-dragging the mouse as you require fractional numbers between 0 and 1) else you will not hear anything even though you can see level in the meters.

4.3.2 Movement and gesture manipulation

It is perhaps at this point where compound effects can (and should) be employed. Panning may well just be amplitude-based but an object might move better with additional Doppler shifts in pitch, varying wet–dry reverberation and low-pass filtering related to distance. And if panning a sound manually, consider designing something that allows the addition of a hardware interface such as a graphics tablet. The manual motion of the hand in a 2D grid reacting to a sound's dynamic characteristics is far quicker than a computational algorithm or a wiggle of the mouse.

The speakerpositions are notated between a 0,0 (bottom left) and 1,1 (top right) grid as coordinates and go clockwise from the top left. The multipan object affords simple circular motion but, as can be seen by the additional randomisation to direction, more erratic motion can be obtained.

4.3.3 Multichannel granulation

The usss.granular8 object splits grains to eight outputs.

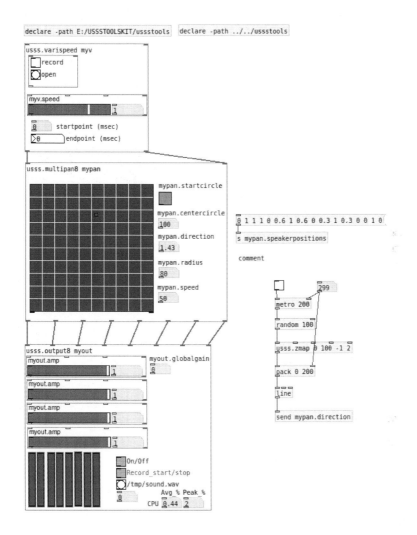

Figure 4.2 `usss.multipan8`

The `usss.granularX` replaces both `usss.granular` and `usss.granular8` as it can have dynamic numbers of channels and grains. It is described in Section 2.2.5. Its output is different to using four `granular` objects with slightly different starting values (so simulating eight-channel undulation) as the perceived undulations are much closer in `usss.granularX`.

4.3.4 Spectral filtering

Filtering across multiple channels can be both subtle and extreme. `usss.fftfilter8` combines four `usss.fftfilter` objects delivering a two-in, eight-out spectral splitter. `usss.makearrays` is a simple extension to set gains for each filter. Of particular interest is the case below where each FFT frequency is randomly multiplied per stereo loudspeaker set. This does give a spectral tilt (though the direction is random each time the tables are filled).

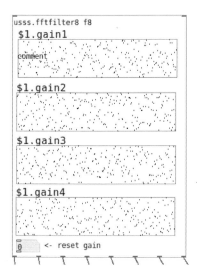

Figure 4.3 `usss.fftfilter8`

4.3.5 Convolution

Convolution of two-in, multiple-out is handled effectively in Blue, building upon the stereo convolution tool either using four stereo files (which can obviously be the same file) or a six- or eight-channel interleaved file. The same convolution file is used for all channels but the start position and slice can be varied. This can be useful for generating a reverberant spread by using very small impulses towards the front and larger impulses towards the rear (similar to using four different reverbs). The visual image of this effect is akin to pinching and picking up a towel laid flat on the floor so that it drapes at different lengths from the pinch point.

4.3.6 *Multiple stereo manipulations*

In an 8.0 studio there is much to be said for repeating the same sound through four stereo effects with slightly different parameters. As the opening quote of this chapter reminds us, the workflow in your programming languages can begin to get a bit messy. You will have noticed that, for the most part, an effect taken from stereo is simply multiplied to fit a multichannel environment.

4.4 The Multichannel Gesture

If we return to the torn flag gestures (Figure 1.14) from Chapter 1 we can assume that components of a gesture will now fade not only in amplitude but in real space. Similarly, 'explosions' may well commence front and centre and evaporate into space, panning and evaporating at different speeds and densities. The potential for a gesture to reverberate away at different durations biased towards the front, side or rear will inform the listener as to the spaces surrounding them. Normally the biggest 'distance' is that receding from the front loudspeakers into a virtual distance, but this need not be the case. Of course the frontal attack with 'fly-away' debris (fast pointillist granulations) can quickly become a cliché. Imagine an explosive firework spreading its debris in the night sky.

4.5 The Multichannel Texture

Assuming a relatively simple multichannel studio of either eight loud-speakers surrounding the listener or 7.1 (six surrounding plus centre and sub), you might simply decide to chop a one-minute stereo granulation into three or four parts and send them to different pairs surrounding the listener. This 'similar but different' approach is often sufficient to create a base texture that, through sheer luck, moves between and across speaker pairs. If you wish to be more precise, you may granulate to multiple channels and then proceed with additional effects (perhaps convolution) across a multichannel file. In a similar way to a stereo texture build, your multichannel texture can take many smaller textures and layer them. Depending upon the level of spectral fusion achieved you will gradually arrive at either a fused complex texture or, as the fusion breaks down, a polyphony.

It is important to remember that the spaces between your loudspeakers in the studio are as small as they are ever going to be. Any performance will extend these distances and may create audible discontinuities in your panning.

4.6 Multichannel Mixing

Here the gestures and textures in mono, stereo, quad, six and eight channels all become 'players' in the creation of a new and increasingly complex environment. The most common multichannel studios tend to remain 'flat' in that their loudspeakers are on one horizontal plane. Therefore, the frontal pairs (main/wide or main/side) are always going to be the best to depict extensions to the virtual distant and the vertical planes. It is always best to consider the side and surround speakers of secondary importance and as you gradually ramp this importance up, note how far you want to disengage your frontal 'view' with sounds appearing behind the head.

This immersion and sense of environment is seemingly one of the most engaging aspects of multichannel composition, and an aspect that has received very little research. As has been mentioned before, *when* the surround environment becomes cacophonous is very much up to personal taste, but there is definitely scope to go beyond the level of sonic polyphony offered by stereo, both in terms of unsubtle accumulations and subtle extensions out of the stereo world.

4.7 Multichannel Performance

Multichannel performance was briefly discussed in Section 2.9.8. Further empirical work has taken place with the Birmingham ElectroAcoustic Sound Theatre (BEAST) where multichannel works have been diffused across multiple loudspeaker groups (Wilson and Harrison, 2010).

4.8 Listening in Multichannel

As we experience new listening environments we can re-educate our stereo listening experience to untangle more complex environments that are squeezed into a headphone space.

Ultimately, listening in multichannel is akin to viewing a film in 3D. The 'wow' factor quickly dissipates: it is not the snowflakes, rain or swords that emerge in front of the screen that impress. Rather it is the depth of field and sense of perspective that makes 3D television worthwhile. This is also the case with audio. The fly-around sounds can quickly become a sickly roller-coaster ride. Instead it is the sense of environment and immersion that make for a more engaging listening experience.

Notes

1. However, this quadraphonic work bristled with naturally sounding spatial articulation as the sounds were naturally articulated and it is perfectly

reasonable to assume that if Stockhausen was listening to the sounds as he spatialised them, he must have felt them to work even though he was following a strict plan of action.

2. See www.dolby.com/us/en/experience/dolby-atmos.html for more information.

3. This unreality is the created soundscape, not the fact that everything is coming from loudspeakers.

4. For more recent and concise work, see Lennox and Myatt (2011). Of particular interest is Plato's Allegory of the Cave where the subject is initially given an outline of the world through shadows and is then invited to experience the real world. We are fortunately not emerging into a fully sensed world from a sense-deprived environment, nor are we leaving our knowledge and experience at the door when we enter the concert venue.

5. In addition Khosravi has completed spectral/spatial tools that use both Csound and Max/MSP. He clearly sees distinct ties between spectral manipulation and our perception of plausible environments and has used theory, programming and composition to investigate these areas during his doctoral studies.

References

Austin, L. (2001). Sound diffusion in composition and performance practice II: An interview with Ambrose Field. *Computer Music Journal*, 25(4):21–30.

Bregman, A. S. (1994). *Auditory Scene Analysis: The Perceptual Organization of Sound*. Cambridge, MA: The MIT Press.

Clarke, E. F. (2005). *Ways of Listening: An Ecological Approach to the Perception of Musical Meaning*. Oxford: Oxford University Press.

Doornbusch, P. and McIlwain, P. (2003). Integrating spatial parameters in composition practice. In *Converging Technologies: Australian Computer Music Assoc. Conf*. Perth, Western Australian Academy of Performing Arts.

Gaver, W. W. (1993a). How do we hear in the world? Explorations in ecological acoustics. *Ecological Psychology*, 5(4):285–313.

Gaver, W. W. (1993b). What in the world do we hear? An ecological approach to auditory event perception. *Ecological Psychology*, 5(1):1–29.

Kendall, G. S. (2010). Spatial perception and cognition in multichannel audio for electroacoustic music. *Organised Sound*, 15(03):228–38.

Khosravi, P. (2012). *Spectral spatiality in the acousmatic listening context*. PhD thesis, City University London.

Lennox, P. (2004). *The philosophy of perception in artificial auditory environments: Spatial sound and music*. PhD thesis, University of York.

Lennox, P. and Myatt, T. (2011). Perceptual cartoonification in multi-spatial sound systems. Paper presented at 17th International Conference on Auditory Display, Budapest, Hungary.

Schnupp, J., Nelken, I., and King, A. (2011). *Auditory Neuroscience: Making Sense of Sound*. Cambridge, MA: The MIT Press.

Smalley, D. (1996). The listening imagination: listening in the electroacoustic era. *Contemporary Music Review*, 13(2):77–107.

Smalley, D. (1997). Spectromorphology: explaining sound-shapes. *Organised Sound*, 2(02):107–26.

Smalley, D. (2007). Space-form and the acousmatic image. *Organised Sound*, 12(01):35–58.

Wilson, S. and Harrison, J. (2010). Rethinking the BEAST: Recent developments in multichannel composition at Birmingham ElectroAcoustic Sound Theatre. *Organised Sound*, 15(03):239–50.

Chapter 5

Examples from the Repertoire

> There can be no synthesis without analysis but you have to do
> something in order to move forward!

5.1 Introduction

This chapter will suggest a number of listening opportunities and relate
works and composers to techniques and theories presented in previous
chapters. It uses the first person in places as the works are described
(often very succinctly) by myself and it is essential that the 'responsibility'
for this interpretation is clear. Compositions are taken in alphabetical
order. Throughout this book I talk about what a sound means to a
composer and to a listener. This is not something the composer injects
into the sound, rather this is something the sound says to us. And
it cannot nor should not be changed such is the force this primary
perception has upon us. Careful construction of sounds go to reinforce
this perception and build a pathway of listening. As time moves from
second-by-second to minute-by-minute we must feel taken on a journey.
One that is permanently in motion or one that leaves us in a place to
explore at leisure. Great music helps you articulate your imagination.
These works exemplify this trait.

5.1.1 Listening to the works

Clearly, it is pointless reading about these works without listening
to at least some of the music mentioned. It is hoped that you can
find many of these works either in their entirety or in 'clip' form
at the Empreintes DIGITALes website (www.electrocd.com and more
recently the streaming site electrotheque.com). Plenty of historic examples can also be found on YouTube and other broadcasting sites.

5.2 Examples

5.2.1 Monty Adkins, Five Panels (2009)

Monty Adkins has adopted the idea of 'the album as work' and in so doing returned to pitch and drone as ground, bleak harmonies of reminiscence and loss, and subtle dream states coming from a beautiful tableaux of sounds. The CD notes from *Five Panels* (2009) neatly contextualise the audio panels with Mark Rothko's work and the links are clear to hear (on a surface level the stasis is there; a certain sense of timelessness). What I ask myself with this set of pieces is why they are so beautiful, time after time? There is more to this than the sense of melancholy set up by minor harmonies and lightly plucked electric bass harmonics, more than the analogy of contemplation that is common between this and Rothko's painting. In fact, Rothko's works are, for me, quite abstract. They are not a Rorschach test of my inner depth in that I do not see myself in them. Instead they suggest shape, colour, texture and time. *Five Panels* articulates its time, no matter how much it might try not to. There may even be some synaesthesia at work mapping colour to sound in *Five Panels*. And notwithstanding the courage of producing such intimate audio works, the album is extremely approachable because of the work's context, pitch rootedness and a well balanced envelopment. This album was very successful and Adkins approached his next album, *Fragile.Flicker.Fragment* (2011), in a similar vein, using the sounds of a musical box to conjure our past in the opening piece *Memory Box*.

5.2.2 Monty Adkins, Memory Box (2011)

There exists a beautiful technique at work in these pieces. What I perceive is a 'many layers' approach. Most apparent is the drone root, though it may not be physically present all of the time. Over this one perceives individual bell hits, some of which are extended by long reverberation or stretching and layering. Consequently the sense of near/far helps set up a huge, but essentially empty, space within which there are many small elements that help cement this environment. Even the addition of mild distortion to some of the drones adds to the worn/sepia-tinted nostalgic feel. It is important to consider the mastering of this work.[1] A work with such sinusoidal drones could feel oppressive. This has grandeur in both breadth, depth and volume. Its envelopment is best when the power of the bass comes through. This, as physics tells us, requires a fair degree of volume. At which point, composers should always be very careful with high frequencies, which require significantly less amplitude to sound as powerful at similar volume. Monty Adkins has this balance just right.

5.2.3 Natasha Barrett, Trade Winds (2004–2006)

Continuing the idea of work as album, Natasha Barrett's *Trade Winds* presents narratives of the sea and returns to a source sound which many acousmatic composers meet at some point or other: water. Barrett is a composer with an enormous body of work. She spends a great deal of time spatialising her material, often using a technique called Ambisonics. One advantage of Ambisonics is that it captures three-dimensionality and is extremely reducible, retaining the essence of the spaces recorded. Therefore this stereo disc takes you to the cold Norway coast, puts you on that boat and gives you all those emotions of the power and enormity of the sea. The additional sound sources, in particular the voice, are granulated with the sense that they are on the sea, slow then fast, becalmed then rough. This disc, whilst delighting in sound as Barrett consistently does, presents its narratives very clearly. To create a piece of 52 minutes duration, one perhaps requires a 'path' that is not just based upon sound and its transformations. François Bayle uses distinct movements, 'climates' and 'scenes', Ambrose Field incorporates live performance and *Trade Winds* gives us folklore and Jules Verne's 20000 leagues, fused with Barrett's own recordings and transformations. It is perhaps an acousmatic opera with all the power of a *Peter Grimes*.[2]

5.2.4 François Bayle, L'Expérience Acoustique (1969–1972)

1. 'L'aventure du cri' (The adventure of the cry)
2. 'Le langage des fleurs' (The language of flowers)
3. 'La preuve par le sens' (Proof by meaning)
4. 'L'epreuve par le son' (Ordeal by sound)
5. 'La philosophie du non' (The philosophy of no)

Bayle's work spans some 50 years or more. His works are often suites and comprise whole discs, so if you are listening you must be prepared for the long haul. And the early work clearly has an analogue 'feel' to it both through its synthesised drones and through its atmospheric 'scenes'. Themes repeat and are slow to evolve but they will haunt you, not least because the synthetic is beautifully merged into the real, making the soundscapes pass as though in a dream. The mixing is so well done that all the high frequency analogue drones feel comfortable. There is a unique 'human' feel to this work.

Despite this, birds open the work in the first movement, 'L'aventure du cri'. In 'Le langage des fleurs' we again perceive instruments, loops (and you can hear the joins, which is a very honest approach) and synthesis. The synthesis has a very instrumental feel to it. I would recommend at this point viewing some of Bayle's collaborations with Piotr Kamler (b.1936).[3] This gives you a sense of the surreality of the music. Surreal in works like *Coeur de secours* (1973), atmospheric in earlier works like *Galaxie*,[4] but in *L'Expérience Acoustique* we have music from the film *Lignes et points* from 1961/1966 where the image and sound appear much more abstract as they depict the title of the work. The music for the film is superposed on top of additional drone-based material (which accommodates these audio interjections perfectly). This work has a very interior feel to it. We are in a closed, slightly claustrophobic, space.

'La preuve par le sens' brings us closer to the world of another of Bayle's monstrous compilations (*Son Vitesse-Lumière*) with shorter scintillating granulations of sound and greater density of mixing allowing for slower textural growth and decay. 'La langue inconnue', the first movement of this section, was first performed at the Bourges Festival in 1971. The pulsating drones articulated by fluttering bird warbles might well have been an influence on Denis Smalley, whose work *Pentes* (1974) has a very similar, nocturnal feel.

And at this point, Bayle takes the idea of evolution even further in 'L'epreuve par le son'. The Bourges festival (sadly no more) used to run its evening concerts in the Palais Jacques Coeur courtyard under a moonlit sky with the bats dancing amongst the stars. This work mirrors this sense of space. Finally, 'La philosophie du non' returns to a more articulated world but is nevertheless dark, mysterious and rather ominous despite the gentle ringing of bells.

I am particularly intrigued by 'Métaphore and lignes et points' which has an eerie simplicity to it and sounds its age whilst at the same time remaining quite novel and engaging.

5.2.5 *François Bayle,* Erosphère *(1978–1980)*

Moving ahead almost ten years, the quality of material and subtleties of language (especially repetition) have improved markedly. In both 'Tremblement de terre trés doux' (Very soft earthquake) and 'Toupie dans le ciel' (Spinning top in the sky) (1980), the focus has shifted somewhat to recorded and manipulated sound interspersed (again in multiple shorter segments or movements) with drone landscapes of unbelievable beauty. Again, a nocturnal environment is suggested, particularly with these dronescapes, which make a nod to the popular music industry in 'Toupie dans le ciel'.

François Bayle's publications

Bayle's œuvre spans some 20 solo discs from his own Magison label alongside a full box-set of the complete works (in stereo only) published by the GRM (2012). For a complete discography see the Empreintes

DIGITALes website.[5] It is important to note that Bayle is now revisiting his key works with the assistance of electroacoustic musicologists and composers like Isabel Pires who are completing fully interactive visual transcriptions alongside extensive documentation. *Erosphère* already exists in this format (book and CD-ROM) and *L'Expérience Acoustique* appeared in 2013.

5.2.6 David Berezan, Baoding (2002)

David Berezan directs the studios at Manchester University and, like Jonty Harrison (with whom he completed a PhD), the starting point for a musical work is quite often one particular sound. For *Baoding* (2002) it is the sounds of Chinese Baoding balls. From here, Berezan conjures the mystical world of China using additional sounds of Beijing and Kun opera. Berezan is a master of accelerating patterns leading to cadences. This is a tried and trusted technique and the basic archetype is described in Section 1.16 with a simple Pd patch to create these gestures in Section 1.17; usss.dynamicdelay will also render some of these shapes. Given that this sonic archetype is also common to Chinese opera, the dynamic fusions created give the work a very strong sense of dramaturgy and sound utterly convincing. The work is in three very distinct sections and starts and ends with its source material.

5.2.7 Manuella Blackburn, Jivari (2012–2013)

It is interesting to compare *Baoding* with *Jivari* by Manuella Blackburn. This work has remarkable similarities to the Berezan not least in its use of accelerating profiles leading to strong gestural hits (this time from a tabla), but also in its sectional form. This work sounds relaxed, despite all the filigree electroacoustic elements that adorn each gesture. The sources are honestly declared throughout yet it is clearly a work for fixed medium playback.

5.2.8 John Chowning, Turenas (1972)

We hear the filigree nature of computer-generated sound as we move to the works of John Chowning. *Turenas* can be called computer music as the computer is central to the calculation of all aspects of the sound. The vast majority of this chapter (and indeed book) pays tribute to Western European electroacoustic music. However, without pioneers such as Chowning not only would the world of synthesisers be a different place but our electroacoustic world would not have evolved as quickly as it did. This piece employs frequency modulation as a musical method.[6] *Turenas* is an anagram of 'natures' and yet it could not sound more synthetic.

However, computer synthesis tended to model the real – notably the voice and bells. If you read the programme notes for Chowning's Wergo disc (1972) you see musical ideas and aesthetic goals but also plenty of technical information and trivia (the use of the music language SCORE and Music IV, the PDP-1 and IBM 7094 mainframes, etc., key identifiers of a modernist approach, something rather avant-garde requiring heavy explanation).

These were times when computer music programming was extremely time-consuming and highly experimental. *Turenas* investigated (for want of a better term) musical sound synthesis and spatialisation and was (for the time) a pioneering work of digital synthesis. It also happens to have a highly balanced sense of space using panning and reverberation, even in the stereo version, and because of the synthetic nature of the sounds, transformations are often seamless.

5.2.9 Francis Dhomont, Forêt profonde (1994–1996)

I have mentioned the unique way certain sounds immediately invoke (for many of us) memories of our past. Francis Dhomont uses music boxes (or something very similar) in the opening of his acousmatic melodrama *Forêt profonde*. Based upon the writings of child psychologist Bruno Bettelheim, *Forêt profonde* confronts us with the adult that relives his or her childhood and remembers the (continued) fascination for the excitement and hidden danger of the unknown (another strong metaphor used in acousmatic music). Bettleheim's work *The Uses of Enchantment* (1976) examined fairy tales for the way they cloak stark emotions behind fanciful, bizarre, monstrous and magical myths and machinations. *Forêt profonde* is an album-sized work in movements, and maintains the listener's interest through the use of multiple voices and texts drawn into and out of 'cotton wool' drones and highly phased granulations. It approaches multiple audiences through the use of numerous languages and, in so doing, reminds us that no matter what the language, we *know* what 'once upon a time', 'it's nothing my child' and 'go to sleep' means.

5.2.10 Francis Dhomont, Novars (1989)

Although part of a larger sequence of works released in 2001,[7] *Novars* (1989) first appeared on the disc *Mouvances Metaphors* in 1991. It is an homage through sound to both the composers and music of the Ars Nova[8] period and Pierre Schaeffer (a man of similar pioneering spirit to the composers of that time). It resamples short sound objects of Schaeffer and has a beautiful sense of open and close through filters and chorus effects. The painterly 'swish' of the brush is also clearly audible (*jetés-glissés*). Dhomont is not afraid to incur grain in his pitch transformations. Indeed, it is this 'rough around the edges' feeling that is sometimes most appealing. No matter what, the soundworld is delicate and exquisite.

Whilst one must not forget Pierre Scaheffer and Pierre Henry, the founding fathers of acousmatic music, Francis Dhomont, François Bayle and Bernard Parmegiani are the great masters in my view. It has been my distinct pleasure and honour to have heard these composers perform live and to have known them personally. It was with great sadness to the community of electroacoustic music that Bernard Parmegiani passed away on 21 November 2013.

5.2.11 *François Donato,* Annam *(1993)*

François Donato's work *Annam* is influenced by François Bayle and the GRM but this is not surprising as Donato worked there from 1989 to 2005. This work is heavily synthetic (but synthetic probably by means of heavily processed natural recordings) and yet very instrumental and orchestral in nature. Donato continues to compose acousmatic music but seems to have embraced multimedia (dance, installations, etc.) over the past decade. His music is well documented at his current blog site.[9]

Annam is a long work at some 20 minutes and it is primarily because of a key trigger sound at 7 minutes in that I enjoy this piece so much. One of the GRM's early pedagogical works was a CDROM entitled *La musique electroacoustique* (Ina-GRM, 2000). It contained a substantial quantity of archive material (including such rarities as Varèse talking about music) and also a 'mini-studio' – essentially a cut-down version of three GRMTools – all for around £20. The CDROM opened with one of Donato's beautiful sound objects drawn from *Annam*. I have consequently heard this sound a thousand times and it is always useful to hear it back in its musical context.

5.2.12 *Robert Dow,* Precipitation within Sight *(2007)*

Like Barrett's *Trade Winds*, Robert Dow's *Precipitation within Sight* is also influenced by the sea and Dow takes us to one of those subtle extremes where sources and transformations mingle in such a way that we are clearly 'there' and yet 'not there'. I would not say that this was another dream scenario, although that sense of disassociation is often easy to create and I continue to do it all the time – it is part and parcel of creating a distance between the composer and listener. Rather, these distances serve to heighten our listening to a cavernous space, an open space, and the influence of the tides and weather. As for techniques, Dow likes to keep his sources very clean so I suspect there's a good deal of equalisation and some convolution. I have always liked Robert's work and like it more as I become accustomed to its stark contrasts. My reading of his work is very similar to other blog-based reviews, which are also extremely positive.[10]

Robert Dow is a close friend with whom I have learned a great deal about composition, performance and academic life. Robert left the University of Edinburgh in August 2013. He will, I am sure, be sorely missed.

5.2.13 Louis Dufort, Gen_3 (2007)

Louis Dufort bridges a divide between historical Canadian acousmatic music (Francis Dhomont at the University of Montreal, followed by Normandeau and his contemporaries) and the modern world of glitch, sound and concept art, and multimedia. Dufort works with diverse forces and also curates large electroacoustic concerts in Montreal. *Gen_3* is therefore perhaps not indicative of his work as a whole. It does however provide a link between the old and the new and a suitable segue from Dhomont's *Novars* as it also borrows from that work (as *Novars* itself was a borrowing). The work therefore has a purpose dictated by its sources; these are not just 'samples'. And whilst Dufort states that *Gen_3* is not an homage *per se*, this intimate act of respect through sound does indeed reanimate the cycle of sound for a third and new generation.

5.2.14 Beatriz Ferreyra, Murmureln (2003)

At just over four minutes this short piece presents something rather magical. It is an excellent example of montage, sound selection and humour in music. A rhythmic dance form normally pounded out by instruments and immortalised by Astor Piazzolla is here exchanged for samples. Were this to be done with arbitrary samples the result would be disastrous. The important point here is that the samples' shape and timing result in the form becoming an audible result, not the driving force. This is an electroacoustic tango! After moving to Paris to complete her musical studies with Nadia Boulanger, Beatriz Ferreyra worked for Pierre Schaeffer at the Groupe de Recherches Musicales and was credited on Pierre Schaeffer's *Solfage de l'Objet Sonore*. Do not expect laugh-out-loud humour, but this might just put a smile on your face. (Where have you heard a cockerel in electroacoustic music before?)

5.2.15 Ambrose Field, STORM! (2006)

Ambrose Field's *STORM!* was described as 'a hard hitting, post-industrial soundscape.'[11] It plays upon musical imagery: drones are 'heavy' and 'dark', gestures are very sharp. The allusion to war is both covert and overt: overt in the use of 'storm' in the title and reference to Operation Desert Storm in the programme notes; covert in the subtle (and not so subtle) incorporation of the real and unreal. It is a highly imaginative depiction of decay, of a 'dysfunctional urban world'. That this music also has strong ties to the soundworlds of rock and roll is also interesting. The cutaways from scene to scene are perhaps a little disjunct but the full sequence as an album of some 40 minutes mirrors the formal structures of the Bayle pieces and with far more surrealistic titles![12] This is a work where identification and imagination all fuse together, and over some 40 minutes we hear a huge variety of sounds, some far more memorable than others. Poignant moments are few and far between but welcome when they come. Movement 10, 'Tombstone catalogue', is one of very few pieces in the genre to generate rhythmically structured passages successfully. The final movement 'Hurricane Ridge' again presents us with sounds and spaces that switch from the vast to the intimate. Trigger sounds stand out in this movement too, notably a very large bass glissando which then permeates the latter third of the work and gives an overall darkness to the piece.

5.2.16 Ambrose Field and John Potter, Being Dufay (2009)

I am breaking with my vow to talk only about pure acousmatic music but this work stands out, not least because it 'reinvents' Dufay and contextualises music of the past with respect, but also because it shows how Field seems to completely reinvent himself as he moves from project to project. Being Dufay is as slick as STORM! is rough and ready, though both are immaculately edited works. I am not talking about process, merely the practicalities of the projects composers are faced with. Field is the last person it seems to ever break the techniques of electroacoustic composition to push boundaries. The sound quality is always crystal clear in all his works. Here, whilst the harmonies might rest upon relatively simple drones, melodic and harmonic progressions are both 'instrumental' and 'electronic', providing an appropriate and approachable fusion of the live and electronic (including the voice of tenor, John Potter, a fellow colleague of Field's at York University). Potter's voice is set against drones that intermingle with synthetic material. The sense of space and contrast through reverberation and convolution, and equalisation of high frequency gestured material, provide an interesting metaphor for the old and the new. The album toured numerous festivals throughout the world in 2009/2010 and though it lends itself to a 'reflective' rather than easy listen, it approaches new audiences and, in so doing, breaks down some of the perceived barriers of electroacoustic music (perhaps most notably, a link with the human body or spirit).

5.2.17 Gilles Gobeil, Ombres, espaces, silences... (2005)

Gilles Gobeil is well known for his industrial soundscapes and the incorporation of live instruments (in particular the ondes martenot) deep within the electroacoustic medium. With *Ombres, espaces, silences ...* Gobeil, in a similar but vastly different way to Field, revisits the music of the past to conjure the music of the future. We are in dark times again: drones, disembodied voices, reverberation and the use of canopies at high and low frequencies suggest the spaces of the distant past (and the title is naturally a giveaway). Gobeil also presents us with real/unreal dilemma scenes where we think we can 'see' in the darkness. That sense of discovery is what drives this work and it is again the result of a highly imaginative and 'visionary' composer. Gobeil likes to paint – and paint big! His performances are often loud and monumental, dark yet colourful. The sense of the industrial clearly applies to *Ombres, espaces, silences...* You can hear the sound forge at work. The pace is for the most part slow and evolutionary, but again, as with the vast majority of these works, the acoustic setting takes you to a new space and, from there, on a journey of discovery. And we notice a common musical thread between some of the works reviewed thus far: looking back to the music of the past (and in particular the distant past).

5.2.18 Jonty Harrison, ...et ainsi de suite... (1992)

Jonty Harrison's work *...et ainsi de suite...* presents us with some very clear examples of the electroacoustic musician's ear at work and is immediately different to those pieces where a distant 'space' was suggested. Here, from the outset the space is very close and personal. *...et ainsi de suite...* is a suite of movements and Harrison is very forthcoming in his programme notes as to the processes and devices employed. The sources, taken from some 'rough-textured wine glasses', are developed through repetition using precursors of the granulation methods mentioned in Section 2.2.5. The programs he used are of historical significance: ETIR, stretch, and BRAG, brassage (granulation with larger grain sizes), from the GRM.

A common technique taught in colleges is to record a sound with close microphones so as to capture all the interior and normally unheard sounds of an object (see Section 1.2.1). Then, through transformation, and juxtaposition, to set this object in relief, highlighting at the same time the propensity of the object for transformation and the composer's skill in transformation. One of the techniques Parmegiani used to great effect in his suites *Dedans Dehors* and *De Natura Sonorum* was to contrast real souds with synthetic equivalents (for example, water drops with filtered attacks in 'Jeux', the second movement of *Dedans Dehors*).

Here it sounds as though Harrison has some glass transformations that are very synthetic and which mix very well with a pool of synthetic pulsed drones and 'swooshes'. Harrison has spent a great deal of time on the details (for example, the interior pitch glissandi when glasses rub together) and there is a lot of raw (though heavily edited) material in *...et ainsi de suite...* Some of the more gritty filter effects seem to be drawn from his previous experiences with the vocoder, an instrument which allowed an input sound to be filtered by a live source (normally the voice). These techniques can be recreated using cross-synthesis methods mentioned in Section 2.2.9 though, as with analogue systems, you may wish to work 'live' with a microphone so that you can alter your voice as you experience the original source recordings.

5.2.19 Jonty Harrison, Klang (1982)

Jonty Harrison is pivotal in the development of electroacoustic music in the United Kingdom. In particular, the blossoming, from the early 1990s onwards, of acousmatic and electroacoustic studies in academia as his students took positions in mainstream universities (Stollery, Lewis, MacDonald, Hyde, Adkins, Berezan, Moore to name but a few examples of composers who have studied with him and gone on to have careers in academia). Therefore it is important to mention his most well-known work, *Klang*. From a simple delight in the sonorous nature of things (in this case a casserole lid and pot) to the need to shape and extend this new world with editing, mixing and analogue manipulations, *Klang* sums up the composition process in a nutshell. The textures created through juxtapositions of the synthetic (oscillating blips) with clear manipulations of the source (a slowed-down version of the lid rocking against the pot) immediately ask the listener to accept the processes involved and understand the hybrid sonic result. Luckily many of these transformations retain a huge spatial dimension, which helps excite the visual senses. And, as another point of contact with an audience unfamiliar with electroacoustic music, the sustained pitch spaces are evidently harmonic (often forming diminished chords) which, whilst ambiguous harmonically, tie the listener to common Western classical associations of multiple augmented fourths.

5.2.20 Jonathan Harvey, Mortuos Plango, Vivos Voco (1980)

This, alongside a number of works in this selection, is a historical masterpiece. It is one work that has had so much written about it and has been played so often (especially on mainstream UK radio) that it requires very little comment. However, its originality is grounded on its solid technique (Harvey worked at IRCAM coaxing sound out of the software

CHANT – a voice synthesis tool – and MUSIC V, the precursor of Csound) and its sensuous soundworld, and perhaps because it has fused the worlds of recorded and synthesised sounds it has crossed barriers between European electroacoustic music and American computer music. Like Wishart, Harvey fused vocal timbres (in this case a recording of a boy's voice) with the partials of a bell. *Mortuos Plango, Vivos Voco* has additional dualities: the deep religious sensitivity of the composer suggested through the programme of the piece and a reverence for the instrumental. Again, it is clear that the composer is making every effort to make his work approachable. The work continues to defy its age (it is now well over 30 years old). Harvey commented upon his own work in Emmerson's *The Language of Electroacoustic Music* (Harvey, 1986).

5.2.21 *Paul Lansky,* Idle Chatter *(1985)*

Paul Lansky's *Idle Chatter* is, in a way, very similar in approach to Harvey's *Mortuos Plango, Vivos Voco*. It uses a relatively new synthesis technique called linear predictive coding (LPC) and is very much reliant upon the computer to (re)synthesise sounds, in this case an IBM 3081 mainframe computer. It also has voice as one of the key source materials. Lansky's notes state that *Idle Chatter* was meant to '...have fun in a musical domain – computer music – which is prone to great seriousness, sometimes bordering on despair'. The work stimulates the cocktail party effect (hearing something stand out from a generally noisy environment). This babble of speech is marked by clear pitches – speech-articulated drones if you like – and underpinned by classical harmonic patterns. As a consequence, this work is extremely approachable, as indeed are many of Lansky's electronic pieces. Lansky himself, in a keynote address at the International Computer Music Conference in Montréal in 2009,[13] considered this work to be pivotal.

5.2.22 *Andrew Lewis,* Scherzo *(1992–93)*

A simple outline of the formal plan of Andrew Lewis' *Scherzo* has been given in Section 3.4 presenting key moments that one can remember even after only one listen (voice, childrens' toys, natural environments – and for those that have seen *The Shining*, something rather eerie). There is one particular process that deserves special mention; something that makes this piece have an almost universal 'darkness' about it despite its use of childrens' voices. Simply put, 'Daaaaaadeeeeeee'. Here Lewis takes a recording of his daughter speaking the word 'daddy', and extends both the 'a' and 'y' into electronic drones. More importantly, as this pitch is extended, its transition from real to unreal is explored. Throughout this work, musical pitches held within the child's voice are brought out, often through a time-stretching process. In 1992 Lewis used a sampler (Akai S1000) to stretch a portion of sound. He then stretched the resulting sound so creating a transition from real to unreal as the end of the processed sound was always increasingly synthetic in nature. We can do this now with time-varying stretches and vocal manipulation tools such as Melodyne[14] but it does not sound quite the same (not least because the Akai time stretch was not FFT-based so a strange, analogue feel was implied).

5.2.23 *Elainie Lillios,* Listening Beyond *(2007)*

Elainie Lillios is an American composer of electroacoustic music and another student of Jonty Harrison at the University of Birmingham. Like Natasha Barrett, Lillios is as 'at home' with instruments being processed live as she is with music that exists solely on support. *Listening Beyond* (2007) is part of a disc entitled *Entre Espaces (Between Spaces)*. Here she creates a very delicate and immersive space using granulations of voice and bell sounds. If you listen to *Listening Beyond* on headphones, you get a very good idea of just how the spaces are used. Panning is both textural and structural. There is a clear division between front/back, top/bottom and left/right. The granulation techniques are quite clear early on but there is very careful mixing as bell pitches cascade with vocal sounds. The second section of the work focuses upon new colours (from filter banks) which also cascade. The key phrase (audible at the end of this section) is 'if you listen carefully, can you hear infinity?' Here I guess Lillios is referring to her friend and colleague Pauline Oliveros, another pioneer of the artform who espouses 'deep listening'[15] as a means of understanding sound in space.

5.2.24 *Alistair MacDonald,* Equivalence *(2007)*

Alistair MacDonald is a composer from the Birmingham stable who moved to Glasgow in the late 1990s and works at the Royal Conservatoire of Scotland. His music crosses numerous boundaries as he works with instrumentalists and dancers. He also improvises live with the laptop. However, it is his fixed media music that is particularly interesting, especially because of its form. The ebb and flow in *Equivalence* and the persistence of sound type (in this instance strongly linked to the source sound of bricks) almost forces us to listen to the changes in sound over time, whilst realising that the emerging structures and the resultant form will be simple but grand in design.

The opening three minutes have short cadences, clear cyclic repetition of material and some individual gestures that sound as if they are

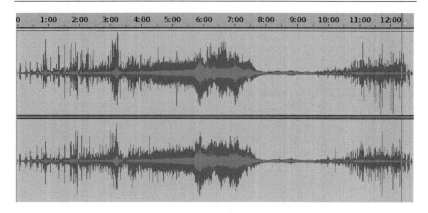

Figure 5.1 Equivalence waveform view

creatures moving quickly in the undergrowth of a dense texture. The waveform tells us to expect something louder and potentially denser after the large build-up of sound at three minutes. This sectionality is reinforced by the sonogram view.

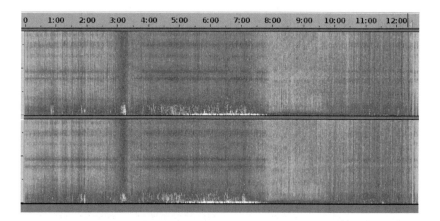

Figure 5.2 Equivalence sonogram view

As has been mentioned before, neither view gives you anything about the detailed repetitions and gestures in the work (which are clearly audible), but we certainly know where we are at eight minutes, from both views. MacDonald has taken us to a relaxed, restful state through sound level, some reverberation and closely recorded sounds suggesting intimacy. His granulations are less from the sound of brick upon brick, less brittle. They appear to sound more like 'air', perhaps a residue from the brick sound. The return to the sounds of the start is evidenced by similar angularity in both views.

Structural principles are accumulation and dissolution. Formally, we hear open–closed.

5.2.25 Michael McNabb, Dreamsong (1978)

I seem to be reflecting upon a vast number of older works, but I was brought up on this piece by Simon Emmerson as he lectured me on his method of analysing electroacoustic music and it is true that *Dreamsong* is a pioneering work. It falls neatly in the centre of Emmerson's grid (see Figure 1.4) as *Dreamsong* has a balance of abstract and abstracted syntax, aural and mimetic discourse. Some sounds clearly identify themselves as human or suggest a space (an airport). Other sounds are very synthetic. However, some of these synthetic sounds are pitched and mirror instrumental sounds. McNabb therefore gives them melodies. Where sounds lose their pitch characteristics, *Dreamsong* re-enters that world of the dream and sounds float, drift and (e)merge. Like Trevor Wishart's *Vox V*, *Dreamsong* takes us from the real into the unreal through careful use of real, synthesised and transformed sounds (again the most obvious being the human voice). Techniques such as comb filtering and phasing are used almost to the degree that they become new source material.[16] *Dreamsong* was premiered in 1978 at the Centre for Computer Research in Music and Acoustics, CCRMA, Stanford University. This work could not be further removed from works such as Chowning's *Turenas*, yet it comes from a similar computer music background. It clearly appealed to Emmerson in addition to explaining his thesis.

5.2.26 Adrian Moore, Rêve de l'aube – Dreaming of the Dawn (2004)

It would be remiss of me not to talk about one of my own works in reasonable detail, if not just to highlight the one aspect of this work which haunts me to this day. *Rêve de l'aube – Dreaming of the Dawn* is both the title of my second CD on the Empreintes DIGITALes label and the title of the work; it comes from a poem by Emily Dickenson. It was the result of a commission by the GRM and was mixed in Studio 116A, Maison Radio France in January 2004 and premiered on 14 March 2004 in Salle Olivier Messiaen. It was a huge honour to have worked in a studio with such a 'history'. The work brought forward (quite by accident) a number of structural – and consequently formal – devices, the most important of which was the idea of '*déjà-écouté*'.

Simply put, instead of taking a foundation and playing it, then repeating this foundation with additional material, creating a build-up of material and indicating quite clearly the mixing process, I reverse this process.

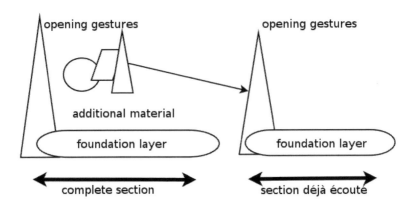

Figure 5.3 Déjà-écouté structure

As the focus in the opening section was primarily upon the additional material (underpinned by the foundation layer) when this layer is presented on its own, the listener feels like they've heard this before. There are at least two moments where this takes place in *Rêve de l'aube*. The sectional nature of the piece is made clear by obvious repetition of an opening 'theme'. However, I felt the work needed a slightly different middle section climax so in came what appears to be an almighty organ chord. My conscience tells me this should go as I do not enjoy this moment when playing the work to others. However, it does fulfil a purpose of clearing the air and, as such, it remains. The work is mainly made from instrumental sources (woodwind sounds), all quite heavily manipulated.

5.2.27 Robert Normandeau, Tangram (1992)

Tangram is both the title of the work and the title of one of Normandeau's many discs on the Canadian label Empreintes DIGTITALes. At almost 27 minutes it is a work of grand scale. Its space is huge too. I first heard this work at its premiere on 19 and 20 May 1992 at the Planétarium de Montréal where the audience all sat inwards (and upwards) and the loudspeakers lined the circular wall. Perhaps this is why, even in stereo, this work presents numerous textures that spiral or circulate around the head. *Tangram* was made at the University of Montreal using a multitrack tape machine. Mixing like this was completely different to the method used at Birmingham where (probably because of cost) most studios used multiple two-track machines that recorded to a master. Both methods were difficult and noise was always an issue (Dolby A helped but you learned very quickly about signal to noise ratios as you recorded and re-recorded).

Normandeau's work was part of his cycle *Cinema for the Ear*. I associate this term particularly with his work, though it appears it was coined in the 1960s. Like many of the pieces in this catalogue, if you shut your eyes (for there is nothing to see), the work is highly 'visual'. Like Parmegiani before him, Normandeau uses natural scenes to frame and heighten the tension of his studio-recorded and manipulated sounds. Normandeau carries on a tradition of electroacoustic music in Montréal after Francis Dhomont retired from the university. The university now has full degree programmes in electroacoustics covering composition, instrument design, software engineering and acoustics. Montréal remains one of the key centres for sound with numerous institutions offering courses and a positive approach to cultural investment.

5.2.28 *Bernard Parmegiani*, De Natura Sonorum (1975)

Bernard Parmegiani's huge cycle *De Natura Sonorum* highlights a number of methodologies that demonstrate how process and compositional style are related. In movement V, 'Etude élastique', we hear 'swirling' sounds and the metaphor of elasticity is tangible. The sound objects pan dramatically and have a whip-like motion. The flow of energy is precise. It is no coincidence that Parmegiani uses filtered noise to create these shapes. The noise can imitate the 'swoosh' very quickly and as a sound with a lot of partials, its motion trajectory is easily identifiable by the ear. The cycle in general and this movement in particular provide the sound diffusion performer with a unique opportunity to create space and dynamism in the concert hall. Here, sounds that pan left to right are clearly meant to fly around the room, filling the space with effervescence. Chapter 8 talks specifically about the art of presenting music on fixed media to an audience.

Parmegiani's liner notes for *De Natura Sonorum* read thus:

> With *De Natura Sonorum* I have begun a new period. After experimenting with the relation between the sound material and the form of its development, I have become interested in the writing of sounds whose ink, so to speak, is taken from materials I try to combine and/or contrast in order to observe their nature [an analysis within itself if you like]. Thus a dialectical contradiction emerges from the contrast between a living and natural sound (that remains diffuse in nature) and an artificial sound (a notion that suggests a

'taste' for improved naturalness as C. Rosset puts it). This music, intended to be as 'general as possible', flows through a continuous metamorphosis, digging its own bed, thanks to successive inductions generating the artificial from the natural. Does listening to this constant transition from one state to another tell us anything about the nature of sound?

'Elastic study' again involves the articulation of a number of instruments (skins, zarbs, vibrating strings) alongside synthetic gestures analogous to this 'playing'. The synthesis is subtractive with white noise clearly the source. Filters give a sense of pitch region but few discernible pitches. The whole movement is in a constant state of flux. But this movement has clear division of phrases where the desolate landscapes of the previous movement, 'Dynamic of resonance' try to appear. And these landscapes take on a decidedly human feel as the low-filtered white noise seems to 'breathe'. The gestures get faster and faster and become texture, articulated now by huge explosions of noise. As the movement closes, pitch emerges and dies, like a beacon of light slowly extinguished.

Parmegiani's method affords freedom whilst maintaining control. He can *process* his natural sounds in one direction and *unsynthesise* his models of said natural sounds in the other direction. There is a real sense of continuity.

5.2.29 Åke Parmerud, Les flûtes en feu (1999)

Swedish composer Åke Parmerud has been working in electroacoustic music for over 30 years and, like François Donato, writes solo pieces, music for installations, ballets and video. *Les flûtes en feu*, like Wishart's *Imago*, imagines the composer as an alchemist, freely able to transform recorded sound with computer technology. In this instance the primary source sound is the flute. The key is in the title of the work: without it, one might imagine a flute sound and perhaps fire, but with the title the metaphor of alchemy is complete. Whilst this may sound obvious, a good title is what a listener will see before they hear anything in concert or before they click a link. Flutes on fire conjures many images and sets the imagination alight. Where this work differs from the Wishart example is that the opacity of transformation is perhaps secondary to the very impressionistic soundworlds being produced. Electroacoustic music has a strong presence in the UK, Canada and Sweden. As is the case with Montréal, Sweden continues to put national support into a number of very high quality institutions, the most well known being EMS (Elektronmusikstudion) in Stockholm. However, the Visby International Centre for Composition's Studio Alpha is also one of the most perfect places to create a work, and my own compositions *Nebula Sequence* and *The Battle* were created there.

5.2.30 Jean-Claude Risset, Sud (1985)

If we look at Risset's biography and employment history – musician and engineer working at Bell Laboratories, IRCAM, the CNRS (Centre National de la Recherche Scientifique) at Marseille – we find a very interesting hybrid of the scientist-musician. Uniquely skilled in music computer programming, possessing an ear that enables him to begin to model real-world sounds and instruments in the laboratory yet equally at home with sound recordings and a sense of play that one finds when confronted by the complexities of natural sound. Hence *Sud*, a work from the composer that helped Boulez create IRCAM, being commissioned from the GRM. As a consequence I hear the creative conflict between some of Risset's strictly programmed sound transformations and his selection of natural recordings.

5.2.31 *Curtis Roads,* Point Line Cloud (1999–2003)

Although a collection of works, *Point Line Cloud* (Roads, 2004b) can be heard as a companion CD to Roads' book *Microsound* (Roads, 2004a). Curtis Roads has, literally, written the book on computer music (*The Computer Music Tutorial*: Roads et al., 1996) and granulation (*Microsound*). The works on this disc are studies in the creative use of one of the most ubiquitous techniques currently available to composers. If one repeats a sound and this sound gradually gets smaller and smaller (until you describe it as a grain) you have granulation. Granulation techniques lie at the heart of many of the pieces in this small selection (and are explicit in Lillios, MacDonald and Smalley). The fascination with granulation is its ability to generate sounds from the repetitive (perceivable chunks) to the iterative (unperceivable chunks) to pitched drones, and from gesture to texture. The musical example I would recommend listening to is *Fluxon* from 2003. It is an explosive, fast and spirited journey.

5.2.32 Stéphane Roy, Crystal Music (1994)

Stéphane Roy's *Crystal Music* presents a unique approach to gesture/texture complexes and reverberation to create a sense of atmosphere. The majority of the sounds are fragmentary in nature and rely upon repetition to progress. Drones exist in a permanent state of flux and undulation. I have always held this piece in high regard.

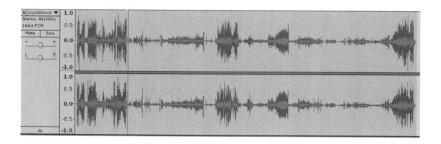

Figure 5.4 Stéphane Roy: *Crystal Music* (1994)

From observing the waveform in Figure 5.4 we can see a huge dynamic range throughout the work's 14:43 duration. Almost half the work sounds distant through subtle and creative use of volume and reverberation. Somehow this work retains its beauty precisely because of this mystery: the environment is as plausible as in Smalley's *Valley Flow* (Section 5.2.34), yet this time it feels hot rather than cold. The textures are primordial and often feel like they are on the verge of getting out of control. There are strong pitch relationships and a considerable proportion of the work relies heavily on pitch, whether through drone or glissandi. It feels as though there are some loop-based mechanisms at work here: bordering on the edge of granularity and with pitch accumulation thrown in, this undulating feel (horizontally through the loop and vertically through the pitch accumulation) heightens the nervous tension. Apparently, Roy used Common Lisp Music (CLM) to create much of the sound in *Crystal Music*. CLM[17] is interesting in that whilst the sound processing modules are similar to Csound (CLM was also developed from the Music V program), one has to program in Lisp and this has always been an interesting language from which to understand music, as Lisp works on lists and nested loops. However, looking at the syntax one can see why many text-based programming languages such as Csound and SuperCollider are so powerful yet difficult to learn.[18]

5.2.33 Alain Savouret, Don Quixotte Corporation (1980–1981)

Alain Savouret's *Don Quixotte Corporation* is a huge 30 minute textual melodrama that presents a rather dystopian view of reality through the eyes and ears of our world-weary hero. Movement II of this work, entitled 'Dulcinea' deconstructs the syllables in the title, and adds the sound of a hen, a horn and a horse to create seven motifs which are then dealt with in a series of variations. Because the sounds are now atomised to around a second in duration, the vast majority of transformations one can think of may well be applied effectively, especially if, as the sound atoms are repeated, the transformation changes over time. The opening transformation is obvious: a bandpass filter. And whilst audible and almost universally understandable, the sonogram of this sound and its modification is unmistakable.

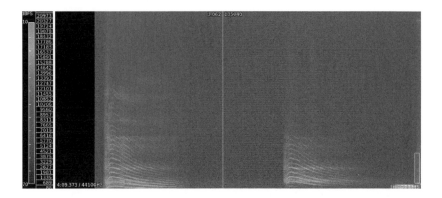

Figure 5.5 Alain Savouret: 'Dulcinea' from *Don Quixotte Corporation* (1980–1981): two opening gestures, the second being a bandpass filtered version of the first

The second instance of the sound 'Ah' is lighter in form, the filter having taken energy from higher and lower (spoken voice) frequencies. As subsequent motifs receive the same treatment, we can begin to hear the theme and variations in process. Voice and horn also receive pitch transformations as there is strong pitch content to each motif. Reverberation extends sibilant sounds and time stretching extends pitches. Of particular note in this example is the very singular panning and separation of elements (very obvious left–right trajectories). One might argue that this is a form-first piece in that the method of transformation and variation is very fixed. However, it is very clear from later sections of the work that this is a 'hands-on' composer (not least because this work was completed in an analogue tape studio) and that the opening statements are there to tie theme to variation. This is an example of how to put a work together because it can be quite easily deconstructed (and has been done so in a wonderful animated analysis on the *La musique electroacoustique* CDROM.)

5.2.34 Denis Smalley, Valley Flow (1991–1992)

We have already talked about the theoretical writings of Denis Smalley. There are potential imprints of his theories in his musical output and these are particularly clear in his work *Valley Flow* (1991). The work opens with one of the most eerie granular synthesis passages, immediately suggesting a cold, desolate space. The pitch swirls in a semi-regulated pulse stream. It breathes. And eventually a 'wash' or 'wave' of sound approaches us. Smalley uses hard hits to cut between motifs. Many of his constituent sounds are 'thin', especially the granulations, which means he can easily mix files to create canopies or floors. Again the 'swirl' motion helps motivate sounds towards and away from us. Precisely how he has created the thin layers of sound is not important (heavy filtering of a noisier sound or through time stretching of his favourite piano string sounds perhaps?) – they attack us like shards of glass. Certainly as shards and wood chimes mix, careful use of filtering allows wood chimes to fade spectrally into the shards. The work is 16:50 in duration and develops this cold landscape for a significant proportion of this time (even when the textures get more excited). *Valley Flow* is a solid example of an environment where a number of key sound types are explored and transformed. It makes enormous use of canopy and floor to define its landscape and utilises granulations and reverberations to further create space.

5.2.35 Denis Smalley, Tides (1984)

Denis Smalley's textural work *Tides* again focuses strongly on filters, especially resonant filters which imbue a pitch upon noisy (although gentle) sea recordings. The processing is quite extreme, in fact it is hard to describe in any detail the other processes involved. There may have been some basic granulation based upon sample and hold loop mechanisms as shown in Figure 2.20. Smalley is developing some very characteristic 'metallic' soundworlds through his resonant filter developments. And in the second movement of this work, 'Sea Flight', even when very natural sounds appear, they have a 'flange' effect giving them a pitched characteristic. We are transported to an interior world where even real-world sounds are 'projected' so as to sound intimate, giving a sense of 'flashback'. A very noticeable feature of Smalley's earlier works is his use of feedback. Feedback offers unpredictability and eccentricity though it sounds quite obvious to the experienced listener. Under careful control it is also extremely useful for creating 'tails'. Feedback is normally related to a delay time and is most obvious when heard in a pitch shifting algorithm (as shown in Figure 2.23). When the delay times are very short (between 10 and 100 ms), the amount of sound fed back into the system blurs to a pitch glissando (rather than a noticeable repetition of a chunk of sound). This is very useful when adding tail spin-offs to further strengthen sound objects. *Tides* continues from where works such as *Pentes* and *Vortex* left off. All Smalley's works are given small yet highly descriptive titles (*Valley Flow*, *Base Metals*, *Piano Nets*, *Clarinet Threads*) that suggest sources and forms. Despite a six-year gap, *Tides* and *Valley Flow* have more in common than I thought.

5.2.36 *Adam Stansbie,* Point of Departure *(2009)*

It was with absolute delight that the University of Sheffield engaged the services of Adam Stansbie in the summer of 2012. Adam is a composer of outstanding ability, with a passion for acousmatic music, a sense of tradition not dissimilar to my own, and an expert in the CDP (Composers Desktop Project) software. He released a disc of works in 2012 on the Sargasso label. The works on the disc are concert pieces spanning some five years of labour in the studio. More importantly, the works range from 9 to 22 minutes in duration so with a dedicated listen it is possible to ascertain how a composer shifts from short form to long form. *Point of Departure* (2009) is long form! It opens with a crescendo reminiscent of Parmegiani's 'Retour de la forêt' from *Dedans Dehors* (1977). Here, Parmegiani brings the forest to a screeching halt after a slow crescendo. Stansbie's crescendo is even larger and fuses drone with noise-based materials. He then leaves us with the drone (almost feeling as though we had lost some of our hearing) which again slowly develops. Smoother textural sounds begin to emerge over this drone which moves from a tonic to a fourth as the density builds again. The use of drone here is entirely pertinent. The engaged listener will hear changes in colour and be thankful that it is there. The listener that recognises it as annoying is the person that says the sky is 'blue' and that is all. Using pitch in this way is extremely difficult. Once on a drone, it is difficult to get out of it. Move to another note and you immediately say 'harmonic shift?' or 'melodic pattern?'. Instead, Stansbie gives us some rather cool *Klangfarbenmelodie* as he 'lightens' the drone with filters towards the end of the work. A spectral decrescendo to close that mirrors the opening leaves one with a form that is, ultimately, *open–close*.

5.2.37 *Pete Stollery,* scènes, rendez-vous *(2006)*

The very opening of this book suggested that all sound was available to us. When a natural sound is recorded in context, it is this context that must be respected in order to abstract the sound and recontextualise it. Pete Stollery has recently shifted a significant proportion of his creative work towards an area which documents, narrates, comments upon and preserves real spaces and places. He is acutely aware of how our sampling of place can become confused depending upon our relationship to the sample (did you record it, were you there when it was recorded, or did you just hear it for the first time in the studio?). *Scènes, rendez-vous* is about cars. But more than that, it is about one particular car at one particular time taking one particular route (Claude Lelouch in 1976). As Stollery retraced Lelouch's steps he recorded his own place, his own space. The personalised reflection of *scènes, rendez-vous* reaches out as Stollery intersperses real scenes with acousmatic 'episodes': new spaces, new places and music very much 'for us'. Stollery works very hard to keep his noise-based material under control. Whilst our first reaction to such noisy material as streets and cars might be to filter towards pitch (which Paul Lansky successfully did in *Night Traffic* by comb filtering a four-lane highway), Stollery battles quite aggressively with his noises using sharp filters and envelope modifiers, imbuing artificial, rattle snake-like rhythms to the opening minutes. Like Smalley, resonant filters do make an appearance and lead one to ask, 'how can a work go from natural soundscapes to such abstract worlds?' It is this very dichotomy that provides the necessary relief (and relief) for the work to have a successful sectional form.

5.2.38 *Hans Tutschku,* Distance liquide *(2007)*

Hans Tutschku has a highly distinguished career as a composer, performer and teacher. He has worked at IRCAM and Harvard University and performed with Karlheinz Stockhausen and Jonty Harrison. One can hear in his music a distillation of French, German and British acousmatic/Elektronische traditions. *Distance liquide* epitomises this distillation. The work has a very clear and focused programme based upon spatialisation of materials and the spectral styling of (mainly) instrumental sources. Sounds are crafted with a real sense of play and vocal sounds are often used to heighten tension. A great deal of attention is given towards spectral division, especially siphoning the strongest sinusoidal components from a sound, giving rise to very pure sinusoidal signals that have a water-like feel. Additionally, and in a similar manner to the Stollery, Tutschku makes use of amplitude modulation to articulate his noisier materials. The vast majority of Tutschku's work is multichannel rather than stereo. Thus, in the stereo version of *Distance liquide* we get but a glimpse of the motion patterns involved.

5.2.39 *Horacio Vaggione, works from the disc* Points critiques *(2011)*

The GRM released a disc of works by Argentinian composer Horacio Vaggione entitled *Points critiques* comprising all their commissions from him. Vaggione's early computer music piece, *Octuor*, from 1982, marked him as a modernist composer that fused the technical skills of the computer musician with the acousmatic composer's sensibility for sound.

He has written extensively about *Octuor* (Vaggione, 1984) and it is possible to trace his style across the decades to this 2011 disc. Vaggione is like a Jackson Pollack of sound in that he will create highly dense structures with very limited means. *Points critiques* comprises five works, 'Points critiques' (2011), 'Arenas' (2007), 'Nodal' (1997), 'Ash' (1991) and 'Phases' (2001). This disc spans some 20 years of work, forms a bridge between earlier experiments and works for instruments and electronics and acts as a well-deserved retrospective. There is an intense granularity throughout these works, reminiscent of the granular practice of Curtis Roads as described in *Microsound* (Roads, 2004a) and heard in *Point Line Cloud* (2004b). What is so magic about all the pieces on this disc is that the vast majority of sounds are crystal clear and whilst the textures may appear aggressive, they always sound engaging. 'Points critiques', the work, finds a unique balance between pitch (often high), duration (mainly short) and density, which weaves through the continuum from dense to sparse and rough to smooth without tending towards redundancy. As sources are often instrumental sounds (but treated very differently compared to Tutschku's *Distance liquide*) we hear clear percussiveness, pitched motifs and a sense of orchestration. And as we are listening to texture after texture the question becomes 'where do sections change and how does he elide one passage into the next?' Some of his works stratify a little more obviously – both horizontally and vertically – than others, but all his works on this disc combine a mathematical rigour with 'gutsy' emotions and a sense of a sculptor's hands at the mouse and keyboard. This is truly original work.

5.2.40 *Annette Vande Gorne,* Figures d'espace *(2004)*

In Section 8.4, I mention a competition for sound diffusion (the presentation of electroacoustic works in concert). This special event was created by composer and teacher Annette Vande Gorne. Coming from the GRM tradition (having studied with Pierre Schaeffer and Guy Reibel), Vande Gorne set up her own tradition in Brussels. She formed the Musiques & Recherches and Métamorphoses d'Orphée studios in the early 1980s, taught at the Conservatoire, created an electroacoustic music department and has produced huge events to promote electroacoustic music (alongside a spatialisation competition and a prestigious competition for composers of all ages). After the demise of the Bourges international festival, Brussels is now one of very few 'Meccas' for composers to go and rub shoulders with all the composers mentioned above. In *Figures d'espace*, Vande Gorne has created a work that is a study in space; a work which demands performance over a multichannel sound diffusion system. The work begins with clear percussive sources (in particular something sounding suspiciously like a

Flexatone) but quickly moves through glimpses of natural soundscapes to something more abstract. In this sectional work, there are clear sounds of 'homage' (the vibrating ruler pivoted at one end) and, like Vaggione, a very dynamic approach to mixing, resulting in extremes of panning and dynamic range. This is a work that also harkens back to Parmegiani's *Dedans Dehors* and *De Natural Sonorum* in its vivid contrasts of real-world versus studio-sampled materials.

5.2.41 Alejandro Viñao, Chant d'ailleurs (1992)

Alejandro Viñao's *Chant d'ailleurs*, like Field's *Being Dufay*, is for voice and computer. It makes it to this list because, like Lewis' *Scherzo*, Viñao fuses the voice and computer in a unique way. Our transition from real to unreal is completed through very clever vocal writing, a unique performer in the form of soprano and contemporary music specialist, Frances Lynch, and simple but effective synthesis drawn from reed instruments and vocal samples, manipulated using the GRM's Syter computer. The voice hits a pitch that is matched by a shawm's sawtooth waveform which is then sampled and filtered in the computer. One has to assume something like a *bishur*, a Mongolian double-reed instrument. The 'exotic' sound and the work's title help enhance the 'other worldliness' of this piece.

5.2.42 Trevor Wishart, Imago (2002)

Imago is mentioned in other parts of this text (Section 7.1.4) as it exemplifies musical transformation and a melding (and unravelling) of musical ideas and computer techniques. In no other work of electroacoustic music can you hear the process of transformation so clearly. This is partly due to the nature of the source sound used – a minute fragment of the 'clink' of two glasses. Therefore any musical continuation requires repetition or stretching of the source. The source is pitched so this is also a clear identifier of change. Thus the electroacoustic music, despite its foreign soundworld, sounds very orchestral.

5.2.43 Trevor Wishart, Vox 5 (1979–1986)

Thirty years ago the computing power we have available on our laptops could only be found in very large, well-funded institutions. One such institution was IRCAM, the Institut de Recherche et Coordination Acoustique/Musique, a centre for experimental electroacoustic music created by Pierre Boulez in 1977. Trevor Wishart was known for his experimental work with the voice and his experimental software for sound transformation; subsequently his work for the CDP (Composers

Desktop Project) and his book *On Sonic Art* (1996). Wishart was invited to IRCAM to write software and continued his *Vox* cycle, producing *Vox 5*. He took vocal samples (relatively atypical sounds, often created through extended techniques) and transformed them using the phase vocoder, now a common means of implementing techniques for spectral transformations. This technique allowed him to morph, very carefully, the spectra of one identifiable sound into another. The most obvious example in *Vox 5* was the vocal sound 'szzzzzzzz' transforming into the sound of bees. *Vox 5* is a highly atmospheric piece, bringing together environmental recordings, vocal sounds and highly processed samples within a poetic narrative.

5.2.44 *John Young,* Liquid Sky *(1998)*

It is very interesting to compare multiple works by one composer. We may recognise a consistent and maturing style and we may potentially recognise similar working methods. The phrase 'it is definitely you' is for the most part complimentary and implies some recognisable actions on/manipulations of sound across a number of works. *Liquid Sky* possesses many similar features to Harrison's work *Unsound Objects* (1995), especially in its use of water and filters. Young's work is challenging yet rewarding. It is crystal clear, yet he does not pander to the listener's requirement for 'something to hold on to', least of all any reassuring pitches. *Liquid Sky* uses the filter extensively, especially in the opening section of the work. Whilst the best way to describe sounds here is through the use of 'grains', smooth granular textures are not present. Instead, everything undulates, sometimes peacefully, sometimes aggressively. In the third section of the work, Young nods towards Smalley, which is understandable given their shared nationality and the close relationship between the two composers. Granulations of this nature if not constrained by a filter would probably sound random and lead quickly to redundancy. Interestingly, in this work Young resorts to a variety of sources and it is for the listener to unravel them from their intertwined textures. Around two thirds in we hear the characteristic sound of the diminished resonant filter chord. This is no longer a clichéd sound. Rather it is a 'tag', perhaps even becoming a new source sound (resonant filters of some kind are present in at least 50% of the works discussed here), and a sign of shared mutual understanding of the processes involved within the electroacoustic community. Similarly, the use of the notch filter to inscribe a pitch on noise-based material can be heard in the Stollery and Wishart examples and the subtle addition of voice or vocal characteristics (often arising from filtering around vocal format frequencies) mirrors techniques found in Tutschku. We treat each work as a separate piece, however, and *Liquid Sky* represents a unique exploratory process.

5.2.45 John Young, Pythagoras's Curtain (2001)

Pythagoras's Curtain retains the subtlety of the earlier work and after the initial 'setting' (opening gestures for approximately one minute) we tumble again to a highly crafted noise-based world where chalk board and water sit somewhat uneasily. One could say that many of these textures are monophonic in that their pseudo randomness (duration, placement in time and space) dictates that not much else could sit alongside them. And so when we have a drone, it is often very thin and ethereal. It is interesting to note the use of accelerating/decelerating patterns within these drones. Young also hints at his sources (around 5:43), a rubbed wine glass. If we were to sum up this work (and *Liquid Sky*) in one word, it might be 'crisp'. Young's work encourages the question 'when is a sound strong enough to be heard *solo*?'

5.2.46 John Young, Trace (2003)

The opening of his work *Trace* comes as no surprise despite its immediate reveal of instrumental sources (the saxophone): the sense of crispness is there alongside intimate attention to detail. But then we have almost one minute of drone-based material and we enter this new, nostalgic soundworld quite easily. Our experience with the sound of the saxophone allows us to be snapped back to quasi reality but then more surprises appear. *Trace* is quite sectional and following a passage of traditional erratic behaviour we have regularity and pitch in full order. Young's drone sections now feature smoothly enveloped material and touch base again with nostalgia though minor mode harmonies. The polar opposites of gesture and texture are explored to the full but the necessity of pitch clarifies the techniques used in previous works and solidifies Young's style as 'dynamic'.

Later works, especially the huge work *Ricordiamo Forlì*, are difficult to compare to these three examples but as with many composers moving from studios with tape machines and outboard gear to computer managed compositions, sounds have become slightly more artificial in design, and in many respects this has also tightened up the perception of form. However, some say that this tighter form comes at the expense of a more clinical feel.

5.2.47 Christian Zanési, Constructions Métalliques (2001)

Currently serving as the GRM's artistic director, Zanési's work bridges 'la musique acousmatique' and the traditions of the GRM with a much younger world of sound art. *Constructions Métalliques* relies upon excellent recordings and transformations but takes techniques of juxtaposition and repetition (conceivably techniques of the Schaefferian age) and brings them up to date using loops, noise and exterior samples of men working/speaking to create a series of tableaux that are very much 'of the time'. The piece does not completely break with its tradition but the documentary feel and sense of 'found art' are, for 2001, quite innovative and perhaps why Zanési is respected amongst today's composers working live with loops and samples.

5.3 What's Left

This section's title sounds too negative for the few remaining works and composers that have influenced me, and clearly the list above and the list below is just touching the tip of the iceberg. The following works were, however, vital during my learning and remain vital in my teaching. They are key works from the pioneers of the avant-garde.[19] As a composer of electroacoustic music, I find it all too difficult to divorce myself from my own preoccupations and listen to the works of others. Moreover, it is often quite difficult to listen with a degree of naivety such that I can enjoy them for what they are and not think about process or criticise as though I'm somehow in a more privileged position. Therefore this particular task has been particularly liberating. Although these paragraphs might be better suited to a blog, the interconnections traced between countries and composers, and fused through techniques and methods, seem to suggest a growing worldwide community that follows many of the motivational principles documented in Section 7.2.

5.3.1 *Karlheinz Stockhausen,* Telemusik *(1966)*

Any mention of the word 'visionary' and I must cite Karlheinz Stockhausen. Like Bayle, Parmegiani and Dhomont, Stockhausen was at the forefront of everything he touched: truly 'avant-garde'. *Telemusik* was one of his finest pure tape pieces which also bridged the worlds of synthesis and recorded/manipulated sounds. The key technique here was ring modulation which not only gave pulse and basic amplitude modulation to some sounds but gave the work a pitch structure and provided the scintillating high frequencies that you hear right at the beginning of the work and throughout its course. Ring modulation (the modulation of one sound by another – often a natural sound like the voice with a synthetic waveform giving rise to your typical 'Dalek' sound) gave Stockhausen the means to fuse the old and the new. For each frequency present in the sounds you get a sum and a difference, which is why – normally – one sound is simple and the other, slightly more complex. However, Stockhausen used two complex sounds delivering very full-bodied results! It is not an easy listening experience, but in 1966 its new sound and bold approach (reinforced by a formulaic structure built upon well-timed 'moments') meant it easily secured a place amongst the great tape pieces of the time.[20]

5.3.2 Pierre Schaeffer, Étude aux chemins de fer (1948)

Credited as one of the first pieces of 'tape' music or musique concrète. A work of short loops using natural sounds recorded at the Gare des Batignolles in Paris.

5.3.3 Pierre Henry, Symphonie pour un homme seul (1950, with Schaeffer)

Very much at the centre of new electronic music, although strangely I never came into contact with him or his later works during my studies. *Symphonie pour un homme seul* was a collaborative work with Schaeffer and exploits the human voice amongst other performed instruments.

5.3.4 György Ligeti, Artikulation (1966)

This exemplary synthetic work, whilst not being made from vocal sounds, explores the nature of vocal language through synthetic sounds that 'act' as though a kind of speech were taking place. It is worth reading the story of Ligeti's flight from Hungary, his apprenticeship at the WDR (West Deutsche Rundfunk – West German Radio) with Stockhausen and his brief spell writing electronic music.

5.3.5 Edgard Varèse, Poème Électronique (1958)

It is fair to say that all the composers in this section wanted to create new sounds and reimagine music differently from Wagner, Strauss and Schoenberg. Nobody felt this need more strongly than Edgard Varèse. He turned initially to percussion (listen to *Ionisation*, 1929–1931) and the theremin/ondes martenot for new sounds. Finally, the opportunity arose to work in a studio. He completed two outstanding works: *Déserts* (1950–1954), which juxtaposed tape music with a chamber ensemble, and *Poème Électronique* for the Paris World Fair. Again, if you can find the backstory of the World Fair commission (about a backup composer recruited to provide music of a slightly more acceptable nature, just in case), the context of the whole event becomes fascinating. Both Varèse and Xenakis had works at this festival.

5.3.6 *Iannis Xenakis,* La Légende D'Eer *(1977–1978)*

Xenakis wrote a very short piece for the World Fair called *Concrete PH* (1958). It was the second of some 15 electroacoustic works written during his lifetime, and whilst short in duration at just over two and a half minutes, *Concrete PH* is completely uncompromising. In fact the vast majority of Xenakis' works present the listener with challenges, none more so than *La Légende D'Eer* which, at 45 minutes, pushes anyone's listening to the limits. It does, however, bring together Xenakis' preoccupations with mythology, philosophy and architecture, and because of this it is worth investigating.

Notes

1. Both albums have been mastered with the help of Canadian electroacoustician, Dominique Bassal (www.dominiquebassal.com/). Dominique works closely with the label Empreintes DIGITALes (www.electrocd.com) which produces a significant quantity of electroacoustic music on disc.
2. *Peter Grimes* is an opera by British composer Benjamin Britten. It was first performed in 1945.
3. www.ubu.com/film/kamler.html.
4. http://fresques.ina.fr/artsonores/fiche-media/InaGrm00826/piotr-kamler-galaxie.html.
5. www.electrocd.com/en/bio/bayle_fr/discog/.
6. Chowning stumbled across this method while modelling the singing voice. Vibrato is essentially frequency modulation. When the ambitus and speed of modulation move from a slow vibrato into audio frequencies, the resulting timbres suddenly become more complex – and, commercially pertinent, at very little computing cost. Writing about the creation of *Turenas*, Chowning (2011) himself acknowledges his fellow pioneers of computer music, Jean-Claude Risset and Max V. Mathews.
7. *Cycle du sons.* IMED 0158.
8. Broadly, the 14th century, with key musical figures of the time being Guillaume de Machaut and Philippe de Vitry.
9. www.struzz.com/.
10. http:// startlingmoniker.wordpress.com/2008/08/20/robert-dow-precipitation-within-sight-white-water- airflow/.
11. Quote originally taken from music.barnesandnoble.com.
12. For example: Silent City, Thor's Hammer, Chinese Whispers, The Alligator, Tombstone Catalogue, Gum and Hurricane Ridge.
13. *Reflections on Spent Time* (Lansky, 2009). Published only locally but cached online at http://paul.mycpanel.princeton.edu/lansky-icmc-keynote.pdf.
14. www.celemony.com/.
15. www.deeplistening.org.

16. A technique used by many composers today where source material is merely a complex block from which new sounds are crafted via invasive procedures.
17. See https://ccrma.stanford.edu/software/clm/.
18. Like Pd and Csound, a number of excellent tutorials and books (Wilson et al., 2011) exist that help ease the pain.
19. Obviously, if you are reading this and do not notice your name in the previous list, sorry. But please contact me. This book is an ongoing project. I would also appreciate your 'recollections' (see Appendix B).
20. The electronic pieces of Stockhausen, in particular the earlier works such as *Kontakte*, deserve much more attention than a short paragraph. Fortunately, literature is abundant, both in libraries and on the internet.

References

Adkins, M. (2009). *Five Panels*. SIG 11063 pub. 2009.
Adkins, M. (2011). *Fragile.Flicker.Fragment*. AB035 pub. 2011.
Barrett, N. (2006). *Trade Winds*. ACD 5056.
Bayle, F. (1978–1980). *Erosphère*. INA C 3002 pub. 1996.
Bayle, F. (2012). *50 ans d'acousmatique*. INA G 6033-47 pub. 2012.
Berezan, D. (2002). *Baoding. La face cachée*. IMED 0896 pub. 2008.
Bettelheim, B. (1976). *The Uses of Enchantment*. New York: Knopf.
Chowning, J. (1972). *Turenas*. Digital Music Digital, WER 2012-50, pub. 1988.
Chowning, J. (2011). *Turenas*: the realization of a dream. *Proc. Journées d'Informatique Musicale*, Saint-Etienne, France, 25–27 May.
Dhomont, F. (1989). *Novars*. Les dérives du signe, IMED 9107 pub. 1991.
Dhomont, F. (1996). *Forêt profonde*. Cycle des profondeurs, 2 IMED 9634 pub. 1996.
Dow, R. (2007). *Precipitation within sight*. personal issue.
Dufort, L. (2007). *Gen_3. Matériaux composés*. IMED 0893 pub. 2008.
Field, A. (2006). *STORM!* SCD 28054.
Field, A. and Potter, J. (2009). *Being Dufay*. ECM Records 2071.
Gobeil, G. (2005). *Ombres espaces silences...* Trois songes. IMED 0892 pub. 2008.
Harrison, J. (1982). *Klang*. Évidence matérielle. IMED 0052 pub. 2000.
Harrison, J. (1992). *... et ainsi de suite...* Articles indéfinis. IMED 9627 pub. 1996.
Harrison, J. (1995). *Unsound Objects*. Articles indéfinis. IMED 9627 pub. 1996.
Harvey, J. (1980). *Mortuos Plango Vivos Voco*. Computer Music Currents 5. WER 2025-2, pub. 1990.
Harvey, J. (1986). The mirror of ambiguity. In Emmerson, S., ed., *The Language of Electroacoustic Music*, pages 175–90. London: Macmillan.
Ina-GRM (2000). *La musique électroacoustique*. Editions hyptique.net.
Lansky, P. (1985). *Idle chatter*. More than Idle Chatter. BCD 9050 pub. 1994.
Lansky, P. (1990). *Night traffic*. Homebrew. BCD 9035 pub. 1992.
Lansky, P. (2009). *Reflections on Spent Time*. Ann Arbor, MI: MPublishing, University of Michigan Library.
Lewis, A. (1992–1993). *Scherzo*. SCD 28046 pub. 2002.
Lillios, E. (2007). *Listening Beyond*. Entre espaces. IMED 11110 pub. 2011.

MacDonald, A. (2007). *Equivalence*. Personal issue.

McNabb, M. (1978). *Dreamsong*. Digital Music Digital, WER 2020-2, pub. 1993.

Moore, A. (2004). *Dreaming of the Dawn*. Reve de l'aube. IMED 0684 pub. 2006.

Normandeau, R. (1992). *Tangram*. Tangram. IMED 9920 pub. 1999.

Parmegiani, B. (1975). *Etude élastique*. De Natura Sonorum, pub. 1990, InaGRM.

Parmerud, A. (1999). *Les flutes en feu*. Jeu d'ombres. IMED 0367 pub. 2003.

Roads, C. (2004a). *Microsound*. Cambridge, MA: The MIT Press.

Roads, C. (2004b). *Point Line Cloud*. ASP3000.

Roads, C., Strawn, J., Abbott, C., Gordon, J., and Greenspun, P. (1996). *The Computer Music Tutorial*, volume 81. Cambridge, MA: The MIT Press.

Roy, S. (1994). *Crystal Music*. Kaleidos IMED 9630 pub. 1996.

Savouret, A. (1980). *Don Quixotte Corporation*. Computer Music Currents. WER 2021-50, pub. 1989.

Smalley, D. (1984). *Tides*. Sources / scènes. IMED 0054 pub. 2000.

Smalley, D. (1991). *Valley Flow*. Impacts intérieurs. IMED 0409 pub. 2004.

Stansbie, A. (2009). *Point of Departure*. SCD 28066 pub. 2012.

Stockhausen, K. (1966). *Telemusik*. Complete Edition CD 9, Stockhausen Verlag.

Stollery, P. (2006). *scènes rendez-vous*. Scenes. IMED 11111 pub. 2011.

Tutschku, H. (2007). *Distance liquide*. Migration. AUR CD 3134 pub. 2007.

Vaggione, H. (1984). The making of Octuor. *Computer Music Journal*, 8(2): 48–54.

Vaggione, H. (2011). *Points critiques*. INAG 6032.

Vande Gorne, A. (2004). *Figures d'espace*. Exils. IMED 0890 pub. 2008.

Viñao, A. (1992). *Chant d'ailleurs*. Hildegard's Dream, INA C 1015.

Wilson, S., Cottle, D., and Collins, N. (2011). *The SuperCollider Book*. Cambridge, MA: The MIT Press.

Wishart, T. (1979–1986). *Vox 5*. Vox, VC 7 91108-2.

Wishart, T. (1996). *On Sonic Art*. Amsterdam: Harwood Academic Publishers.

Young, J. (1998). *Liquid Sky*. La limite du bruit. IMED 0261 pub. 2002.

Young, J. (2001). *Pythagoras's Curtain*. La limite du bruit. IMED 0261 pub. 2002.

Young, J. (2003). *Trace*. Personal issue.

Zanési, C. (2001). *Construction Mètalliques*. INA La muse en circuit n10 pub. 2002.

Chapter 6

Space and Time

Space and time are inextricably linked. But how?

This chapter will speculate upon the nature of space and time in electroacoustic music, how the theory of opposites (Chapter 3) can assist with thinking about space and time when composing, and how composers cited in Chapter 5 use space and shape time. It may be possible to investigate whether space and time can be tied down (or drawn apart). Thinking about space and time as entities in themselves in any philosophical sense is daunting (see Chapter 7). However, music may help as an intermediary to understanding.

Whether sitting at an instrument playing music, sitting at a computer making sounds or just listening to sound, we have a tendency to move or be moved. This movement may be real, it may be felt, it may be be situated in our own physical space or it may be transportation to a new space. It is our movement, small or vast, with or against the sounds we hear that informs us that we exist in space and makes us feel human. A physical movement and our metaphorical 'I was moved' are ultimately one and the same thing.

6.1 Space (and Time)

The final frontier.

Jonty Harrison's (1999) article on imaginary space and the performance of electroacoustic music presents a worthy reminder as to the multidimensionality of space.

> Firstly, the intrinsic 'musical space' of sound material has a bearing on spatial considerations. This includes: (a) spectral space (the vertical axis, embracing both pitch and timbre and which can, as we know send out strong psychological signals to the listener about

'height'); (b) temporal space (the horizontal axis; incorporating our ability to connect temporal structures with 'distance'); (c) dynamic space (the axis of amplitude, which encodes cues about the implied (physical) 'size' and/or proximity of sound objects); and (d) 'spatial' space (the position, which may be static and/or dynamic within the (recorded) soundfield – this last point is important, for space is thereby encoded as an intrinsic part of a sound object).

Secondly, we have the notion of 'placement' of a sound object in a compositional and/or listening space. I mean this in the sense of actual perceived physical location, though it is, of course, linked to our ability in the studio to place sound in a virtual acoustic space (passing a signal through a reverberation unit, for example).

Thirdly, we have the idea of 'environment' – that what we capture in, for example, a field recording, is not only the sound we are trying to record (a bird, a stream, a passing locomotive), but also the wider sonic context in which that target sound exists. We are thus dealing here with real, pre-existing spaces, in which other events may occur. This dimension is most likely to have a strong referential aspect, at least as much because of the totality of the environment as because of the nature of the target sound itself.

Finally, we have the realisation that whatever the composer's intentions involving the other three aspects of space, the moment of public performance is crucial; here, everything can be destroyed - though good diffusion can also (fleetingly) improve a mediocre piece! It seems clear that the acoustic of the performing space must be taken into account in the public presentation of acousmatic music; denying the existence of this acoustic is futile, but admitting it as part of the sonic equation of the work on that occasion offers the creative possibility 'to sculpt the sound in the space and to sculpt the space with the sound' (Harrison, 1998), which is actually an extension of an organic compositional process. (Harrison, 1999)

Denis Smalley's article, 'Space-form and the acousmatic image' (Smalley, 2007), runs to definitions of some 50 different types of space. It is *the* definitive text for discovering the spaces of electroacoustic music. Of particular importance are *personal space*, *proximate space* and *distal space*. These are the spaces of distance in relation to the listener. When it comes to identifying sound shapes, *spectral space* is clearly important. *Spectral space* is defined by our understanding of how sounds are made and how we listen to them. Consequently, a very low bass rumble accompanied by a very shrill whine will normally define a large spectral space with low density (nothing in the middle). Similarly, broadband noise will also (in theory) define the same space but the density is such that we do not perceive height or depth, rather simply 'quantity'.

Spectral space is closely related to *perspectival space*, which engages with the 'tracking' of a sound and a closer understanding of it (potentially outside of the course of time's flow). Smalley cites Bayle's notion of environment (with horizon, temperature, climate and the predominance of high to low defining gravity). Plausible sonic environments where agents interact and where nature's rules such as gravity are followed can be found in numerous pieces of electroacoustic music. Examples include: the bouncing ball archetype, the Doppler effect, the tendency of higher frequency sounds to require less amplitude to be heard and for these sounds often to have more agile spatial movement. Smalley situates these environments and agents within a navigable *gestural space* – the perception of source-cause – interacting within an *ensemble space* – a 'scene' – and focused within an *arena space* – a frame. The above examples clearly enable us to grade quantity and quality and position ourselves within and without the space. And it is here where time perhaps plays a role.

6.2 Time (and Space)

Tick tock, tick tock.

Smalley writes: 'Time becomes space' (Smalley, 2007, 39). It is clear that time and space are closely related, almost interchangeable. We know this from an everyday understanding of the term 'light year'. We can wonder in awe at space and time, but when listening to music or composing with sounds it is our proximity to the world of sound that is perhaps the easiest relationship to grasp. From there, the imagination triggered by sound represents timelessness. (We can imagine what a light year is without having to experience it.)

In *real space*, we are closely located (in time) to the sounds around us. We perceive them as they pass us. We are in the moment. Our memory is working very quickly. Time is an arrow moving in but one direction. We are using echoic memory[1] to feature-extract and group events that may eventually become connected in short-term memory. Music psychologists and cognitive scientists have carefully documented the evolution of the ear, brain and mind concerning listening.[2]

In *distorted space* time is more variable; an arrow moving in at least two directions (backwards and forwards). Time is also flexible (we can appreciate and anticipate). We are not there. Better still, we can understand our relationship to the sounds in time (like being in an 'out-of-body experience' and looking down at your sleeping body). This is the 'sensation' of larger-scale features of a work (a feel). And it does not have to happen once the piece is over.

This is a huge simplification of Smalley's view in 'Space-form and the acousmatic image' (2007) which is so detailed that it deserves picking apart (as well as reading in its entirety). It is Section 9 and onwards of Smalley's text which resonates so well with the listener's imagination. Section 9 documents *perspectival space* and Smalley rightly references the world of two-dimensional art (and the way it represents three-dimensional space). Throughout this text the relation of sound to sight has been unavoidable. No more so than in our *visualisation* of sounds and the worlds they inhabit. If asked to 'imagine an expansive space' we might immediately conjure a view of an unpopulated space, a distant horizon in a hot or cold climate. Looking back at our tables of opposites (Tables 1.1 and 1.2) we find these descriptors to be woefully inadequate for this larger-scale task.

Table 6.1 Table of spatiotemporal metaphors

Table of spatial and temporal metaphors		
Space	Time	Relationship
Expansive (sparse), desolate	Unstructured	unpatterned, under-populated space, hot or cold, (post-apocalyptic if a city view), light or dark
Contracted (dense), desperate	Structured	patterned, no matter how erratic, as population must move in some order (even if this resembles chaos!), temperature-free or perception of getting hotter, pressure high
Real	Structured	some population, some evidence of 'gravity', a sense of the natural
Unreal	Structured time(s) – there is some disruption because...	...real objects may be existing in unnatural spaces or vice versa
Surreal	Unstructured	we find it difficult to describe the space with any term

The spaces here are perhaps best described by Smalley under the term 'prospective space', from 'prospect':

> a view of landscape that implies a vantage point from where one looks forwards, scanning and exploring the scene to take in the identity and proportional relations of the shapes observed, and the dimensions, extent and depth of the image. (Smalley, 2007, 49)

And this view incorporates the multidimensionality of time in that by zooming in on features within the landscape we implicitly understand that time is 'more of an issue'; we begin to feel the moment of time rather than the enormity of time.

In practice, a canopy or rooted setting (through solid drone or high frequency granular particles) can immediately be seen to mirror land and sky and therefore give us a clue as to the horizon. The density of the high frequency granulation might emulate clouds. The amplitude of both might suggest proximity or immensity. The population may (necessarily) be dictated by the space (or we are heading towards the unreal). If the temperature is extremely 'hot' or 'cold', we would not expect a solidity of life – images would be fleeting. We might imagine the movement of sand or snow in the wind. Our sounds would be nonlinear (mainly exponential, see Figure 1.5 and we might use the swish–swipe motion shown through Figure 1.15). The overall focus of the scene would be occluded and there may be reverberation involved. To bring the scene into focus we could take away the landscape leaving only the populace (in thin air), or make the swish so extreme that it breaks free of the landscape and, through increased amplitude, becomes a solid, audible event with sufficient energy to trigger something new.

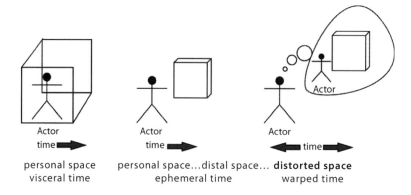

Figure 6.1 Being *in* and *out* of time

Imagine being close to loudspeakers listening to a multitude of dry, crisp, aggressive sonic gestures. Our position is defined by our avoidance of these sounds (as though they were throwing punches at us). This situation is like landing in the middle of a dense forest. It is us that have to move. Our situation is defined by what we bump into. Time feels more of a challenge.

However, consider a similar environment when our acoustic space is viewable and experienced from within but felt to be 'distant'. This is the environmental approach and is especially prominent in multichannel pieces where loudspeakers are playing vastly different sounds or granulating across multiple channels. It is also the case where we perceive a landscape in the stereo field. We feel like we could rotate in our seat and appreciate another perspective as though we were in a boat in the middle of a lake (Figure 6.2). Normally, the components of the soundworld are distant from us. The trees and wildlife are at the periphery of the lake: we can't reach out and touch them but we can appreciate their movement from afar. Time is ephemeral.

Figure 6.2 Peripheral surroundings

Finally, there is the moment when we take what we have heard, predict what we might hear and feel either lost in the moment or very self-conscious. It is possible that when we get lost in the moment (the out-of-body experience, the dream moment) our perception of the duration of a work is considerably shorter than it actually is. This does not mean the work must be dream-like (and this dream state is not the same as that associated with the perception of surreality): if we are engaged in the work, we are less likely to notice ourselves. When we are self-conscious we feel the passing of time acutely and as a result may not end up liking our listening experience. (The 'when will it end?' scenario.)

6.3 Wave – Particle Duality

Through avoiding the lattice as codified in the regulated structures of pitch and duration, electroacoustic music can make time appear continuous – a wave model. It can also *mark* time through regulated repetition and lattice-like characteristics – a particle model. The *visceral* time of Figure 6.1 will have distinct object edges. Sonic gestures that flow (no matter how aggressively) will normally have a more natural temporal flow; and we flow with it. Regular repetition presents us with a picture not of the sounds sitting in the lattice *but of the lattice itself.* We can become imprisoned by this rigid structure both as composers and listeners.

6.4 Quantum Theory of Opposites

Our perception of time within a work can be compressed to a large moment (two minutes of continuous music or a heavily reverberated space felt as *'the expansive section'*, yet still a discrete moment). It can be a dynamic flow (continuous) like riding a wave or it can be a numerical experience (discrete). The closer we are to realising the particular nature of time (particular as in 'tick-tock' as we count the seconds), the less we can engage with the sounds around us. The more we engage with the sounds around us the less control we have over the flow of time, and this can be equally worrying. The feeling of a past (or future) time is even more hazy. This is our perspective influencing the way we eventually structure our composition or listening experience. In real life, one would (probably) not sit and relax for two minutes enjoying a glorious view *without* moving one's view; scanning and zooming. Therefore, a composer will normally invite the listener to do exactly the same by populating their scenes with occasional moments of focus. Thus the quantum theory of opposites becomes rather like the focal ratio of a camera and consequent depth of field produced in a picture. Clarity of foreground often comes at the expense of the background; clarity of background often comes at the expense of the perception of hierarchical structures such as gesture and texture. Luckily with a time-based art form like electroacoustic music, the quantum theory of opposites can be explored.

At the end of the day (a useful temporal phrase, not normally used in academic prose), for music that is *fixed* to a medium and played back over loudspeakers, we are given a *fait accompli*. Some may ask whether time flows differently for composers (in the studio or sitting in a concert) than for a listener who is less engaged. Perhaps it is best to assume that some will have more familiarity with electroacoustic music than others. They may (most probably will) be more amenable to giving their time to experience the time of the music in front of them. Familiarity with sonic art does not need to take a long time and by actually making some music (perhaps using this book and its free tools) listeners can quickly acquire an understanding of how sound can be manipulated and share similar frames of reference.

6.5 Time and Space Equals Energy

If we think back to the first time we placed a sound in a DAW, saw a waveform yet *did not* actually listen to it, we are seeing an image of energy over time. As we layer sound upon sound, we perhaps notice a little red light appear on the mix track indicating overload. We compress or lower the amplitudes of some waveforms yet we somehow keep the energy constant. The entropy of the situation is the tendency of our composition to sway out of control as soon as we start. Making too much of the sound/science metaphor is perhaps dangerous but our pieces (of whatever finite duration) are enclosed entities where we have taken control of and shaped sound energy. The fact that the ear/brain then converts this energy into hierarchies of chunks, themes, transformations, images, spaces, meanings and emotions over time, and after the work is finished, is a reminder that we must always be in control of the energy in our music.

6.6 The Practicalities of Time

6.6.1 Composing time

If the composition process is boiled down to Figure 6.3, composers tend to spend the vast majority of their time generating and accumulating. The recording process may provide the inspiration for the work and normally happens before any other work. The start of the mix varies from composer to composer. Some may start with the very first sound and then their 'where from here?' will direct their development and accumulation process. Many accumulate sounds into families and generate large quantities of material which they then review before beginning a mix. This process can happen quickly or it can be laboured. As composers develop (and this comment is drawn from personal experience), finding what we think are 'new sounds' becomes increasingly difficult. Works do not require new sounds all the time, however. It really is a matter of 'it is not what you have, it is what you do with it' that counts. But perhaps you need at least one sound that, when you listen to it every day, excites you to continue composing (the work that you are on and the ones to come!)

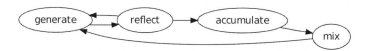

Figure 6.3 The work–reflect process

6.6.2 Duration of electroacoustic music

A number of chapters have strayed from the practical necessities of making, presenting and performing electroacoustic music. As this book began as a resource for students at the University of Sheffield, the question 'how long does my piece need to be?' had to be answered. If students are taking a credited course then it is right that there be parity of commitment and assessment between a practical module and a theoretical one. Therefore if a duration is set, it is an unfortunate parameter that you must work with and turn to your advantage. Hopefully you have some room to manoeuvre (a duration plus or minus something). If your work must be between three and six minutes you have an opportunity to create something that might be very quick throughout its course and be spent by three minutes. Equally you may granulate some extreme textures or landscapes that require six minutes to develop. But at six minutes you also have the possibility of combining the two and demonstrating that you can move from the fast to the slow. *De Natura Sonorum* by Parmegiani (see Chapter 5) presents some excellent examples of small, self-contained movements. The final movement, 'Points versus fields' is almost a mini-piece in itself and at eight minutes has a very solid form. Short-form works of three minutes duration have been commissioned and published on the Empreintes DIGITALes label in two discs, *Électro Clips* (1996) and *Miniatures Concrètes* (1998). Shorter than the modern 'pop' single, this particular style of electroacoustic music is often very focused upon one sound or technique. In a genre normally devoid of quantified pitches and rhythms, texts and speech, and built from unfamiliar sound in nebulous frameworks, three minutes goes by all too quickly.

6.7 The Practicalities of Space

6.7.1 Recording, spatialisation and performance

The practicalities of space are dealt with in Chapters 8 and 9. Headphones are very portable but present a completely different listening experience to loudspeakers. Recording and working in stereo will require at least stereo playback. This stereo image can then be duplicated with multiple loudspeaker systems for larger concerts. The more loudspeakers one has in concert, the more difficult it is to set up and control in performance. There will be less rehearsal time, and expense increases with every additional pair of loudspeakers (physical and financial). If you make an ambisonic work your piece will have portability but you require very regulated performance conditions. If your composition is in a 5.1, 7.1, 10.2 or other cinema-style format you may have the opportunity to receive very accurate representation in a number of venues where the sound systems are already installed – cinemas! Sonic art has not approached cinemas in a major way even as a pre-film experience or concert in its own right as it does not appeal to the masses. However, more and more cinemas are playing opera and independent films to maintain diverse audiences. Sonic art can travel here, and for little or no expense! Cinema configurations in concert or multichannel from 8 to N (normally a multiple of 8) are hugely expensive. Works of this nature have 'research' value in that they will investigate something most of us will not normally hear and the composers can report their results. Performance is vital; the presentation of your work to an online audience especially so. Whilst real spatialisation of sound is a wonderful experience, a good work should present its spaces, times, meanings and emotions without recourse to such expensive infrastructure.[3]

6.7.2 Space in sound, space through sound

Back in the studio, how might we investigate space more practically through sounding models? This is not a recapitulation of techniques of up–down, left–right, near–far, close–diffuse. Rather, it is space as environment, something mentioned way back in Section 1.8. Referring back to the spatial metaphors of Table 6.1 we find the following.

Expansive (sparse), desolate

As a fixed space, the best solution might be to create a 'canopied' or 'rooted' setting with either a high frequency drone, a low frequency drone or both. Using both affords a more dramatic enclosure. Both drones or textures can be created using granular methods or synthesis. Drones crossing through numerous frequencies may need to be notch filtered.

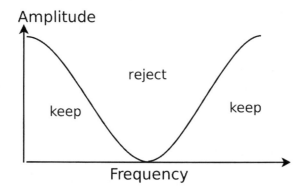

Figure 6.4 A notch filter passing high and low frequencies only

The Csound unit generators for this are Butterworth filters (bp for pass, br for reject) requiring a centre frequency and a bandwidth.

```
aout1 butterbp ain1, <frequency>, <bandwidth>
aout2 butterbr ain2, <frequency>, <bandwidth>
```

You can use bandpass or reject filters in the Blue `bandpassreject` `effect` (see Figure 6.5).

Figure 6.5 The bandpass/bandreject effect in Blue

In the sonogram below, the white area is noise. Over time, the white is pushed to the extremes of the frequency spectrum creating our canopy. We hear the extremes and visualise what is missing – and this is *vast* (and affords the potential to be populated/filled).

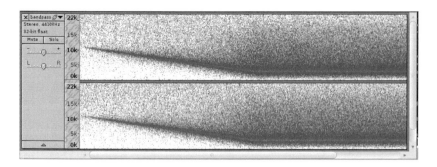

Figure 6.6 A canopy forming from band-rejected noise

Contracted (dense), desperate

It is more difficult to create this space synthetically. This contraction could represent itself in many ways. It could be a compression of fast-paced sounds that lack direction, although this might be described as dense and expansive: the audio equivalent of the kettle full of (almost) boiling water. It could also be a sound that verges towards a very fixed frequency and becomes quite sinusoidal, almost piercing (emulating the tinnitus effect, for example): the audio equivalent of the pain caused by a needle.

Real

Despite sounds coming from loudspeakers, we note the actions of the laws of physics and nature, potentially recognising human agency. A real space is best suggested by a live recording or a real-world sound that feels like it has been played by someone. Artificial reverberation only accentuates the perception of the real if the sound itself continues. It is, however, possible to fake a real space using synthesised environmental models. Andy Farnell's Pure Data examples of environmental sounds in his book *Designing Sound* (Farnell, 2010) could quite easily evoke a sense of real space. Quite often we make the necessary leap of faith to make a texture suggest a real space. Cicada-like sounds can often set up the sense of a hot environment (and it does not take much to trick the brain into thinking that any repetitive click sound could be said cicadas). Wind noise (even a varying-pitched whistle or whine) can suggest a real space. Normally, though, real spaces have more than one object interacting over a period of time and as a consequence some delay or reverberation is required to give a sense of reality. Human agency is often suggested by the sounds either side of the sound itself (take breathing, for example, prior to and after playing a note on the oboe). Filters that peak around vocal formants can quite easily imbue 'human' characteristics and, as a consequence, make foreign sounds more approachable. Anything recognisably non-mechanical (even though machines are real) suggests a reality.

Unreal

Unreal is the opposite of real; something synthetic. Imagine you have set up your reverberation but instead of raindrops or cicadas, you have sinusoidal 'blips'. It is difficult to relate this to anything we hear in the real world. There is a tendency for the unreal to imply an aural discourse where we look for patterns based upon simple sound types and their repetition/transformation. Our perception of space can then become arbitrary (and meaningless). The dissolution of space and its disruption through the chaotic mixing of sound or randomised montage of materials creates a redundancy that destroys reality. Here, unreal equals unwanted.

It is actually quite difficult to imagine unreal spaces, or sounds for that matter. Given that we have a tendency to create relationships quickly, once a lone, unreal sound is joined by another sound, a 'reality' of sorts begins to form.

Surreal

The surreal is fantastic and is often caused by the exaggeration of the real, the unreal disguised as the real – a potential dream-like state. Trevor Wishart talks about surreal spaces in his chapter on landscape in Simon Emmerson's *The Language of Electroacoustic Music* (Wishart, 1986). Imagine your dry, hot environment with cicadas in the background and whalesong. The audio equivalent of a Dali painting.

Notes

1. Echoic memory is part of our sensory memory that can hold sound for around three to four seconds prior to further processing.
2. See Bob Snyder's excellent book *Music and Memory: An Introduction* for a detailed explanation of memory and neural activity when listening (Snyder, 2001).
3. Whilst a 24-channel work may never work in stereo, the stereo work plus spatial imagination is often an excellent alternative to mediocre works over multichannel speaker systems.

References

Farnell, A. (2010). *Designing Sound*. Cambridge, MA: The MIT Press.

Harrison, J. (1998). Sound, space, sculpture: some thoughts on the what, how and why of sound diffusion. *Organised Sound*, 3(2):117–27.

Harrison, J. (1999). Imaginary space: Spaces in the imagination. Australasian Computer Music Conference Keynote Address. http://cec.concordia.ca/econtact/ACMA/ACMConference.htm [Online; accessed November 2009].

Smalley, D. (2007). Space-form and the acousmatic image. *Organised Sound*, 12(01):35–58.

Snyder, B. (2001). *Music and Memory: An Introduction*. Cambridge, MA: The MIT Press.

Various Artists (1996). *Électro Clips*. IMED 9604.

Various Artists (1998). *Miniatures Concrètes*. IMED 9837.

Wishart, T. (1986). The relation of language to materials. In Emmerson, S., ed., *The Language of Electroacoustic Music*, pages 41–60. London: Macmillan.

Chapter 7

Philosophical Reasonings

A sound always sounds like something else.

7.1 Understanding Sound and Understanding Sound

7.1.1 A basic viewpoint

We need to have a stronger understanding of how and why sound exists and how and why we might want to transform it creatively. Even if a sound is wholly abstract we attempt to come to terms with it. If, upon repetition or transformation, we recognise a bond between A and A' we begin to realise the potential for some ideal sound 'parent'. This is the Platonic/Kantian philosophical approach. It is a search for order out of chaos, but in the practical dimension when creating sound associations in the studio it is easier to know when you have it wrong than right. But as mentioned before, it is often easier to learn by making mistakes, to learn by error, as it more clearly presents a reason for moving forward.

In Figure 7.1 we see a 'squaring off' and a reduction of area as transformations become more extreme. Points become exaggerated, and finally it is the points that define the object. Conversely, our transformation backwards is one of going from sharp to smooth (and a filter on a metallic sound texture might aptly represent this shift from source to transformed sound).

7.1.2 The phenomenology of sound

Pierre Schaeffer was obsessed with the phenomenology of sound. This is dangerous philosophical ground for a composer, as phenomenology has a history going right back to Plato so it is terribly difficult to summarise in a way that enables a greater understanding of sound within the practice of making sonic art.[1]

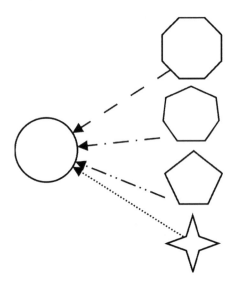

Figure 7.1 Comparison of four shapes with degrees of separation from an imagined ideal

Don Ihde (2007) has, however, made a meticulous study of the phenomenologies of sound. His introduction sets the scene.

> The examination of sound begins with a phenomenology. It is this style of thinking which concentrates an intense examination on experience in its multifaceted, complex, and essential forms. Nothing is easier than a "phenomenology," because each person has her experience and may reflect on it. Nothing is more "familiar" than our own experience, and nothing is closer to ourselves. Potentially anyone can do a "phenomenology".

> But nothing is harder than a phenomenology, precisely because the very familiarity of our experience makes it hide itself from us. Like glasses for our eyes, our experience remains silently and unseeingly presupposed, unthematized. It contains within itself the uninterrogated and overlooked beliefs and actions that we daily live through but do not critically examine. (Ihde, 2007)

Ihde builds his research upon the key ideas formulated by Edmund Husserl (1859–1938) and Martin Heidegger (1889–1976). Husserl is best known for introducing us to phenomenology: the study of experience (and in particular the understanding of our subjective experience). In short, a way of objectifying subjectivity.

The *Stanford Encyclopedia of Philosophy* describes phenomenology as 'the study of structures of consciousness as experienced from the first-person point of view' (Smith, 2011). It encompasses the sensation of seeing and hearing and their associated meanings. The interesting thing about our experiences is that **we** *experience* them.[2] Moreover, having experienced them, they become and inform our ongoing experience. We change what we experience by experiencing it! Smith continues: 'This field of philosophy is then to be distinguished from, and related to, the other main fields of philosophy: ontology (the study of being or what is), epistemology (the study of knowledge), logic (the study of valid reasoning), ethics (the study of right and wrong action), etc.' (Smith, 2011).

We may be able to use a phenomenological approach when analysing something as inexpressible as electroacoustic music. Perhaps there is a meeting point between the phenomenological approach of understanding through knowing (a holistic approach) and a more clear-cut (Cartesian) approach of dissected objects reformed through analysis to create relationships.

Husserl's method of 'bracketing' allows us to avoid dissection and instead suspend our judgement of the object (Emmanuel Kant's *noumenon*), considering instead our interpretation of our experience (Kant's *phenomena*). The idea of 'bracketing' sound led Schaeffer to propose *reduced listening*. The ElectroAcoustic Resource Site (EARS) defines reduced listening as follows:

> In Schaefferian theory, reduced listening is the attitude which consists in listening to the sound for its own sake, as a sound object by removing its real or supposed source and the meaning it may convey. More precisely, it is the inversion of this twofold curiosity about causes and meaning (which treats sound as an intermediary allowing us to pursue other objects) in order to turn it back on to the sound itself. In reduced listening our listening intention targets the event which the sound object is itself (and not to which it refers) and the values which it carries in itself (and not the ones it suggests). In "ordinary" listening the sound is always treated as a vehicle. Reduced listening is therefore an "anti-natural" process, which goes against all conditioning. The act of removing all our habitual references in listening is a voluntary and artificial act which allows us to clarify many phenomena implicit in our perception. Thus, the name reduced listening refers to the notion of phenomenological reduction (Époché), because it consists to some extent of stripping the perception of sound of everything that is not "it itself" in order to hear only the sound, in its materiality, its substance, its perceivable dimensions (Landy and Atkinson, 2004).

The problem here is that as we bracket, the listening process gets more difficult: we step back from engagement with the sound itself, we suspend the moment where we give in to assigning a sound, gesture, texture or object a name. Moreover, despite the fact that we only hear the sound in terms of its 'materiality, its substance, its perceivable dimensions' we begin to suspend the moment where we even assign anything remotely objective like 'fast', 'hard', 'rough' and move a sound from episodic memory to short-term memory.[3]

We are used to thinking that reduced listening was the process of assigning shape, colour, character and not source or cause, but it could be that reduced listening is actually impossible!

Add to this the idea that the sound object we hear is but a perspective (remember Figure 7.1, and consider your appreciation of a two-dimensional painting representing a three-dimensional scene). The more perspectives we hear the more we get a grasp on the object itself. With repetition (and potentially with transformation) comes increased understanding of this ultimate object. Hear a sound once = X; sound played twice = Y; the sound played 20 times could tend towards *the sound itself*. Repetition helps us divorce ourselves from making hasty judgements. Repetition plus transformation affords a progression as the perspectives are changed for us. We see the object in a new light. We imagine an object that might not be there.

The result of all this stepping back, coupled with active and engaged listening, is that we better understand the objects being put in front of our ears and our ability to engage with them.

Ultimately, the problem with associating a source or a cause as Schaeffer defines them may come down to the time we spend playing the sound, and the key trigger moments in it. Take the sound of a bus door or the departure of a tram or underground train. If part of a large 20 minute cityscape it could be a real moment. But perhaps it is simply a metaphor for entry–transfer. It may just be a prolonged 'swish'. It may be all three!

And beyond the understanding of the essence of things we move towards an ontology of Being; existential philosophy that fortunately is beyond the understanding of this author!

7.1.3 Schaeffer's theories in practice

In the latter stages of Michel Chion's *Guide des objets sonores* (1983), a reduction of Pierre Schaeffer's huge *Traité des object musicaux* (1977), he outlines Schaeffer's process for generating a typomorphology – a catalogue of sound types and their change over time. Reducing sound to manageable units through editing; classifying them into rough characteristic types (almost impossible); describing their characteristics in detail (futile). It transpires that from Schaeffer through to the electroacoustic compositions of today, *pitch* is unavoidable. Therefore, to be able to consider a sound object's degree of pitched-ness is important and fortunately we are predisposed to do this! This is clarification vertically (low to high). Continuation, separation and segregation are required to clarify horizontally. Schaeffer defines the vast majority of his terms via extreme poles and continua roughly similar to those mentioned in Chapter 1.

7.1.4 Gestalt principles

Gestalt theory was developed in psychology to enable theorists to talk about how items, segments or chunks might group together, how they might relate to one another and to describe a general context. They are global principles that might apply to sound objects, phrases or complete pieces and can be divided into three distinct areas:

- figure and ground
- similarity, proximity, continuity
- closure, area, symmetry.

We have talked about foreground and background, motif and accompaniment. In gestalt terms this is *figure* and *ground*. Texture-set gestures (gestures that just appear above the surface of a more enveloping texture) play with this idea of figure and ground in that the figure is dominated by the ground.

Similarity (we mentioned the principle of 'similar but different' when processing sound sources) allows for items to be joined and developments to be understood. If you put two completely different soundfiles next to one another (or on top of one another), especially if they are natural sounds that we recognise, you are asking us to think they are related. This is the principle of proximity. If the car and the whale sound don't eventually find a meaningful coexistence, their original mix, surreal though it may be, will be for naught. (Though before you drop this idea, consider how convolution might assist you here. The drone of the car or its energy profile – probably quite noise based – could be coloured by the pitches of whalesong forming a whale-shaped car!)

Continuity is vital in electroacoustic music, especially in fades. It is sometimes the case that you make a fade out and hope that the new material 'covers the exit' of the previous material. When listening back, try to listen just to the fade to really make sure that its exit is almost imperceptible. Continuity, however, is a red herring as we know material must start, change and stop. Glitch music obeys the principle of continuity. Many composers may hear a click in a piece and note this down as an error. If, however, your piece is 'about clicks' you need to use this principle to convince the listener that the clicks are the objects of attention, not errors.

Closure, area and symmetry are perhaps better explained with visual examples, but in audio, closure applies to ADSR envelopes. The principle of symmetry would definitely apply when thinking about durations of objects and when using specific pitch glissandi. In a number of Blue tools, you can apply your process over any duration, so you can have a shape with parameters that go from X to Y over 20 seconds, 10 seconds and 2 seconds, thus creating a symmetry. Self-similarity (a fractal quality as documented in the well-known Mandelbrot set) is sometimes seen as a holy grail of structure and form. Unfortunately, playing a five-second sound over five-seconds, then playing a variety of time-stretched variations (self-similarity to a point) is futile *unless* the sound itself, when stretched or compressed, *reveals* this self-similarity to us. Normally this principle would involve us composing some additional material to direct the listener to the self-similar aspects of the transformations (which is an interesting compositional task).

An addition to this small list of relationships, and related closely to the idea of continuity, is perhaps one new gestalt theory (or principle) and that is *transformation*. Trevor Wishart talks extensively (and openly) about the necessity for transformation in his book *Sound Composition* (Wishart, 2012). This recent book exposes some of the secrets of Wishart's language from early works such as *Red Bird* (1977) to his most recent masterpiece, *Encounters in the Republic of Heaven* (2009).

He talks about compositional methods and implements computer music techniques to develop them. As many of his works involve the voice, its own vast array of sounds often obscure a clear description of method as techniques are already very closely intertwined with highly complex extended vocal techniuques. However, works such as *Imago* (2002) with a very abstract source sound give us a greater insight. *Imago* uses only a single clink of two whiskey glasses from *...et ainsi de suite...* by Jonty Harrison (1992). All subsequent sounds are derived from this very tiny fragment. It ought to be possible to define a number of clear techniques and relate them to the methods of composition.

Wishart writes, 'As with *Tongues of Fire* I began by systematically exploring the source. In this case the sound is less than 1/10th of a second in duration. The most obvious initial approaches were to time-stretch the sound in various ways' (Wishart, 2012, 101). This statement of the obvious resonates with my own theory of opposites. Given a short sound, the method is to make it longer; the recipe is repetition (from complete repetitions of the object to repetitions of grains).

Wishart concludes that as time-varying transitions assert themselves over 10–100 repetitions of the object, transformation itself becomes a method. As the principle of transformation dominates the music, the sound itself must be sufficiently malleable (one might say functionally neutral) to enable the transformation to be heard. At this point, Wishart may be verging towards what Pierre Boulez required of the note: a neutrality that afforded serial manipulation. But I think Wishart always has at the back of his mind a sense of the magic of transformation, and because of that he is always thinking about the sound, not the process. The argument that we may be listening because we like the sound is unfinished and weak. We are listening because we like the sound, want to understand where it has come from and want to know where it goes.

7.1.5 Dark Arts?

The word 'magic' has cropped up a few times in this text. If we are to assume that our object betrays a source of hidden (higher) power, one that can perhaps never be revealed, then our sound as heard is like a totem, an emblem with spiritual significance. We are normally drawn to that which we do not understand. Think Harry Potter and the 'Dark Forest' or 'don't look behind you'; our fascination often gets the better of us. Acousmatic listening must take us beyond magic, lest 'magic' itself just become a source. It is either Alice's 'Wonderland' and we leave it to her, or, *we explore it too.*

7.1.6 An ecological perspective

Building on the theoretical work in ecological perception and vision by James Gibson (1986) and the early works of William W. Gaver on everyday listening mentioned in Chapter 4 (Gaver, 1993a, b), theorists and composers such as Eric Clarke (2005), Luke Windsor (1995) and James Andean (2011) have considered how our direct understanding of sounds as we hear them can affect meaning in music in general and acousmatic music in particular. As you fill up a watering can, you can hear a rising pitch proportional to the size of the resonant space left in the can. It helps us (admittedly reinforcing sight) in preparing to turn off the water. Clarke, a keen cyclist, uses the sound of his back tyre rubbing against the frame to suggest a problem is imminent. Recognition of the sound (something in this case which should not be there – and that is interesting in itself) leads to identification of the problem.

The ecological theory of Gibson is a unifying theory of natural and social sciences and suggests that we 'resonate' with information received aurally or visually. How we get 'tuned in' to this myriad of information is presumably through experience and failure. Clarke mentions the relationship between perception and action, adaptation, and perceptual learning (Clarke, 2005, 19). Our action stimulus with electroacoustic music can actually be quite sharp. We will not be dancing in the aisles but the often natural shapes created through logarithmic and exponential paths (consider the unfolding of a whip or the flight of a fly-fishing line) lead to cumulative motions of the head or hand.

Clarke is at pains to demystify the ecological approach:

> One of the complaints that cognitivists make about the ecological approach is that it appears "magical."[4] By rejecting the dominating role of internal representations, and with it the idea of explicit processing stages that are intended to explain perception and cognition, the ecological approach seems to retreat into a quasi-mystical belief that perception "just happens" as a result of a miraculous tuning of perceptual systems to the regularities of the environment. That charge is based on a fundamental misrepresentation of the ecological approach – one that completely ignores the central role of perceptual learning. The tuning of a perceiver's perceptual systems to the invariant properties of the environment is no happy accident, nor the result purely of some kind of Darwinian biological adaptation: it is a consequence of the flexibility of perception, and the plasticity of the nervous system, in the context of a shaping environment. Perceptual systems become attuned to the environment through continual exposure, both as the result of species adaptation on an evolutionary time scale, and as the consequence of perceptual learning within the lifetime of an individual. (Clarke, 2005, 25)

In short, we are attuned to becoming attuned and it is through repeated exposure to sound (music) that we become accustomed to it and gain an ability to discern it. No wonder then that electroacoustic sound born out of 60 years of the ability to record and transform is having a hard time against over 2,000 years of indoctrination to pitched instrumental music! However, we know that 'when listening to the sounds of an unfamiliar foreign language [we] notice the huge variety and specific qualities of the sounds that make up the language – to be quite acutely aware, in other words, of continuously variable acoustical features but to understand nothing' (Clarke, 2005, 34). Can this be applied to electroacoustic music? A delight in the play of sound (for a limited period of time perhaps) but no understanding as to 'what's going on' (dictating the time one might stay with the music). An understanding of the syntax, methods and discourse consequently and conversely might engender a harder time simply enjoying the music.

And thus Gibson introduces the idea of affordances and invariance. Invariance is the fixed and logical within a sea of continuity. Affordances are what bring object and subject together and whilst these tended to result in physical action, our cultural appreciation of music (of all kinds) is often appreciated sitting down. However, as the changing nature of performance of electroacoustic music brings in more diverse audiences so the affordance of more physical interaction outside of the 'face-forward' approach increases. The acousmatic position therefore is ideally suited to affordances, invariance and resonance. There are no codified structures in between the listener and the sound; many works offer the natured and nurtured (sounds that feel 'right' or feel 'wrong' when something does not go to plan and sounds that require time to bed in such that their future repetition or development is understood); there is a requirement to attempt Schaeffer's 'reduced listening' *and* attach as many sources, causes, labels, identifiers and tags as you need, to work out 'what's going on'.[5]

7.1.7 Intention and reception

Readers have already been recommended the work of Robert Weale and Leigh Landy at Leicester DeMontfort on precisely this subject (Weale, 2005; 2006). Many of the relationships between composer (as listener and creator) and audience (as listener and re-creator) can be drawn from the semiotics research of Jean-Jacques Nattiez (Nattiez, 1990) – the study of signs and symbols. For Nattiez, a *sign* comprises a *signified* ideal and a *signifier* or sound image. Meaning is derived when objects, pointed to by signs, are drawn into our experience (phenomenology). The words *poietic* and *esthetic*[6] are used to describe the process of creating and receiving. And somewhere between these two poles lies the *neutral level*, which for instrumental music normally implies the score. For electroacoustic music without such an inanimate object, the neutral level is more difficult to find. It is probably the ones and zeros of the soundfile itself. This soundfile can be probed scientifically for frequencies, amplitudes and phases, *and that is all*. Once the human element is brought into play our experiential baggage serves to aid (and confuse) our interpretation (which is understood here to mean highly informed reception).

David Huron places similar importance upon expectation as he defines his ITPRA theory (Huron, 2006). ITPRA stands for the Imagination–Tension–Prediction–Response–Appraisal theory of expectation. During the elaboration of this theory, Huron talks about *schemas*; essentially a framework. He cites the frameworks of major and minor tonalities and how we develop multiple schemas so that major and minor can work both with baroque music and reggae. If electroacoustic schemas began with texture and gesture, we might further imagine that textures are easier to enter into than gestures (due to continuity potentially trumping repetition) and that multichannel composition enables very powerful textures (environments) out of which (very few) gestures might ever emerge. Ultimately the Imagination response requires the listener to drum up potential future events based upon what they have already heard 'accompanied by feelings that make the various outcomes emotionally palpable' (Huron, 2006, 305). If a sonic world does not afford easy predictability based upon our previous casual listening (some hint of pitch or rhythm) or set up an environment where predictability can take place (ideas of repetition), it is no wonder we neither know nor care 'what comes next'.

For intention and reception to align, the segments of analysis become (potentially) the brackets/segments of composition. Pierre Schaeffer documented the sound object, the components that make it and the integration of the sound object into a structure in his *Traité des object musicaux* (1977). He was deeply concerned that the composer's intentions be heard by the listener. This is as impossible as hearing the 'thing in itself' (if the opening gambit of this chapter is anything to go by) but there is no cause to be pessimistic. It is surely the job of the composer not to assume but to guide the listener and if they want to make something abundantly clear, *it must be made abundantly clear*.

There may be a way of finding a neutral level in electroacoustic music as we begin to record (and keep) everything that a composer does (a tracking score of sorts). Composers and software developers at the University of Sheffield are in the process of writing software[7] that records all the data required to recreate a composition, leaving you with starting sounds and a long list of processes. Additionally, it leaves a trace of every action that went wrong. This for analysts is pure gold. By comparing the path taken with all the dead ends, a fuller understanding of compositional method may be gleaned. Readers are encouraged to look at the *Journal of Music, Technology and Education*, volume 6, number 3 for a fascinating discussion of compositional methods in electroacoustic music, including an article authored by the team at Sheffield (Moore et al., 2013) outlining why it is so important to document our compositional decisions.

7.1.8 Emotion and meaning

Patrik Juslin has written extensively about emotion in music, how we feel it and control it. He lists a number of emotions:

Happy, relaxed, calm, moved, nostalgic, pleasurable, loving, sad, longing, tender, amused, hopeful, enchanted, expectant, solemn, interested, admiring, angry, ecstatic, lonely, content, desiring, empathic, proud, spiritual, curious, relieved, bored, indifferent, frustrated, tense, disappointed, surprised, honoured, regretful, contemptuous, confused, anxious, afraid, jealous, disgusted, guilty, shameful, humiliated. (Juslin, 2005, 101)

Emotion and meaning are often intertwined and therefore confused. Emotion can be as simple as minor chord–sad; major chord–happy; excited–fast; calm–slow. But we know it is rarely that simple and, after all, is creating an emotional response in others really the be all and end all in music?

Emotion is strongly linked to form and structure and we notice this most acutely in classical and romantic music as we have been culturally attuned to it for centuries.

I prefer to read Wenger's (1999) description of meaning, which is still a little ephemeral but which is linked to practice (doing), participation (experiencing), reification (objectifying) and ultimately our community of practice as composers and listeners, one and the same.

From a practical point of view, emotion is hard enough to embody let alone produce in others. Meaning is even more difficult. In music, if you work the structure and form to be cohesive and if meaning is drawn by the listener, you are in luck! There are, however, many ways of structuring the work such that the form (the meaning of structure?) is understood.

The strongest emotions are those involving humans. Reifying these in classical music is hard enough: in electroacoustic music it is almost impossible. But this is where opera and film (supported by film music) has managed to twang the heart strings of even the most steadfast viewer. When we see humans *giving* we are blessed with the spirit of something righteous, something that invokes the strongest of emotions and meanings – that there is a purpose in life and that some are willing to give (ultimately their all) to that purpose. And that this giving takes place in real life denotes a certain truth to this purpose. There is an emotional strength in bonds between people (family, lovers, friends) that is as intense when it is working as it is saddening when it breaks. You can gauge your emotional response to your music. The more *you* feel it, the more likely others will too.

7.1.9 Form and structure

Just as there could be confusion between emotion and meaning so there is an equal confusion between form and structure.

As we listen to Bruckner's third symphony we note that Bruckner lays his forms and structures very clearly. Both are related to *repetition*. Repetition at the note level is predominantly structural: phrases, motifs, developments. Repetition at the phrase level is a hybrid and is more dependent upon time. The sensation of an emotion arising from a structure (a shape, colour, dynamic combination) – an emotion we produce by reifying (personifying, objectifying) a chunk of music, a structural element – is reinforced (or repelled) as the music progresses.

The form then becomes a global culmination of our emotional journey aided (or hindered) by the way the music was structured. Form in classical music and its relation to emotion and meaning has been well documented by Leonard Meyer (1994; 2008).

The structure of music can dictate moments of tension and release, especially between moments of repetition, development and recapitulation. Stéphane Roy (1996) has drawn upon Meyer's theories when analysing the music of Francis Dhomont's *Points de fuite* (1982). Roy then draws in the semiological models proposed by Nattiez (1990) in his text *L'analyse des musiques électroacoustiques: modèles et propositions* (2004). Of particular interest are his ideas of rhetorical functions which relate explicitly to transformations of statements and the interruption of discourse, ideas closely related to a phenomenological 'bracketing'.

7.2 A Social Theory of Learning

This section is particularly of relevance to advanced composers. It helps explain why composers playing their works to each other in concert understand the nuances that make electroacoustic music sound the same to some but completely different to others.

We may think that the vast majority of electroacoustic music is conducted in solitary isolation in the studio then placed on the internet for whomever may happen by. This is incorrect. There is an historical community of active participants who have forged a tradition of sonic art. We must not be afraid of the words *history* and *tradition*. They are as useful to be part of and something to react against. Etienne Wenger has written extensively about communities of practice (1999) and it would be useful to reflect some views of the past 60 years of sonic arts practice through his writings.

The process of composition is ultimately a learning process with the end results shared and experienced by others: it is a social act, something Christopher Small calls *Musicking* (Small, 2011).[8] Wenger begins by putting forward four premises (Wenger, 1999, 4):

1. We are social beings. Far from being trivially true, this fact is a central aspect of learning.
2. Knowledge is a matter of competence with respect to valued enterprises, such as singing in tune, discovering scientific facts, fixing machines, writing poetry, being convivial, growing up as a boy or a girl, and so forth.
3. Knowing is a matter of participating in the pursuit of such enterprises, that is, of active engagement in the world.
4. Meaning – our ability to experience the world and our engagement with it as meaningful – is ultimately what learning is to produce.

These premises are made real through (Wenger, 1999, 5):

1. *Meaning:* a way of talking about our (changing) ability – individually and collectively – to experience our life and the world as meaningful.
2. *Practice:* a way of talking about the shared historical and social resources, frameworks, and perspectives that can sustain mutual engagement in action.
3. *Community:* a way of talking about the social configurations in which our enterprises are defined as worth pursuing and our participation is recognisable as competence.
4. *Identity:* a way of talking about how learning changes who we are and creates personal histories of becoming in the context of our communities.

The common theme here is 'a way of talking'. This book is trying to facilitate a conversation about the sonic art we make and further understand the sonic art practice of others.

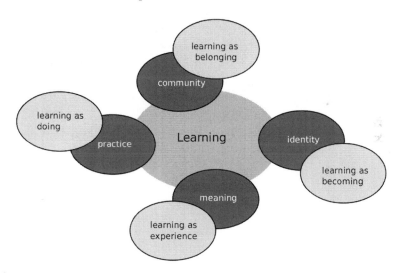

Figure 7.2 Components of a social theory of learning: an initial inventory (Wenger, 1999, 5)

7.2.1 Sonic arts practice

The concept of creating sonic art in a way that contributes to the knowledge and understanding of yourself and the communities within which you work can include:

both the explicit and the tacit. It includes what is said and what is left unsaid; what is represented and what is assumed. It includes the language, tools, documents, images, symbols, well-defined roles, specified criteria, codified procedures, regulations, and contracts that various practices make explicit for a variety of purposes. But it also includes all the implicit relations, tacit conventions, subtle cues, untold rules of thumb, recognizable intuitions, specific perceptions, well-tuned sensitivities, embodied understandings, underlying assumptions, and shared world views. *Most of these may never be articulated*, yet they are unmistakable signs of membership in communities of practice and are crucial to the success of their enterprises. (Wenger, 1999, 47, my emphasis)

Which is why your solitary composition *must* be made to engage with a community and why you as a composer *must* engage in performance, documentation, explanation and sharing in real situations as these unwritten cues are audible, visible, sensed in the moment but not written down. And this leads to a central philosophical question: *How closely is process related to product?*

Given the very qualitative descriptors in Chapter 1, the uses of particular transformations in Chapters 2 and 4 and the connections between transformations and descriptors in Chapter 3, my personal view is that process and product are inextricably linked, though in order to talk about them we must untangle sounds and processes, or better still, relate them so closely that it is impossible to talk about one without the other.

7.2.2 A community of practice

The physical embodiment of a community of practice might well be those organisations or social network groups that are born and die as a practice develops. Communities such as the Canadian Electroacoustic Community (CEC) are discussed in Chapter 9. Communities of practice encapsulate the thoughts and ideas of their members over time. They help us negotiate the past. Wenger again helps us understand why communities might be useful and how they maintain their existence. When we create a thing that has any relation to another thing already extant, we must remember in order to continue the existence of the object (reification). This provides continuity to a community's collective understanding. Similarly, when we know we are individuals within a community, our actions will rely upon shared knowledge but break free from boundaries of convention. As Wenger puts it, 'we can shred documents, but it is not so easy to erase our memories. We can forget events, but the marks they leave in the world can bring them back to us' (Wenger, 1999, 88).

There are aspects of this text that are clearly set forth to explain sonic art practice to those that wish to learn. However, we are all learning and it is only through learning that a community evolves. That is especially true in sonic art. Although we mentioned the process was inextricably tied to the product, the tools of sonic art have changed dramatically since composers used tape recorders, analogue filters and tone generators in the 1960s. However, the methods have remained very similar and processes like delays and filters are the same now as they were back then. The discovery of the Fourier transform has enabled spectral modifications, but even here these modifications often emulate analogue alternatives (such as filtering). The practice of sonic art on fixed media has remained relatively unchanged over the years: the consumption and production of it has sped up. In other genres, particularly installation and interactive music, the influence of technology has been more aggressive. And it is here that the technology community has perhaps strayed somewhat from the sound community. There are few that will deny that technology has been both the servant and the master, the tool and the inspiration. However, there are times where the technology itself is of greater interest than any secondary output (sound, image or interaction).

Wenger charts these connections through community boundaries. Boundaries for the sonic arts community relate to 'idiosyncratic ways of engaging with one another, which outsiders can not easily enter ... complex understandings of their enterprise as they define it, which outsiders may not share ... and a repertoire for which outsiders miss shared references' (Wenger, 1999, 113).

But as we have argued before, the best way of understanding sonic arts practice is to join the community through practice. Wenger cites three methods of expanding communities: through boundary practices, overlaps and peripheries (see Figure 7.3).

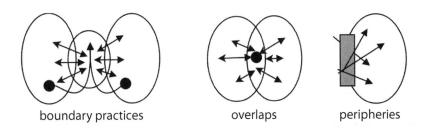

boundary practices   overlaps   peripheries

Figure 7.3 Types of connections provided by practice (Wenger, 1999, 114)

One can easily see how sonic arts communities translate to these states. The boundary practice example is perhaps the composer working in a hybrid medium like mixed music (for instrument and electronic sounds). They will traverse both the sonic arts community and the instrumental community but will be a part of neither. One could say the same of visual artists dabbling in sound and sonic artists creating visual music, but this is perhaps more of an obvious case of 'overlap'. For the most part the artist lives in a primary community but shares a small degree of experience with a secondary community. The periphery is best explained through the outreach work of many composers bringing in non-community members, many of whom will, through practice, eventually enter fully into the community.

7.2.3 Identity in practice

Section 3.5 talked about originality. Originality is the obvious marker of identity but it is a quick identifier. Other identifiers take a lot longer to permeate and if you are part of a community of practice then your identity will emerge as people get to know you. Wenger states,

> There is a profound connection between identity and practice. Developing a practice requires the formation of a community whose members can engage with one another and thus acknowledge each other as participants. As a consequence, practice entails the negotiation of ways of being a person in that context. This negotiation may be silent; participants may not necessarily talk directly about that issue. But whether or not they address the question directly, they deal with it through the way they engage in action with one another and relate to one another. Inevitably, our practices deal with the profound issue of how to be a human being. In this sense the formation of a community of practice is also the negotiation of identities. (Wenger, 1999, 149)

Read most biographies and you will see the words 'studied with'. We identify with our teachers and, whether we learned a great deal from them or not, they are part of our trajectory of learning (Wenger uses 'trajectories of identity') and part of our community of practice. I spent many years at Birmingham University studying with Professor Jonty Harrison. I value his works highly, look to them for inspiration and sometimes expect to use them as a springboard from which to move on. Whilst the 'Darmstadt school' is a well-known community of mainly instrumental composers that sprang up after the Second World War, community evolution does not require such radical catalysts as war and a smaller community began in the 1980s that was built up around

BEAST, the Birmingham ElectroAcoustic Sound Theatre. Whilst Jonty Harrison never taught specific rigorous methods, a style of composition has emerged that has been so strongly influenced by him that others find common audible traits in the music of his students. My personal community also attempts to embrace the works cited in Chapter 5, and whilst we can often more easily describe what we think does not work than what does, I am not going to describe works in Chapter 5 that I do not find inspiring (as this book is focused upon inspiring composers who work with sound, after all).

Identification of 'you' can sometimes also be better achieved by non-participation and non-conformation. This is neither a good nor a bad thing but striving for this is perhaps best once you have come to terms with your own trajectory of identity.

Ultimately it may be better to identify with others and leave your own identity to others. This is a chapter on philosophical reasonings and there are times we think about the nature of self. However, this is also a text about practical solutions and negotiating the self can become bit of a blind alley!

7.3 An Historical Perspective

Of all the composers that made a concerted effort to represent what they did in their works (albeit without real reference to the techniques they used), Pierre Schaeffer and Denis Smalley have been the most open about their activity.

- Schaeffer's *Traité des objects musicaux* (Schaeffer, 1977) was the major analytical work in this area. It is due to be given an English translation very soon.
- Michel Chion's *Guide des objet sonores* (Chion, 1983) acts as a companion to the large Schaeffer volume and was translated by Christine North and John Dack in 2009. In the guide, Chion highlights Schaeffer's programmes of research. Whilst they appear to be analytical it is difficult not to think Schaeffer was desperately trying to reverse engineer his theory to produce music. The guide is still quite detailed and also relies heavily upon descriptors based around extreme poles.
- Schaeffer's *A la recherche d'une musique concrète* (Schaeffer and Molès, 1952), which has recently been translated by Christine North and John Dack (2012), is fascinating because it reads as a real-time journal, presenting all the trials and tribulations of Schaeffer's vision; what was working and what was not, not just in terms of the development of a theory but in terms of producing

the music, equipping the studios, staging and managing concerts and advocating for concrete music.
• Smalley's 'Spectromorphology' is now one of the most cited papers in electroacoustic music. It is also better suited to analysis than synthesis.

We might consider how the rules of Western classical music kept it secure for centuries yet afforded huge changes in the system leading to the breakdown of tonality and atonalism/serialism. It is not that there are no shared understandings or theories in electroacoustic music; Schaeffer and Smalley have clearly articulated the scene. However, in today's fast-paced world, rules or standards once suggested are given no time to bed in. Moreover, such is the pace of change that a shared grammar can neither migrate nor mutate.

It is only through our social fostering of identity (see Section 7.2) that a vast majority of unwritten guidance passes amongst practitioners. The consequence of this depth of study and experiential learning through practice is that there is a place for electroacoustic music in teaching institutions throughout the UK and beyond, both as 'music technology' in secondary education and as a specific avant-garde practice in higher education. Not least because one has the time to contextualise, join or form communities of practice and take the time to develop an emotional intelligence for the meaningful reception of sound.

7.4 The Brain on Electroacoustic Music

Numerous attempts throughout this text have insisted upon a highly active state of arousal, strong participation in listening and a focused search for structure and form whilst creating electroacoustic music. They go against an observation that when listening we are 'moved', often to a new space or place and that said place is inhabited with agents that work in plausible ways (perhaps obeying, in a simple fashion, some of the laws of nature) and that this movement takes us away from self-conscious states. When listening to a work and so moved, try focusing upon something else – reading, email. It may well be that the sound that draws you back in is the sound that *should not have been there*.[9] Recent psychological research is indicating the importance of the default-mode-network (DMN; Vessel et al., 2013) during an aesthetic experience. The emergent field of neuroaesthetics uses brain-imaging studies taken during aesthetic experiences (such as listening to music). DMN is also associated with self-referential mental processing and our mental projection of identity and sense of 'self', though not necessarily our self-conscious awareness of being in the space as mentioned in Chapter 6. Clearly there is a great deal more research to be done to map out our active engagement with sound, our mind-wandering, our introspection, our 'selfish-ness' in music, and we return to an even greater understanding of listening modes (see Section 1.2.5).

Notes

1. Schaeffer wrestled with philosophy to a far greater extent in his writings than I ever will in mine. As a composer not a philosopher I look forward to understanding these concepts in greater depth.
2. It is difficult to extrapolate these three words. In short: any one without the others would be meaningless in any musical situation.
3. Do not worry: thinking about sound is more complicated than actually doing it (listening). The hard and fast rules of the real-world listening experience bring us down to earth with a bang rarely experienced by the philosophers of ontology.
4. Please do not make any links between this magical activity and the magic of listening to the unknown mentioned in Section 7.1.5 either. (Yet. . .)
5. This last statement sounds like electroacoustic music is the apogee of all musical experiences: something that could be both visceral and intellectual at the same time. I would not have written this entire book if I did not think this to be the case!
6. Not to be confused with poetic and aesthetic!
7. SCMake will comprise an interface to scripted software such as Csound and the Composers Desktop Project and an innovative mixer that delivers XML output.
8. Small personifies musical works (especially the symphonic repertoire) as masculine and suggests that we identify with the characters presented. There is a growing body of work on gender and music. Although we can examine the electroacoustic music of male and female composers, it is doubtful that there will be extensive work on male/female symbolism in this genre. It is potentially asexual unless it borrows stereotypes from other genres. And perhaps it cannot help itself here as it is almost impossible to avoid pitch and pulse.
9. Certainly, this is how I often listen to works by my students. I find that my attention is drawn when something is wrong: otherwise, I am content to let the music happen. Clearly this is after numerous auditions focusing on specific topics and tasks!

References

Andean, J. (2011). Ecological psychology and the electroacoustic concert context. *Organised Sound*, 16(02):125–33.

Chion, M. trans. Dack, J. and North, C. (2009). *Guide to Sound Objects*. http://monoskop.org/log/?p=536[accessed18December2015].

Chion, M. (1983). *Guide des objets sonores: Pierre Schaffer et la recherche musicale*. Paris: Editions Buchet/Chastel.

Clarke, E. F. (2005). *Ways of Listening: An Ecological Approach to the Perception of Musical Meaning*. Oxford: Oxford University Press.

Dhomont, F. (1982). *Points de fuite.* Cycle de l'errance. IMED 9607 pub. 1996.

Gaver, W. W. (1993a). How do we hear in the world? Explorations in ecological acoustics. *Ecological Psychology,* 5(4):285–313.

Gaver, W. W. (1993b). What in the world do we hear? An ecological approach to auditory event perception. *Ecological Psychology,* 5(1):1–29.

Gibson, J. J. (1986). *The Ecological Approach to Visual Perception.* London: Routledge.

Harrison, J. (1992). *...et ainsi de suite...* Articles indéfinis. IMED 9627 pub. 1996.

Huron, D. B. (2006). *Sweet Anticipation: Music and the Psychology of Expectation.* Cambridge, MA: The MIT Press.

Ihde, D. (2007). *Listening and Voice: Phenomenologies of Sound.* Albany, NY: SUNY Press.

Juslin, P. (2005). From mimesis to catharsis: expression, perception, and induction of emotion in music. In Hargreaves, D. J., ed., *Musical Communication,* pages 85–115. Oxford: Oxford University Press.

Landy, L. and Atkinson, S. (2004). Ears: Electroacoustic resource site. www.ears.dmu.ac.uk/.

Meyer, L. B. (1994). *Music, the Arts, and Ideas: Patterns and Predictions in Twentieth-century Culture.* Chicago, IL: University of Chicago Press.

Meyer, L. B. (2008). *Emotion and Meaning in Music.* Chicago, IL: University of Chicago Press.

Moore, A., Moore, D., Pearse, S., and Stansbie, A. (2013). Tracking production strategies: identifying compositional methods in electroacoustic music. *Journal of Music, Technology & Education,* 6(3):323–36.

Nattiez, J. J. (1990). *Music and Discourse: Toward a Semiology of Music.* Princeton, NJ: Princeton University Press.

Roy, S. (1996). Form and referential citation in a work by Francis Dhomont. *Organised Sound,* 1(1):29–41.

Roy, S. (2004). *L'analyse des musiques électroacoustiques: modèles et propositions.* Paris: Harmattan.

Schaeffer, P. trans. North, C. and Dack, J. (2012). *In Search of a Concrete Music.* Berkeley, CA: University of California Press.

Schaeffer, P. (1977). *Traité des object musicaux: essai interdisciplines.* Paris: Seuil, second edition. Originally published in 1966.

Schaeffer, P. and Molès, A. (1952). *A la recherche d'une musique concrète.* Paris: Editions du Seuil.

Small, C. (2011). *Musicking: The Meanings of Performing and Listening.* Fishers, IN: Wesleyan.

Smith, D. W. (2011). Phenomenology. In Zalta, E. N., ed., *The Stanford Encyclopedia of Philosophy.* Fall 2011 edition.

Vessel, E. A., Starr, G. G., and Rubin, N. (2013). Art reaches within: aesthetic experience, the self and the default mode network. *Frontiers in Neuroscience,* 7:258.

Weale, R. (2005). *The intention/reception project: Investigating the relationship between composer intention and listener response in electroacoustic compositions.* PhD thesis, De Montfort University.

Weale, R. (2006). Discovering how accessible electroacoustic music can be: the intention/reception project. *Organised Sound*, 11(02):189–200.

Wenger, E. (1999). *Communities of Practice: Learning, Meaning, and Identity*. Cambridge: Cambridge University Press.

Windsor, L. (1995). *A perceptual approach to the description and analysis of acousmatic music*. Doctoral thesis, City University.

Wishart, T. (1977). *Red bird: Anticredos*. October Music, Oct 001.

Wishart, T. (2002). *Imago*. EM153 pub. 2004.

Wishart, T. (2012). *Sound Composition*. York: Orpheus the Pantomime Ltd.

Chapter 8

The Presentation of your Work in Performance

This is your work. How is it shared with others in concert?

8.1 Prior to the Concert

8.1.1 Sound diffusion systems

Throughout this book it has been suggested that in order to fully understand the process of composition with sound, it is best if you become fully immersed in the process 'chain' which includes composition, thinking, documenting, publishing, talking and performing.

Stereo sonic art that is fixed to media (hard disk files now being the most common) is often presented across multiple loudspeakers in concert situations. The majority of the processes presented in Chapter 2 deal with stereo soundfiles and can be expanded to include multichannel operation where the polyphonic nature of the transformations may be explored. For example, consider eight slightly different filters on a moving soundfile, granulation with grains spaced across loudspeakers or frequency spectra of a sound object distributed across loudspeakers. It is easy to see how the spatial effect could play a far more important role 'as an effect' than as a contributor to the overall shape of the sound. Multichannel composition has been briefly mentioned in Chapter 4: compositional methodologies are not dissimilar to working in stereo, and indeed multichannel pieces do not defy diffusion.

Sound diffusion has a history that was born out of the GRM (Groupe de Recherches Musicales) and the work of Pierre Schaeffer and Pierre Henry. In the UK it is the work of Professor Jonty Harrison (1998; 1999) who founded the Birmingham ElectroAcoustic Sound Theatre (BEAST) that has inspired directors of many UK sound diffusion systems (the University of Sheffield included) to create their own concert series. Just as technology has influenced the development of composition, so too has it impacted upon performance. Surprisingly, these diffusion systems are all very different in terms of quantity and quality of speakers, displacement through very different concert spaces and human–computer interface.

The GRM's system is called the *Acousmonium*. It has now become a generic term for an orchestra of loudspeakers or sound diffusion system. In addition to the GRM Acousmonium and BEAST, established systems can be found in Belfast, Brussels, Karlsruhe, Leicester and Manchester. Many smaller ad hoc systems exist. The Sheffield system is a combination of PA and studio speakers controlled by a bespoke computer program.

8.1.2 What is sound diffusion?

For some time now, the term 'sound diffusion' has been used to encapsulate what is typically a duplication and subsequent distortion or exaggeration of the stereo image over multiple symmetrically placed loudspeakers. This is somewhat akin to mixing in reverse (two in, many out).

Figure 8.1 The BEAST-style diffusion rig (SEAMUS 2000, UNT)

Diffusion has often implied the invisibility of the loudspeaker. There are times, however, when the image to be presented requires focus: if a work had a spoken text, for example. At these times the unwritten rule was to present the sound at the front on a 'main' pair as though someone were talking to you. Moreover, if the text is to be audible, it is vital that it is clear. Front and centre would be the best approach. The need for this clarity is of course exemplified in the centre speaker in all cinema systems. At times, then, it was almost unavoidable not to focus upon the sound's source (the loudspeaker) as the 'diffuse' in 'diffusion' had disappeared. The image was still virtual and always will be, but the focus was strong enough to draw the attention towards a specific pair of speakers. Sometimes attention is drawn to the visibility of the loudspeakers when it is inappropriate to do so – a mistake in diffusion perhaps. This presence is made explicit in the French-school acousmoniums with one offset pair of loudspeakers (or mono sum) acting as 'soloistes' and, at times a non-symmetrical placement of loudspeakers further strengthening the sense of an 'orchestra' and perhaps affording a more human feel to these otherwise heavy, static and emotion-free transmitters of sound.

We are encouraged to compose for the potential of a diverse range of speakers positioned throughout the venue. This was at least the position 10 to 20 years ago when loudspeaker ensembles were all shapes, sizes and conditions. It is less the case now where a vast majority of loudspeakers are often by the same manufacturer.[1] Such is the possibility for reanimation through sound diffusion that works composed explicitly for live performance can sometimes sound less good in living room conditions (two loudspeakers). The opposite is also true: works with strong scenes and lots of focused stereo detail are often too dense to separate in diffusion. The current tendency to master electroacoustic music quite heavily also affects diffusion.[2]

8.1.3 Traditional diffusion practice

The 'main eight' is Jonty Harrison's term for four sets of loudspeakers called 'mains', 'wides', 'distant' and 'rear' in the BEAST system. This is normally sufficient to give both a rendition of a variety of near/far spaces and afford some sense of agitation in diffusion when there is considerable movement in the stereo master. James Mooney has commented extensively on the BEAST sound diffusion practice in his free to download PhD thesis.[3]

The main pair mirror the studio image and generally focus at the diffuser who is normally seated somewhere in the middle of the audience block. The wide pair focus behind the diffuser. They give a good expansive feel to those sitting near the diffuser and a tighter stereo image for those sitting near the back. The distant pair focus to a mono image in the centre of the stage. You will notice a huge gap between the wide and rear pair. It is advisable to bridge this gap by placing a side pair halfway between the wide and the rear. The sides and rears then give an extended headphone feel and a sense of surround respectively. Some say that the rear speakers give you a sense of foreboding as we are often apprehensive of sounds appearing behind us. If you are getting that feeling and you are sitting at the diffusion console, imagine the poor audience member sitting next to the loudspeaker on the back row! Mostly, the side and rear are

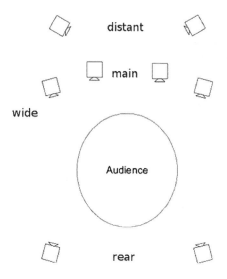

Figure 8.2 BEAST main eight (Mooney, 2006, 135)

used as surround speakers. Many years ago, each loudspeaker had its own fader on the console. The diffuser tilted the balance of sound this way and that in accordance with what they heard. If the sound was a 'scene', the faders were generally moved in pairs. If the sound scurried around, there was a chance to perform what was humorously termed 'wiggly wiggly', a gentle or aggressive agitation of the main faders, four faders per hand, essentially swinging the sound around. Clearly this motion only works when this kind of 'swish' or 'whiplash' gesture *is implied in the music*. Which it most certainly is in Bernard Parmegiani's *Etude élastique* from *De Natura Sonorum* (1975) – see Chapter 5 for a description of the work.

Diffusion then becomes a matter of orchestration, making the louds louder and the softs softer; articulating the movement implied in stereo in a three-dimensional space, bringing the piece to life for you as diffuser, the person on the front row and the person on the back row. You must not think you are diffusing for yourself. You have to be considerate, especially of frequency and volume, for all listeners. This almost certainly will mean compromising your diffusion and, in rehearsal, setting a balance then moving to the front and back to see whether you – as audience member – can stand it!

Diffusion of stereo repertoire is enormous fun and it is recommended that every composer has a go. This is difficult to do because of the sheer logistics of moving a minimum of eight loudspeakers into a room and rigging all the necessary cables. For the most part the stereo repertoire is fixed (it is a soundfile that you play from computer and matrix out to multiple dac~ outputs). It is often the case that through sound diffusion composers gain a greater understanding of the composition process. This could be because:

- Time in a larger space is potentially more fluid (this could mean it travels faster or slower than you expected in the studio).
- You are hopefully communicating to a crowd. Compare talking to the person next to you with engaging with 50 people. You don't just have to be louder: you need to be clearer, more profound, more direct, and if nuance is your signature, you need to make sure there is time for this to be understood.
- The performed space is so vastly different to the studio space. Chances are the reverberation time is longer. More loudspeakers in the space offsets this but your sense of intimacy is all the more difficult to create in a larger space.

Consider then the opening of a classic piece of electroacoustic music such as *Klang* by Jonty Harrison (1982). This work opens with a statement, a re-statement and continued development of material. It is traditional, though by no means necessary, to present the opening statements in an elemental and incremental fashion, commencing with sounds from the main loudspeakers and gradually opening out the theatre of sound (like drawing back curtains) as the work proceeds. It is almost impossible to place individual sounds in different pairs of loudspeakers – that's multichannel composition, not sound diffusion – but there is an opportunity to heighten the dramaturgy of the work through explicit selection of a small number of speakers. Clearly there are some sounds that migrate to speakers because of their frequency content (bass to any subwoofer in the room, high frequencies to smaller tweeters in loudspeakers).

Klang gradually mixes synthetic sounds with recorded samples and builds to a cadence. This expansiveness can be heightened through focus, and gradual addition of loudspeakers, so enveloping the audience and making the crescendo louder.

We have mentioned cases where sounds may be pulled towards a specific set of loudspeakers. Another case where diffusion is difficult is at section ends. Imagine a scenario where a sound drifts away (tails in reverb, panning, spectra and amplitude), but before it is completely finished it is interrupted with a loud sound object that requires front-and-centre exposure. In the past, the technique has been to increase the amplitude of the distant loudspeakers to make the closing sounds physically move there and increase the main loudspeakers in such a way that they do not overpower the distant pair. And at some point, one can then begin to lower the distant loudspeakers.

This also stems from a general technique of diffusion. Rarely do we effect change through addition of loudspeakers but by withdrawing loudspeakers from a composite. Sound 'heard' through loudspeaker identification is less effective than sound which 'magically' disappears from one set of loudspeakers (effectively appearing somewhere new – the loudspeakers that remain).

Where overlap is required, multichannel separation would be pertinent. Given that we can dynamically matrix our inputs to outputs, we can arrange for our end of section material to move out of the main pair. This has implications of course for the spatialisation system used and the potential prescription of diffusion.

Say 1 and 2 = distant, 3 and 4 = main, 5 and 6 = side, 7 and 8 = rear:

- matrix in12–out12/34/56/78 – same material
- (delay) matrix in12–out34/56/78 – fade out
- matrix in34–out34/56/78 – new material
- (delay) matrix in34–out12 – fade up

as shown in Figure 8.3.

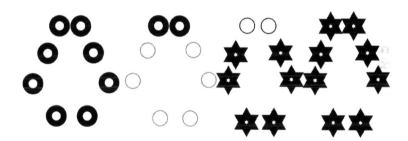

Figure 8.3 Simple polyphony with matrix fades

This practice-based research into the fusion of composition and performance is currently occupying my thoughts as I endeavour to merge sound diffusion with the performance of segments of pre-composed music. By making this practice more intricate we can investigate how diffusion can be automated, controlled more pragmatically in concert, linked more securely to the music it supports and deliver a more overriding sense of performance to the audience. We can even begin to consider how diffusion and performance, becoming a more fused object, need to be notated so that from one performance to the next there is more coherence *and* more structured opportunities for play, alongside the demonstration of interpretation and virtuosity.[4]

Chris Rolfe's *A Practical Guide to Diffusion* (Rolfe, 1999) mentions 'collapsing all 8 channels onto a single front speaker as an exit strategy.' He continues by talking about automated diffusion patterns. The case where declamatory material is static while textured material is diffuse is another example where multichannel composition and performance merge. This highly dramatic separation can be achieved both through standard multichannel practice and also through matrix diffusion with stem-based audio.

A further example is Smalley's concept of canopies (Smalley, 1997). It has been difficult in the past to physically separate droned or textured canopies from material that inhabits that zone.[5] By splitting canopied material to specific loudspeakers we can create interesting 'real' polyphonies as visualised in Figure 8.4. Here we see four loudspeakers above the audience, reflecting a sky canopy, and four reflecting a ground. Diffuse material that occupied these loudspeakers would envelop the audience. Meanwhile, the six mid-height speakers could emerge from and articulate a more intimate space. This is harder to do when the diffuse and distinct are mixed to stereo. Moreover, the compositional decisions that emerge from the knowledge of this separation (when to introduce distinct material, how to make it emerge without focusing necessarily upon the six loudspeakers being used) are of key importance and are, again, something that warrants extensive practice-based research.

The requirements for sound diffusion systems vary enormously, therefore it is vital that any computer-based system have the flexibility to be programmed quickly and scale up or down to any size of system. It is important to stress that this is not strictly speaking a multichannel model as mentioned earlier. Rather, a 'fractured acousmatic' (Moore, 2008), where a work comprising multiple files is given a new freedom via a dynamic matrix to speaker network.

We have suggested that stereo diffusion over multiple loudspeakers enables a real-time rendering – almost an analytical dispersal of the two-channel source by the diffuser. When the diffuser is not the composer a graphic score must be made. This normally presents key moments in the piece against a basic time line so that the performer can prepare themselves ahead of time. See Figure 8.5 (Moore, 2004).

The graphic score documents attacks, identifies a number of key sound types that might map to specific themed placements or similar fader gestures and highlights moments of intense left–right panning and far–near panoramas. The level of description is kept to a minimum and the key terms relate directly to a standard loudspeaker rig as in Figure 8.2. Far to near will be a profile that gradually removes the distant loudspeakers from the mix; L/R will imply a possibility to fluctuate

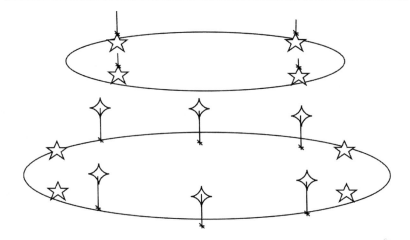

Figure 8.4 Canopied separation allowing diffusion over at least six speakers with four upper static and four lower static

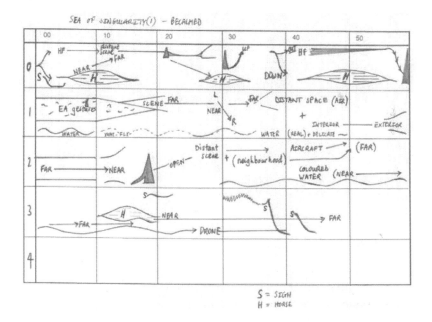

Figure 8.5 A graphic score of Adrian Moore's work *Becalmed* from *Sea of Singularity, 2001*

the balance of stereo pairs (and if using mains as a root whilst gently undulating the wides and rears, a left–right pattern with front–back articulation will create motion patterns that occupy the complete space).

Graphic scores are excellent for performance and equally good for analysis as they filter out all but the salient aspects of the work. When making a score, one starts listening in a much more time-oriented manner, looking for sections, highs–lows, gestures and textures instead of being drawn into the spectormorphological flow of the work. A layered approach might be useful for analysis, taking the bones of Figure 8.2 then adding in progressively more detail.

8.2 The Rehearsal

Rehearsals for electroacoustic music are notoriously short. Therefore, you should be well prepared. If it is not your piece that you are diffusing you should have a score ready to go. If you already know the layout of the sound diffusion system you may already have noted in specific directions (near, far, fast, slow, high, low). Remember to keep your score detailed enough to know what to prepare for and when, but not to have too much spectromorphological detail. If there is a block of sounds that all 'swirl' together, you may just draw a block and write in 'swirl'. Leave room to add additional markings during rehearsal. Your 'swirl' may be articulated through rapid fader movements or you may decide to place the passage in the roof loudspeakers to give the effect of being 'in the sky'. Which means, make a fair copy of your score then photocopy it so that you can scribble all over it in rehearsal.

If you can, use the clock on the DAW to give you times starting at 0:00. If this is not possible, you are going to have to guess or bring a stopwatch. The more you know the piece, the less you will require a score to guide you. Performance then becomes a structured improvisation where from time to time you aim for specific goals and in between you react to the sounds you hear, augmenting them with the instrument in front of you (the mixing console and loudspeakers).

8.2.1 The performer of electroacoustic music

As a performer of your own music, you will present it as you want to hear it. As a performer of music composed by someone else, the situation is completely different. You are responsible for knowing how the composer would like it (and if they are present in the audience and not diffusing you can bet they will not like what you do – so ask them to attend the rehearsal). But you are also the interpreter and an artist in your own right. Again you have to gain an intimate knowledge of the work through repeated listening and the construction of a score. That way you are probably well justified in your actions.

You are responsible not only for the piece and its composer but also for the audience, who must be given the very best possible performance. As stated earlier, you may need to compromise on the best possible performance 'for you' in the middle as you may have audience members on the front row (getting blasted by the 'main' loudspeakers) and on the back row (likewise with the 'rears'). The best compromise is not to give everybody an average all of the time but to decide when something may be more interesting for those at the back and use wides, sides and rear loudspeakers. The people sitting at the front will hear sounds coming mainly from behind them but they should know that it will not last long. Then give the people at the front a quality listen with main, wide and distant. This will all sound very far away for the person sitting at the back.

You may need to introduce the work and talk about the programme if there is one. You might wish to explain how you are going to diffuse it. At the end of the work (and this may sound terribly obvious), if people applaud please acknowledge the audience. If you are diffusing the work of another and they are in the audience, find them for a bow. Take your bow too – you have done a huge job of work. Sound diffusion is not just about fiddling around with a bunch of faders. A large number of performances where diffusers with little experience, limited knowledge of the system or the work and no rehearsal time, have given diffusion a bad name.

8.3 The Concert

8.3.1 Introduction

At the heart of this book is a need to communicate: normally a work by one composer to numerous listeners. Historically this has taken place in the concert hall. Despite technological advances, concert hall presentation, with all its formalities and traditions, provides an ideal opportunity to reinvent the work through *performance*. Performing your work or the work of others over a sound diffusion system is hugely exciting. Whilst it is nice to be invited to play over different systems, setting up your own system and curating your own concerts affords an opportunity to tune your system to the way *you* want it to sound. Inviting others to come and play then becomes an absolute privilege. There are always financial and logistical 'obstacles to progress' but once these are satisfied, you can begin to find your audience and create a concert.

8.3.2 Setting up your system

Look at your space and try to visualise where you might place loudspeakers. Your artistic design will always change once health and safety have been considered. Traditionally, your main loudspeakers will be of the highest quality. This is often a pair of studio monitors. However, depending upon the size of your hall (and the size of your budget) you may require high-quality PA loudspeakers that have similar fidelity to studio monitors but with considerably more power. Then think about the wide and side speakers. These may be closer to the audience than the mains so may not need to be as powerful. Rear loudspeakers may be of a lesser quality as they are often turned through 180 degrees to point at the back wall (to give a reflected sound). Distant loudspeakers can also be of a cheaper PA variety if needs be. If you have the budget, try to get an LFE loudspeaker and place this somewhere in the middle of the stage (or one at either side if you are splitting the stereo signal to two bass units).

It is not necessary to split the bass signal as it rarely defines itself and can be mono. If you also have some high-frequency tweeters, try to place these somewhere above the audience (high frequencies feel like they are coming from .... on high). BEAST and the Edinburgh Sound system suspend their high-frequency loudspeakers on poles or from a gantry. They are very lightweight and have no amplifiers in them (amps are off-stage) so easily comply with health and safety. It will be rare to get an opportunity to suspend heavier loudspeakers above the audience. However, many halls have balconies, so use them. Put loudspeakers high at 'side' and 'wide' positions, giving you a variety of floor-level and head-level positions. If you have stereo pieces and multichannel works, you may already be compromised for speaker placement. Other compromises include cost, time for setup and time for rehearsal. The 24-channel rig for the University of Sheffield Sound Junction series takes at least half a day to set up with six people. It takes considerably less time to take it all down!

8.3.3 Programming a concert of electroacoustic music

If you are fortunate enough to create your own concert you need to think very carefully about what kind of pieces you programme and where in the running order you put them. There are too many pieces that are 'full on', because composers often want to get the audience's attention and shouting loudly is sometimes the easiest means of achieving this. Some pieces may have specific narratives or an overall emotional feel. Remember the traditional classical concert of overture (something to get people settled), concerto (something for the star soloist), interval (time for a drink) and then symphony (concentrated 30–40 minutes). Increasingly, electroacoustic music can be found in every shape, size and duration. It might be good to place one or two short pieces against one longer work. Clearly the more works you have on the programme the more composers you might get coming along. If you just schedule your own one-hour masterpiece, you might find fewer people in the audience. Programming your own concert of works, whether themed or just handsomely selected, will no doubt delight the composers concerned and annoy those you have not selected. At Sheffield we try to do a number of smaller concerts that introduce our larger events. These events often have lunchtime and evening concerts. We undertake these events once or twice a year, and take a week in a theatre space that has the most perfect, dry acoustic for electroacoustic music. As a consequence we programme a lot of work. Ideally we'd have one smaller concert per month. Logistically, however, this is impossible until we have a dedicated space with the vast majority of the sound system permanently installed.

8.4 The Art of Sound Diffusion

The art of sound diffusion is highly underrated. It used to be the case that composers only played their own works in concert and travelled with their works. There are now a number of respected diffusers that will interpret your work and a number of courses where 'interpretation' and 'diffusion' are taught and encouraged. It is important that your work is performed as you would wish it. The growing importance of sound diffusion is reflected in an increasing number of diffusion artists, often composers that start by collecting together a small number of loudspeakers and a console and who begin by staging a number of concerts. Also, there is an increased popularity in the *L'Espace du Son* spatialisation competition held biannually in Brussels. The competition is the brainchild of composer and pedagogue Annette Vande Gorne. Finalists at this competition are preselected by their skill in producing a graphic score. They are then asked to present a programme of works including one set piece, and run a complete concert. I was fortunate enough to share the first prize in 2004.[6]

8.5 Further Reading

Two important articles appeared in the *Computer Music Journal* in 2000 and 2001 featuring interviews led by composer Larry Austin with Denis Smalley and Ambrose Field (Austin, 2000, 2001).

Austin's interview with Smalley begins by focusing on the practicalities of sound diffusion and an understanding that an audience has come to hear a concert so the presentation must be different to that of the studio or home environment and be at an equally professional level to concerts of classical or rock music. Smalley also focused upon the challenges of moving a work from the studio to the concert space, from the loss of sonic intimacy to the need to recognise the relationships between the spatial characteristics of sound as heard in stereo and the spatialisation methods employed to enhance that sound in concert. All in all a very practical article.

Austin's interview with Field mentions Ambisonics. Ambisonics is achieving something of a comeback since its invention in the early 1970s as its ability to store spatial information in a form which is then decoded on the fly to suit the delivery method is extremely powerful for the games industry. It also enables very accurate recording of environments. Field neatly captures the latent power of Ambisonics by revealing that because all the loudspeakers in the system are working together to represent an environment, 'where the speakers actually are has absolutely nothing to do with where the sound is coming from' (Austin, 2001, 27).

Finally, the fusion of multichannel thinking, multichannel compositional methods and sound diffusion techniques is documented in an excellent article by Scott Wilson and Jonty Harrison (Wilson and Harrison, 2010) where they 'rethink the BEAST', take a step back from the explicit placement of materials and consider how sound diffusion and composition can be more dynamically implemented.

Notes

1. To the point that some digital diffusion systems now incorporate EQ to artificially 'colour' loudspeakers!
2. Diffusion retains a sense of 'live' mastering, especially of sound pressure level (SPL): this is more difficult to do when dynamic range is reduced. In fact a non-mastered work will normally be compressed in performance and a fully mastered work will be expanded.
3. See www.james-mooney.co.uk/research/sound_diffusion/JM_Sound_Diffusion_Systems.pdf.
4. www.academia.edu/3782058/The_fractured_acousmatic_in_performance_a_method_for_sound_diffusion_with_pre-composed_materials.
5. Composers rely upon the material splitting itself purely by its spectromorphological qualities.
6. In the spare room in my house, where I'm writing this text, hangs my certificate from the 2004 competition. It is notable for the fading handwritten signatures of the jury: Patrick Ascione, François Bayle, Francis Dhomont, Beatriz Ferreyra, Bernard Fort, Bernard Parmegiani and Annette Vande Gorne.

References

Austin, L. (2000). Sound diffusion in composition and performance: an interview with Denis Smalley. *Computer Music Journal*, 24(2):10–21.

Austin, L. (2001). Sound diffusion in composition and performance practice ii: An interview with Ambrose Field. *Computer Music Journal*, 25(4):21–30.

Harrison, J. (1982). *Klang*. Évidence matérielle. IMED 0052 pub. 2000.

Harrison, J. (1998). Sound, space, sculpture: some thoughts on the what, how and why of sound diffusion. *Organised Sound*, 3(2):117–27.

Harrison, J. (1999). Diffusion: theories and practices, with particular reference to the BEAST system. *eContact*, 2.

Mooney, J. R. (2006). *Sound diffusion systems for the live performance of electroacoustic music*. PhD thesis, University of Sheffield, Department of Music. www.james-mooney.co.uk/publications.

Moore, A. (2004). *Dreaming of the Dawn*. Reve de l'aube. IMED 0684 pub. 2006.

Moore, A. (2008). Fracturing the acousmatic: Merging improvisation with disassembled acousmatic music. In *Proceedings of the International Computer Music Conference*, Belfast.

Parmegiani, B. (1975). *Etude élastique*. De Natura Sonorum, pub. 1990, InaGRM.

Rolfe, C. (1999). A Practical Guide to Diffusion. Issue 2.4. http://cec.sonus.ca/econtact/Diffusion/pracdiff.htm.

Smalley, D. (1997). Spectromorphology: explaining sound-shapes. *Organised Sound*, 2(02):107–126.

Wilson, S. and Harrison, J. (2010). Rethinking the BEAST: recent developments in multichannel composition at Birmingham Electroacoustic Sound Theatre. *Organised Sound*, 15(03):239–50.

Chapter 9

The Presentation of your Work Outside Performance

It must sound nice *and* look nice!

This chapter is about presentation and as a consequence it is rather dry, and may read a little like common sense. But it is here because in a vast majority of cases, common sense does not seem to prevail. This chapter is aimed at students at undergraduate and postgraduate levels but may also be of use to anyone wishing to submit their works for consideration at concerts, competitions and festivals.

9.1 Presenting your Work for Submission

9.1.1 Hard copy and electronic copy

It is always worth having a backup copy of your submission 'off-site'. Today this means placing a digital copy in the cloud. Google Drive, Dropbox, YouSendit and SoundCloud are a few examples. If you have created a stereo work and you are short of space then compress your file to MP3, or better still, FLAC.[1]

At many institutions there may exist an opportunity to host your own website or upload your file via an online submission system. Most online submissions systems, however, only accept written documents (pdf, odt, docx) as they then filter through to something like Turnitin for plagiarism assessment.

Most courses (and course leaders) will probably want consistency in submission (and potentially high quality audio). In which case you may still be submitting on CDR or DVD. It is rare to submit an audio CD. Most people want to see a file and then open it in a program of their choice. The data disc should have a copy of your folder with the notes and piece inside. The outside of the disc should be clearly labelled. The disc should ideally be in a hard jewel case. At which point you might

Table 9.1 Submission of multichannel zip on USB stick with identification of bit depth and sample rate

Your name, Your submission	
as one zip file on	mypiece2444-L.wav
	mypiece2444-R.wav
	mypiece2444-C.wav
	mypiece2444-Lfe.wav
	mypiece2444-Ls.wav
	mypiece2444-Rs.wav
	testsound2444-L.wav
	testsound2444-R.wav
	testsound2444-C.wav
	testsound2444-Lfe.wav
	testsound2444-Ls.wav
	testsound2444-Rs.wav
	myprogramme-notes.pdf
	mybiography.pdf
	mypicture.jpg

wish to create a cover. What you place on the cover may depend on the regulations of your institution if you are a student (you may not be asked to put your name on the submission). However, given that composition is such a personal activity and you are (hopefully) proud of the work you have completed, why not make the submission look as close to professional as possible?

Irrespective of whether you are producing a data or audio CD, look at www.electrocd.com/ under CD or DVD-Audio or www.sargasso.com/ to see how they approach labelling, liner notes and overall profile.

At the University of Sheffield, we tend to prefer materials on a USB stick which is much quicker to copy over to a hard drive. Here, presentation becomes more difficult. However, would it not be beyond the bounds of possibility to encapsulate your work inside an offline webpage, Powerpoint slide or interactive pdf?

If your work is multichannel, you will need to zip all your files together. For example, a folder called *Your-name-mypiece* might look like Table 9.1:

This should be self explanatory to many. You may still add a pdf comprising a speaker diagram of a 5.1 setup and confirm that L, R, C, Lfe, Ls, Rs are left, right, centre, low frequency effects, left surround, right surround. You may also include a test sequence so that who ever is listening can align their outputs correctly: one soundfile that repeats through all speakers and which should essentially sound the same in each (save for the sub).

9.1.2 Writing about your work: the anatomy of a programme note

This text is about writing about music. Your programme note should help the listener contextualise your work irrespective of whether it is for public consumption or for an academic assignment. As an example see Denis Smalley's notes for his work *Valley Flow* (1991) (Table 9.2).[2]

As can be seen, the notes romanticise the work a little but take in aspects of date and place of composition, inspiration for production and allude to technical methods. In very few words Smalley gives a brief glimpse of his preoccupation with space. You have a rough idea what to expect – in terms of quantity at least – from these notes (force, volatility, turbulence). But also that there will be delicate moments (floating, flying contours). Note also that Smalley creates a space within which to describe his compositional methods using polar opposites (stretched versus contracted motion). What he does not do is give us a blow-by-blow account of the work, nor talk about the kinds of techniques he used to implement 'flying contours' and 'broad panoramic sweeps'.

There are some works that are not so programmatic in design. Compare Smalley's notes to my 1996 work, *Junky*.

> *Junky* is 'electroacoustic ambient.' The few discernible sound sources were quickly processed to form pitch and rhythmic motives in simple melodic and harmonic structures. The work has three main sections – A (slow), B (fast), and A+B – with a coda and a more detailed structure of introductions leading to static passages, developments and returns in each of the primary sections. The opening minute introduces the gesture-types and the pitch center of the work. Many sound events appear, accelerate towards the ear and recede into the distance. One such event cascades into the first real occurrence of the dominant drone that contributes towards its ambient feel. As the drone becomes lighter section A proper begins. Sweeping drone-like gestures act as cadence points for the essentially static experience of section A and pave the way for section B with its more aggressive material and continual stretching and compressing of a rhythmic device, into and out of drone. There is a clear pitch outline and a sense of stability remains. A falling drone heralds the return section A+B where, through pitch alignment, both sound-types (drone and rhythm) merge, either sequentially or through mixing. A coda ends the work.

Table 9.2 Programme note for Denis Smalley, *Valley Flow*

	Denis Smalley, Valley Flow
Composer:	Denis Smalley
Title:	*Valley Flow*
Date:	1991–92
Duration:	16:50
Commission:	BEAST with support from West Midlands Arts
Premiére:	February 27, 1992, Pebble Mill Studios – BBC (Birmingham, England, UK)
Programme notes:	The formal shaping and sounding content of *Valley Flow* were influenced by the dramatic vistas of the Bow Valley in the Canadian Rockies. The work is founded on a basic flowing gesture. This motion is stretched to create airy, floating and flying contours or broad panoramic sweeps, and contracted to create stronger physical motions, for example the flinging out of textural materials. Spatial perspectives are important in an environmentally inspired work. The listener, gazing through the stereo window, can adopt changing vantage points; at one moment looking out to the distant horizon, at another looking down from a height, at another dwarfed by the bulk of land masses, and at yet another swamped by the magnified details of organic activity. Landscape qualities are pervasive: water, fire and wood; the gritty, granular fracturing of stony noise-textures; and the wintry, glacial thinness of sustained lines. The force and volatility of nature are reflected in abrupt changes and turbulent textures.
Performance Details:	*Valley Flow* was composed at The Banff Centre for the Arts (Canada) in 1991 and was completed in the composer's studio in Norwich (UK) in 1992. It incorporates sounds created at IRCAM in Paris (France) during a previous research period (1989) and further materials subsequently developed at Simon Fraser University in Vancouver (Canada) in 1991. *Valley Flow* was premiered on February 27th, 1992 in a concert broadcast live from BBC Pebble Mill Studios. This piece was commissioned by the Birmingham Electroacoustic Sound Theatre (BEAST) with funds provided by West Midlands Arts.

Here again, the notes mention key points about the work and try (perhaps not very successfully) to outline the formal shape. More recently, I have begun to contextualise my own work in programme notes by referencing key aspects of the works of others. For example, my 2012 work *Nebula Sequence* has a strong programmatic vibe but also a section where I was mindful of the works of others.

> Creative motivations: Wednesday November 30, 2011 was the first day in my working life that I went on strike. I thought I was being hypocritical taking my recording equipment with me but with hindsight I experienced a sense of place, a feeling that I was personally doing the right thing, and an enormous sense of the support that those on strike were giving to their colleagues under pressure. I also captured elements of the primary sound source of this piece and in so doing continue to reflect upon the reasons why I was out that day. The vast majority of this work was made during April 2012 at the Visby International Centre for Composers, Gotland (Sweden) in their 5.1 Studio Alpha. Being away for a month allowed me to work consistently and freely: I was able to take stock of a wide variety of materials and develop a number of spectral surround sound manipulations. I was also able to pay homage to composers whose music has influenced the way I work.
>
> Secondary sources included stones and bricks (after Jonty Harrison and Alistair MacDonald), and ball bearings (after François Bayle's majestic *Tremblement de terre trs doux*) and my thanks to simply-bearings.co.uk for accepting the fact that I only needed to buy two of each size (ranging from .5 to 2 inches in diameter). For the 'dissolve' at the close of the piece, I am always reminded of Andrew Lewis' *Scherzo*. Finally, thanks to the Groupe de Recherches Musicales for producing some great new tools that helped me deliver some very unique (if easily identifiable) sound nebulae. And it is these sound spaces that drive this work. Nebulae present us with the sense of the unknown, a sense of the future. There is a space there that is vast and distant and within the nebula a cloud of swirling dust and gas. Vast, but not a void. We can place ourselves inside this space and explore its very details.

Again, formal aspects such as a closing 'dissolve' are mentioned but not described in any detail. Ultimately the programme note should whet the listener's appetite by setting a scene and giving an idea of a composer's motivations. Practically, one starts to read the notes just before the lights go down, so oftentimes the shorter, the better!

9.1.3 What examiners are potentially looking for

The University of Sheffield student handbook lists some criteria for assessment of compositions. It is not a checklist: a piece of work does not have to fulfil all the criteria listed to gain a particular classification. Examiners will form judgements based on the predominant character of the work.

Marking something with definite right or wrong answers is considerably easier than putting a mark to a composition. Even in a mathematics problem, some *working out* often needs to be shown for partial marks. Examination of compositions is normally graded on the finished product. Rarely is preparatory composition work taken into consideration. Notwithstanding this, assessing composition is notoriously difficult as subjectivity, no matter how logical, must, at some point, show its hand. A potential grading system might look like that show in Table 9.3.

As you can see, it is not a checklist and cannot be reverse engineered to generate a piece! But there are pitfalls that can be avoided and this begins with technique. Glitches, when expressly used, are probably welcome but the context must be abundantly audible else any glitch may sound like an error.[3] Similarly, distortion at 0 dB or above. If you require distortion it is advisable to normalise or compress the squared-off wave so that examiners know (i.e. can see on the submitted waveforms) that you wanted distortion. For the most part, in electroacoustic music, distortion is unwarranted. Therefore, if you limit your work to a maximum amplitude, do not limit at 0 dB; go for between −0.1 and −1 dB.

Other common 'failings' include cutting the final edit when reverberation still has time to run (an abrupt stop) or starting a work with too much silence (indicating no final editing). These are technical errors that can be easily avoided. It is also *normally* the case that poor balance in a work is both audible and visible. If, during the course of a work, you or someone else have to reach for the volume control (either to make something louder and/or then to decrease volume) this indicates a balance problem either due to amplitude or frequency control (or both). This kind of error creeps in when you compose your piece solely over headphones which have a very specific frequency response and, because of their size, under-emphasise low frequencies. It is important if at all possible to listen over loudspeakers (and good ones at that). When the resultant headphone-composed work is auditioned over loudspeakers, you might expect to hear excessive low frequency content.

Many subjective comments will often be related to a listener's experience and understanding of past works. This assumes quite a lot can be learned simply through listening (and as a student perhaps emulating – though not copying).

Table 9.3 Potential composition grading scheme

A grade	Very original work demonstrating the ability to generate and develop musical ideas into a coherent and meaningful structure. The work is imaginative and there is evidence both of independent thought and of an active engagement with, and an understanding of, the prevailing stylistic tendencies in the music of our time (or, for stylistic composition, the music of the appropriate historical period).
A grade one star	The work demonstrates a thorough understanding and command of the medium (whether instrumental, vocal or electroacoustic) and confidence in harnessing it to creative ends. There is a sense of personal communication through the music, with ideas clearly expressed and presented. While the work displays excellent standards of imaginative, creative and technical achievement, this is not sustained throughout.
A grade two star	An excellent level of imaginative, critical and original thought. The work demonstrates independence of thought as well as a thorough technical command of the medium and the materials used.
A grade three star	Work that is outstanding in all respects, showing the ability to pursue advanced composition at a level beyond that expected of undergraduate students. Publishable material.
B grade	Denotes carefully structured and well presented work revealing a strong background and understanding of the broad principles of composition. There will be clear evidence of an awareness of the prevailing stylistic tendencies in the music of our time (or, for stylistic composition, the music of the appropriate historical period), but the work may fall short of sustained original thought. Few technical errors. A mark towards the top of the range suggests a well developed and clearly presented submission with some touches of originality and personal expression. A mark towards the bottom of the range suggests a coherent and well presented submission but rather lacking in imagination and originality of invention.

Table 9.3 (*continued*)

C grade	Competent work which conforms to the broader demands for coherence and soundness of technique, but without much evidence of original thinking or imagination. There may be lapses in coherence and some errors in presentation (e.g. unidiomatic writing for instruments or studio glitches). Evidence of limited knowledge of the music of our time (or, in the case of stylistic composition, the music of the appropriate historical period). A mark towards the top of the range suggests fair technical accomplishment and competence, with some attempt at musical coherence and expression, but this may be insufficiently developed or inadequately sustained. A mark towards the bottom of the range suggests a less cogent presentation with a number of technical errors and lapses.
D grade	Evidence of some background knowledge of compositional technique and some attempt at developing a coherent piece of work. However, the work is superficial and technically flawed, with lapses and errors of judgement in writing for the medium. There is little evidence of imagination or originality in the work and there may be serious weaknesses in organisation and presentation. Little evidence of an awareness of the prevailing stylistic tendencies in the music of our time (or, for stylistic composition, the music of the appropriate historical period).
E grade	Only elementary evidence of compositional skills. There may be several technical errors in the manipulation of musical materials, in writing competently for instruments or in the handling of studio resources.
Fail	Failure to carry out the task assigned. Negligible content. There may be evidence of plagiarism or collusion (it can occur even in electroacoustic music). 0 indicates work either not submitted or unworthy of marking.

But what if you 'wanted it that way'? What one wants must be justified within the broader context of works demonstrated in any learning situation and/or perhaps the volumes of work mentioned in this document if you are planning to compose in an acousmatic idiom. There is no substitute for experience, and Chapter 5 is a good place to start. It is entirely possible to demonstrate this understanding within the context of an original piece. The vast majority of the works in Chapter 5 have a certain clarity of sound and even if they use noisy sounds, they are a result of the recording itself (the sea, for example) or result as part of a spectromorphological journey (a noise that is, over time, filtered). Some composers *use* noise as a metaphor or as a means to encase us in sound. For the most part I do not find this satisfying as noise itself is difficult to listen to and 'finding the hidden beauty' or 'navigating the structure' through very noisy environments is arduous. Also, noise almost demands to be played at high volume as its metaphor is 'massive'. Trouble is, at this volume, noise is also dangerous (and thus we get to the composer's tautological 'this work is dangerous'). There is a whole genre of *noise music* that emanates from Japan, spearheaded by composers such as 'Merzbow' (Masami Akita). In the electroacoustic domain, Ben Thigpen's *divide by zero* presents an interesting hybrid of noise and sound sculpture (2011).

It is vital to understand that examiners will find it impossible to distance themselves from a submitted piece to such an extent that they can review it dispassionately. This would assume a checklist and assume that listening is merely a sonic experience to be noted and experienced as vibrating molecules reaching the ear, rather than a communicative experience to remember. Taking into account all the activities of Chapter 7, ask yourself the question: 'why do I *like* this passage of music; why would someone else *like* it?' The very honest composers' recollections in Appendix B provide examples of when to ask this question and what to do when you do not know why anyone would *like* anything you have done.

9.1.4 What makes a sound, sound nice?

Quite a number of the repertoire examples from Chapter 5 exploited resonant filters of some kind. This could be because of the need to derive pitch from noise, a shared mutual understanding between a practising community of composers or because there is something unexplained but 'nice' about the resonant filter sound. The highly ringing resonant filter (whilst appropriate in certain situations) is often too resonant. The dry percussive sound of, say, stones, bricks, Styrofoam – any short series of clicks is too dry. The colour imbued by a resonant filter that has very little decay appears to bring otherwise redundant material to life. Is it just because there is some semblance of pitch? The comb filter affords similar colouration, yet has seemingly gone out of fashion. This is but a personal opinion based upon 20 years of using, not using, and using (but hiding) this quite obvious technique. However, in a similar vein, phasing and flanging (again, remaining quite dry but often adding internal pitch inflections) remain popular. So too swept filters, which are essential in dance music. This is beginning to sound like a checklist! It is, however, one of those important questions that composers ask as they click 'save' and, as has been stated before, I think it is vital to have at least one sound in a piece to which you can turn at any point, feel inspired and know 'this is my sound'. The concept of colour in electroacoustic music, our personal relationship to the sounds we make and our understanding of 'nice' are also areas of music psychology research that seem to be underdeveloped.

9.2 Presenting your Work for Competitions and Concerts

9.2.1 Essential documents

A work, once completed, needs both optimal concert presentation and physical presentation or delivery and, as stated at the beginning of Chapter 9, your presentation matters. Recently, however, when presenting works for concerts, we have noticed a marked change in formats. A lucky few now work at much higher sample rates and channel counts. Many do not. This can sometimes lead to tricky situations where a sound system running at 44.1 kHz in stereo is required to play eight channels at 96 kHz.

A recommendation to concert promoters:

1. Be very clear about the specification of the system so as not to receive the unexpected.
2. Do not compromise on quality if you can afford it.

A recent festival of electroacoustic music in Sheffield[4] played multi-channel works, stereo works with instruments and live electronics and some huge high definition (HD) video files. There was little or no compromise and the composers were most appreciative.

A recommendation to composers:

1. Be prepared to compromise on quality. The difference to most audiences between 96 kHz and 48 kHz is not the same as the difference between a normal TV picture and HD.

2. As part of that preparation, have your work in numerous formats. Most players will read a WAV file, though for Mac users sometimes an AIFF file is required.
3. If you are not prepared to compromise or do not provide a concert promoter with different sample rate options, you may face being removed from the programme of events.
4. Therefore, for multichannel works at high sample rates, include a 'standard' (44.1 kHz – 24 bit, 48 kHz – 24 bit).
5. It is easier for a promoter to chose from your selection of formats than for them to take your no-compromise original and reformat it without your knowledge.

9.2.2 What competition and conference juries are looking for

Competition and conference juries are somewhat similar to any examining body save for the fact that they probably come from a wide variety of artforms and, as a consequence, have very different tastes (and, from time to time, agendas). Since the rise of competitions such as the Bourges festival[5] (sadly this competition is no more) and Prix Ars Electronica,[6] entrants realised that works that began aggressively and were between 8 and 13 minutes tended to secure the attention of the jury. More recent competitions such as Jttp[7] in Montréal have accepted works with video and works of long duration. Jury members for this competition were asked to rate works according to the following 'categories':

• Technical skill (in some combination of recording: synthesis, processing, sequencing, mixing, oral narrative structure or other techniques used in the piece)
• Compositional skill – the evident use of approaches appropriate to the genre
• Overall technical quality (of result)
• Formal/structural success
• Articulation/clarity of ideas.

Again, this is no checklist and relies heavily upon the experience of the jury members. Many composers use a variety of processes (often as many as they can get their hands on). However, it is clear from the above that demonstrating mastery of a particular method might be useful. And perhaps the most obvious and ubiquitous skill may be mixing and montage (especially micro-montage) using the power of a DAW. This process is normally very time-consuming and often very noticeable in performance as small elements of sound fuse together. Compositional skill implies a contextual understanding. Technical quality relates to errors in editing and mixing. Formal/structural success and articulation/clarity of ideas remain undefined. In the former, ask yourself about the duration of the work, the flow from fast to slow, loud to soft, tension to relaxation. In the latter, ask yourself about the 'chunking' of material. Are there enough tangible relationships between sounds 10 seconds apart, 30 seconds apart, 8 minutes apart?

Conference juries may work to a theme and may select pieces that reflect certain avenues of endeavour. They may also select work precisely to be contentious and raise questions. These questions may or may not be based around the satisfactory nature of the music itself. Instead, they may be tangential questions concerning concept or construction. A similar approach is taken in academia where works may be used to explain a concept or answer a particular 'research question'.[8]

Competitions are not like educational assessments as feedback is rarely given and criteria such as mentioned above are held to very loosely. Moreover, whilst we all liked feedback as students, if you enter a competition, you must be confident of your work *but* be prepared to fail and receive little or no distinction as to why. Ultimate control is not held by any body conforming to national or international laws, merely the conference or competition organiser. Much fuss is made over competitions that restrict according to age, duration or format of work, date of completion and pedigree. Many also express concern over competitions that require an entrance fee. The entrance fee is becoming increasingly the norm as funding diminishes. Entering your piece was a gamble in the past but came at the cost of preparation of materials and postage. It may well be the case that a small fee engenders a much more strategic approach from composers towards competition entry and this may be no bad thing.

9.3 Backing Up and Recording your Progress

Whilst we would not recommend this to anybody, many have learned the lesson 'back up your materials' the hard way by losing data and either vowing henceforth to keep records (no matter how disparate and disorganised) or to learn to accept a degree of loss and move on. Recording your progress is something that most composers do but often in a very unstructured way (normally a diary, notepad or sketchbook) and normally linearly (day 1, day 2, etc.) Different methods work for different composers. You may wish to develop an ongoing mind-map or Venn diagram (interlocking cells detailing connections between materials, ideas and techniques). Sometimes workflow improves most where we not only have a notebook to hand but also have a large overview (on a wall) that presents in diagrammatic form some of the key 'aims' or 'goals' of the work. With storage becoming ever cheaper there is no reason not to store everything. And once doing this it becomes even more vital to document where things are.

9.4 Presenting your Work on the Internet

Depending upon your copyright situation (whether you have published works for purchase) you may not wish to place complete works for download. However, most composers wishing to market their compositions have their own space and you resist advertising at your peril! Also, you do need to be flexible and responsive to change. The example of MySpace is indicative of the swift changes that flush through the internet from time to time. As the internet changes, so your own personal space must adapt.

A recommendation for composers:

- Host your soundfiles in a compressed format either on your own web domain[9] or link back to a well-known audio storage site such as SoundCloud.
- If you host a complete MP3, make it very clear that upon request you can provide uncompressed audio.
- If you are not willing to host a complete MP3, host the opening few minutes.
- If the opening few minutes do not adequately represent the work (the opening begins very quietly and builds very slowly), construct your own 'trailer' of beginning (cross-fade); middle (cross-fade); end, or other such construction.
- If your work is multichannel, host a stereo reduction and point to where multi-channel files may be found.
- Link soundfiles with programme notes, a short biography (100 words) and some photos of you that concert promoters can sample.

9.4.1 Your website

It is now quite easy to make your own website and to possess your own domain name. This gives you personalised online identity and individuality. Looking at the variety of designs of personal pages, I would suggest starting with something simple, something that documents your past, present and future, contextualises your works and which points effectively to your soundfiles, programme notes, biography and publicity photos. As your site becomes more complex, consider linking away from the site to social media and other 'following' opportunities. A site that works really well here is that of American composer Elainie Lillios[10] – a really easy-to-navigate interactive menu and a colourful and dynamic web site.

9.4.2 Social media

Social media, including of course Facebook and Twitter, will enable 'following' and 'friend' opportunities and give you easy mobile access for instant updates. The 'store everything' nature of these sites also enables you to keep a timeline of sorts, though you may well not wish to publish everything to your friends all of the time.

9.4.3 Working with communities of practice

The power of the internet and social media has somewhat diminished the strength of local, national and international communities of practice. However, there comes a time when you realise that sitting at home publishing MP3s and timeline updates just does not cut it any more. Normally meeting in Yorkshire, the Sonic Arts Forum has a Facebook page[11] with some 700 members worldwide. It meets once or twice a year and is a very open forum for the presentation and sharing of music and ideas. Sound and Music[12] is the United Kingdom's national organisation for sonic art with a mission to promote 'fresh and challenging new music and sound'. The remit here is very broad and, as a consequence, the community is quite disparate. On the international stage the International Computer Music Association is an organisation rooted very much in academic circles.[13] If you have read this book you probably have access to all of the above and are a fluent internet user!

Notes

1. On the Linux command line, type *flac infile.wav* or *lame -V0 infile.wav outfile.mp3*.
2. If your submission does not have details such as commission and prémière performance, do not include them. Programme notes taken with permission from www.electrocd.com/en/oeuvres/select/?id=14132.
3. I am clearly of a certain age when clicks were the result of bad tape edits or incorrect synchronisation between digital devices. I continue to make a distinction between wanted and unwanted digital sounds.
4. From Tape to Typedef: Compositional Methods in Electroacoustic Music 30 January–2 February 2013.
5. http://imeb.net.
6. www.aec.at.
7. http://cec.sonus.ca/jttp.
8. Electroacoustic composition as *research* often gives rise to heated debate. Here a 'piece' may test a concept or question yet be generally understood not to be an excellent 'piece of music'. This is solely a question of purpose and it is quite easy for compositions to answer an external research question. In the vast majority of cases, composition presents us with a 'chicken and egg' scenario in that a work, once completed, suddenly presents the composer

with fresh, new challenges (questions). You need this chicken first (a piece of music). And if things proceed as planned, this then gives rise to numerous follow-up questions and thus a search that can take weeks, months, years.

9. Such as www.adrianmoore.co.uk.
10. http://elillios.com.
11. https://www.facebook.com/groups/sonicarts/.
12. www.soundandmusic.org.
13. www.computermusic.org.

References

Smalley, D. (1991). *Valley Flow*. Impacts intérieurs. IMED 0409 pub. 2004.
Thigpen, B. (2011). *divide by zero*. SR317.

USSS Toolkits

A.1 Downloading and Installing Software

This book uses a number of pieces of software to develop sounds, all of which are cross-platform and freely available:

- Pure Data (http://puredata.info/). The USSS toolkits use Pd-extended.
- Csound (http://csound.sourceforge.net/). which is required when you use.
- Blue (http://blue.kunstmusik.com/), a fully programmable composition environment for Csound.

If these graphical and text-based languages inspire you, you might wish to look at:

- Max/MSP (www.cycling74.com/). The USSS toolkits began their life in Max but it is not free.
- SuperCollider (http://supercollider.sourceforge.net/). Now a very popular and powerful language.

And these just touch the tip of the iceberg. Even http://en.wikipedia.org/wiki/Audio_programming_language remains incomplete and undocumented.

Additionally, we have often used two free cross-platform audio editors/DAWs:

- Audacity (http://audacity.sourceforge.net/). A very solid two-channel editor with multichannel capability.
- Ardour (http://ardour.org/). A more powerful multichannel DAW.

If these DAWs inspire you and you have access to funds, the most common commercial DAWs are:

- Cubase and Nuendo (http://www.steinberg.net/)
- Logic (www.apple.com/logic-pro/)
- Pro-Tools (www.avid.com/UK/products/family/Pro-Tools/)
- Reaper (www.reaper.fm/)
- Ableton Live (https://www.ableton.com/en/live/new-in-9/).

The USSS toolkits that work with this book can be downloaded from www.shef.ac.uk/usss. Patches come without any guarantees and are licensed under the Creative Commons Attribution-NonCommercial-Share Alike 3.0 Unported License (http://creativecommons.org/licenses/by-nc-sa/3.0/).

Appendix B

Composer Recollections

> ...But I am giving away my secrets!
> ...Nothing is secret for long.

B.1 Kevin Austin

When mixing, consider: the first principle is your hearing. Does your work reflect refined, detailed hearing and listening? Do you hear inner parts in pieces? Are you able to both integrate and segregate elements of sounds? This is a continuous study. The work will not be able to rise above the level of your capacity to hear. Do you have a complete understanding of the metrics and psychometrics of sound and hearing? This requires research and study, and provides the foundation for further work.

The second principle is that of 'where are you listening?' Speaker quality is important. Room acoustics, essential. If your speakers are $300, it is difficult to rise above the limits of $600 speakers. If the speakers are (simply) placed in a room where they will look best ... the sound may also look best. This phase requires a reasonably detailed knowledge of acoustics, which relates directly to the first principle.

There are lots of introductory sources out there, and for someone starting out who does not wish to progress beyond the $600/pair speakers, they are generally adequate. Beyond that, it is necessary to go to more technically detailed studies, often found on university sites, as university electrical engineering departments don't have making a kick-ass bass as an aim.

How good is the source? For acoustics, among the words I check is 'standing wave' to see whether it is applied to two- and/or three-dimensional conditions. I see whether the term 'overtone', 'harmonic' or 'partial' is used in describing spectra. For loudspeakers, I check for an explanation of 'near-field'. For me, these separate the sheep from the mountain lions quite well.

Detailed knowledge of equipment and its limitations follows in assuring that the quality stays in. This is much less of an issue now that real and virtual equipment is less expensive and better than 10–20 years ago. In the actual 'mix' situation, the first question for me is 'What am I not hearing?' If there is a filtered, gated, two-second delay on a signal, is it always audible to me? Get the basics in place!

Kevin Austin is a composer, educator and arts animator based in Montreal. http://music.concordia.ca/people/faculty/full-time/kevin-austin.php. This text was originally sent to the CEC-conference Google Groups mailing list on 28 May 2013.

B.2 Jonty Harrison

B.2.1 All sound is potentially musical

There is no such thing as a completely unmusical sound, a sound that could never, ever play a part in a piece of music; it all depends on the musical context in which it occurs. It is the job of the composer to create that context by investigating sound material in the studio, working in partnership with it to discover and develop its unique qualities and characteristics, to be elaborated in 'a piece' – a broader context of other sounds, shaped and interacting in time and space.

B.2.2 Listen! Keep your ears (and your mind!) open and your batteries charged

'All sound is potentially musical', so whatever you are doing and wherever you go, try to be aware of the sonic events around you. Keep your ears open for interesting sounds and carry a portable recording device with you at all times, just as you might carry a camera on holiday.

- Listen *out* ... for unique or unusual sound materials, or for more familiar sounds behaving in a way you hadn't noticed before. Hit the 'record' button – they may not happen like that again!
- Listen *in* ... by focusing on the individual sound and by trying to get your microphones closer to it than you might be able to get your ears.
- Listen *around* ... to the real-world context of the sound – how much is this informing your interest in this sound (and how much or little of it do you want in your recording) and, if you change this context for a different one, how might this affect 'meaning'?

- Listen *within* ... the different spaces (open or enclosed, and with unique landscape or architectural features and materials) and places (such as other countries with unfamiliar languages and wildlife) in which you discover your sounds.
- Listen *through* ... to anything in the sound's behaviour that strikes you as particularly rich for more 'abstract' musical development (changing spectrum, iteration, pitch content, spatial characteristics).
- Listen *beyond* ... to how the sound's energy trajectory might interact with other material to generate musical structure.

Keep listening and keep recording, BUT... don't make any decisions yet! Wait until you are back in the studio. Listen again, critically and reflectively – you are no longer making the recording in real time so the context has changed and you have changed, too, so the sound has also changed.

B.2.3 Listen again

Tease out the bits that you find particularly interesting/intriguing; work with them (and I mean with them: this is a partnership, and both parties – you and the material – need to agree on what's happening!), develop them, transform them. Prune out what isn't working, but don't delete it: as it may work in another context or another piece ('all sound is potentially musical ... it all depends on the musical context in which it occurs'). Change the order; change the balance; change the timing; tweak this; alter that. Try to listen with new ears – you are the first listener; bring new ears (other people's) into the studio. Discover what other events need to happen before/after/with/around the sounds and what other sound materials you might need to pull in to this developing organism. Go back through your sound archives; record more if you need to – either out and about or in the more controlled environment of the studio. Repeat the process(es). Listen again, and again, and again – you will know when the piece is finished.

B.2.4 Keep listening; keep composing

Your piece will always be a slice of time, a frozen moment (though that moment might in truth be a period of weeks or even months of composition) that somehow encapsulates its composer and its component material (even though you might have recorded that material years before you finally found a compositional use for it!). But as you – and other people – listen to the piece over the years, it will also always change ... because circumstances change, listeners change and you change. This is not something to mourn but to celebrate, and you can always make another piece.

Jonty Harrison is a composer based in Birmingham (and occasionally Italy). He is the founder of BEAST and Emeritus Professor of Composition and Electroacoustic Music, University of Birmingham.

B.3 Andrew Lewis

B.3.1 First I find, then I seek

I try not to be too intentional too soon. In choosing and recording sounds, and in transforming them, I aim to have a completely open mind, and just go with the flow. I see what I can find, almost by accident, without worrying too much what I am going to do with it. I stumble across things, and allow myself to be surprised by unexpected revelations. This is 'finding'. I try not to compose at this stage, except in the sense of putting things together to make individual objects or phrases. If I do try composing too early, it is usually very bad and very frustrating.

Then comes 'seeking': this means I start actively looking for specific things, trying to realise certain kinds of ideas, exploring and developing the latent possibilities of the stuff that I have 'found'. This applies to transformation, but is also when the real composing begins, in the sense of trying to shape a whole piece. Of course, 'finding' can also continue in this stage, as unexpected possibilities present themselves. If they do, I try to be prepared to abandon my previous plans, and even material that I spent a long time on, and instead let this new 'finding' take my 'seeking' in a new direction.

B.3.2 The trash can is your friend

I find that it is important to reject material, both at the development stage and when composing. In the same way, muting tracks in a mix or regions (segments of sound) can be a revelation. Sometimes I have made the texture so rich that really beautiful things are hidden away. Thinning things out a bit often produces surprisingly good results.

B.3.3 Listening

I agree with Alistair MacDonald about listening with someone else in the studio. It really is a revelation (usually a negative one, because you stop being able to kid yourself that 'it's OK really'!)

I try not to listen too much. My ears become quickly jaded, I try not to have processes droning on while I am working on something else. I also don't listen to large chunks of the piece too often, but treat it as something special. The first listen through to things on entering the studio is crucial – I can hear everything at its clearest, both sonically and musically.

On a related point, I do not play around too much with real-time processes without recording them. If it sounds good I record straight away, otherwise I find I end up playing around with different possibilities for an hour, at the end of which I (a) have no results, and (b) cannot really hear properly any more, or decide what's good or what's bad.

B.3.4 Time

Acousmatic music is MUSIC, not just 'sound art', and the main distinction here is its use of time. It is not just that the material is 'time-based', but that the artistic ideas themselves are shaped by and shape time. This is different to most gallery-based 'sound art', where the material is still time-based, but the overall artistic conception is not – it doesn't make too much difference in what order you hear things, or at what point you start and stop listening. In acousmatic MUSIC you must start listening at the beginning and stop at the end, and it makes a huge difference in what order things happen, and how quickly they follow. I spend a lot of time changing the order of events and their pacing, without changing the sounds themselves. To me, ordering and pacing is as transformational to sounds as processing or dynamics. Another way of thinking about this is that I am trying to shape the listener's perception: I put sound B after sound A, because sound B will take on certain special qualities if I lead the listener through sound A first, and thus create a particular perceptive space. This involves things like expectation, tension, fulfilment, contrast and so on. These are all changed by different orderings and pacings of material.

Andrew Lewis is a composer based in Bangor.

B.4 Alistair MacDonald

Top tips:

- Listen with somebody else in the studio (it always sounds different).
- Think about space and dynamics for each sound from the start (do not add dynamics and spatialisation later – they are part of the identity and character of each sound).
- Think about energy and move around the studio when you are listening (does the music move you?)

- Think about shape – you may need to add simple layers to underpin/orchestrate the overall shape that the surface layer is articulating.
- Think about EQ, a common but very powerful tool. Consider using EQ on every sound, partly just to see what is there (or not there).
- Editing is probably your most powerful tool – isolate bits of your sound; decontextualising bits will tell you things you did not know.

Alistair MacDonald is a composer based in Glasgow.

B.5 Adrian Moore

I have tried almost every technique under the sun, and if I had one piece of sound advice it would be that as soon as you think you have happened upon a sound that is particular to you (to the best of your knowledge this is currently your 'signature' sound), write down how you made it. Despite the supposed rigour of creating toolkits in all manner of software, when it comes to manipulation, we as composers are often switching between software and soundfiles at a rapid pace, and sometimes we forget to note down what went with what. I remember (or should I say, failed to remember) how I made the opening sounds in my work *Dreaming of the Dawn*. There was a strange foldover sound to them. However, I have since found a method for creating drone-based material using the Partikkel opcode in Csound/Blue. Again, I'm not quite sure exactly why the transpositions are such that my drones have quite strong full spectrum colour, especially in the upper ranges (I always tend to roll off the frequencies above 15 kHz by up to 12 dB) but these drones interest me enormously and I have used them in recent pieces such as *Tapeworm* and *Click*.

Additionally, I absolutely love using convolution and spectral cross-synthesis in whatever language (convolution and vocoding in Csound/Blue, cross-synthesis in Max/MSP or Pure Data using the Shapee plugin). Ever since I used convolution and cross-synthesis in *Junky* these techniques have been essential in developing my works. Simply put, cross-synthesis fuses sound A and sound B, creating a hybrid. If sound A is pitched and sound B is articulated, suddenly your pitched sound is not only articulated dynamically but is spectrally filtered through sound B. In one easy step, you have used filters and amplitude modulation and given life to an otherwise static drone.

When undertaking a concentrated period of work one may be developing and mixing at the same time. When mixing, try not to immediately listen to what you did the previous day. It may too rigidly direct your thoughts going forward and has the potential to confirm that

that day's work was all good. Reflection later may more strongly confirm or deny the potential of the previous day's work.

Adrian Moore is a composer based in Sheffield.

B.6 Louise Rossiter

B.6.1 Good choice of sound materials

I always keep my ears open for new and interesting sound objects: things that are perhaps not as commonly heard within acousmatic music. My own work *Black Velvet* (2010) used a can of Guinness as a source sound. The whole idea came about from having a curry night with good friends!

B.6.2 Recording: microphones

Think about what kind of piece you want to compose. Is it to be highly gestural? Textural? In the listeners face? Consider microphone type and the placement of those microphones. Experiment with different types of microphones in different arrangements: a circle of four or eight perhaps? Or a middle side placement. I try to create movement in my recordings and create effective panning effects within the recording itself.

B.6.3 Listening

My next step is to listen to what I have just recorded – in a closed room with no distractions. This is my reduced listening. I edit out any junk (clips, etc.) but also write notes about the properties of the sound. Are they gestural? What do they remind me of? Then, I start to edit the snippets of sound I definitely want to use. I am very picky. Typically I might record one or two hours of material, but end up using five minutes in my final work. However, I never throw anything away permanently. Rather, write it up and store it in a folder. You never know when it will come in handy for another piece five years down the line. Like the other composers writing here, I like to listen with someone else in the studio and learn to be critical of my work.

B.6.4 Play – compose

I personally think that play is a crucial part of the compositional process. I improvise with the sound object and mine it for every conceivable sound. Quite often I am surprised by the sounds that come out. I make sure I record all my improvisations. I find this stage of the composition is rather like an onion, peeling back the layers to reveal new sounds that can then be used later on.

I also improvise a great deal with programs and plugins and note everything down. That element is crucial (see below). However, I try to avoid presets wherever possible. I like to stack one plugin on top of another and then try something completely bonkers that I would not normally dream of trying out. These can sometimes produce some really interesting results.

B.6.5 Composition diary

You have no idea when you will want to go back to that recipe for the epic drone you made three years ago so it is always a good idea to keep some sort of record of your work. I also name all my sound regions effectively so I do not end up with a document full of files entitled Audio 1, Audio 1.1, Audio 1.11!

B.6.6 Performance setting

I try to think where my work will be performed. Will it be listened to over headphones or on an eight-channel sound system? If it is primarily to be played in stereo I think about how the work might be diffused. Compositional approaches for each situation can vary slightly.

B.6.7 If you get stuck

1. *Never* throw anything away, put it to one side and do something else.
2. Listen to lots and lots of other pieces by other composers.

   Lousie Rossiter is a composer based in Leicester.

B.7 Pete Stollery

B.7.1 Listening

As a composer working with sound objects, you always need to have your ears open – at all times of the day. Listening is one of the most important things that you do and doing it properly means that you are able to keep tabs on things at all stages of the compositional process. Listen to sounds before you record them, listen to them again in the studio over and over again to find out what they are capable of achieving, and listen to them again once they're part of a completed composition. Also, get others to listen at all stages; this will confirm your thoughts about a sound's potential as well as provide new information you hadn't thought about.

B.7.2 Capturing

With your ears always open, make sure that you are always ready to capture sounds whenever you can. Try to carry some kind of recording device with you at all times, even if it's only your phone, but always make sure that you record at the optimum level available to you so that you don't encounter problems later on. If you can take the sound object into the studio then go to town with it when recording. Make sure that you mine the sound for every possible nuance and, above all, improvise with it and work it.

B.7.3 Manipulating

Once the sounds are ones and zeros in the computer, then there's more improvising to be done editing, processing, manipulating the sound. At this stage I always think of Francis Dhomont's idea of working with sound like a potter works with clay. Of course you will have some ideas about what you want to do to the sound via various processing techniques but always spend time improvising with sounds within plugins to create new sounds.

B.7.4 Creating

You will inevitably get stuck during the compositional process. If you do, zoom out and look at your work from a distance – contemplate the bigger picture. Then zoom back in and tackle the issue afresh. Also, don't be afraid to throw anything away – even the sound that is so, so precious to you – don't try to force it into a piece when it just doesn't want to be there. It might be that it needs to be in another piece.

Pete Stollery is a composer based in Aberdeen.

Binary Representations

Binary is the 'language' of the computer or electronic gizmo. It is used for the storage and processing of everything that is inside the computer. We can use binary codes to represent any data structure we like, but in the studio we commonly see binary representations of audio signals, control data and measurements. A single binary digit (bit) is represented by the state of one electronic switch inside the computer. Bits can be grouped together to form a 'word'; word lengths of 8, 16, 32 and 64 are common. For example, we might talk about a 64-bit CPU; this would be a CPU that uses a 64-bit word length for the majority of its operations. eight bits is one byte (and more amusingly four bits is a 'nibble').

Table C.1 Names for multiple bytes

Name	Symbol	Number of bytes
Kilobyte	KB	10^3
Megabyte	MB	10^6
Gigabyte	GB	10^9
Terabyte	TB	10^{12}

In audio and video applications we often deal with very large numbers of bytes and single projects often require gigabytes of data storage. So how can we represent numbers? Are the numbers whole numbers (integer) or fractional (floating point)? Are they signed, either positive or negative? How do we store text or even audio?

C.1 Decimal (Base 10)

Let us take a look back at the number system we are all familiar with. We are used to working with numbers in base ten, the decimal number system. In decimal, each digit represents the number of ones, tens, hundreds, thousands and so on. Each digit column is based on successive powers of ten from right to left:

Table C.2 Decimal column values

10^4	10^3	10^2	10^1	10^0
10000	1000	100	10	1

In decimal we have ten symbols to represent column values and we know these as the digits $0,1,2,3,4,5,6,7,8,9$. Large values are represented in decimal by placing the digits in appropriate columns, e.g. 345: three hundred and forty-five. You remember your early school maths? 'Three hundreds plus four tens plus five units'.

$$3 \times 100 + 4 \times 10 + 5 \times 1 = 345$$

Note that a column value is given by the base raised to the power of the column index starting from zero, i.e. the thousands column is three to the left from the units column (zero index column) and we see that $10^3 = 1000$.

C.2 Binary (Base 2)

As with decimal, the columns represent multipliers but in this case they are based upon successive powers of two from right to left:

Table C.3 Binary column values

2^5	2^4	2^3	2^2	2^1	2^0
32	16	8	4	2	1

A simple way to remember the columns here is to start with the units column and repeatedly multiply by two until your have the desired number of columns.

C.3 Counting in Binary

The following table shows the numbers 0–9 translated to binary equivalents:

Table C.4 Decimal numbers represented in binary

Decimal	Binary
0	0
1	1
2	10
3	11
4	100
5	101
6	110
7	111
8	1000
9	1001
10	1010

C.4 Bits, Bytes and Leading Zeros

The number of digits in a computer representation of a binary number is the number of bits. When we specify a number using a certain number of bits we fill all the bits with 0 or 1, so 3_{10} is 00000011 in 8-bit binary. Modern computers typically use 32-bit or 64-bit representations, i.e. 3_{10} would be 00000000000000000000000000000011 with all the leading zeros filled in.

C.5 Adding Binary Numbers

In the following example we can see how the same methods for adding numbers column by column work equally well for binary numbers:

Table C.5 Adding binary numbers

Binary	Decimal
101_2	5_{10}
001_2	1_{10}
110_2	6_{10}

C.6 Representing Negative Numbers

By using one of our bits to specify positive or negative we can represent negative numbers. The method used in computing is called two's complement. To go from a positive number to a negative we invert all the bits and add one.

C.7 Fractional Numbers

In decimal the digits after the decimal place (.) are negative powers of 10:

Table C.6 Decimal column values extended

10^4	10^3	10^2	10^1	10^0	10^{-1}	10^{-2}	10^{-3}
10000	1000	100	10	1	1/10	1/100	1/1000

In binary we can do the same with 2s:

Table C.7 Binary column values extended

2^5	2^4	2^3	2^2	2^1	2^0	2^{-1}	2^{-2}	2^{-3}
32	16	8	4	2	1	1/2	1/4	1/8

C.8 Floating Point

Floating point numbers are essentially a way of representing an extremely large range of numbers with a smaller number of bits and a 'floating' point. You have almost certainly done this in decimal when you used scientific numbers: $0.001 = 1.0 \times 10^{-3}$. In this case the mantissa is one and the exponent is negative 3. In binary we use a base two representation for the mantissa and exponent: $0.125 = 1/8$ in decimal and 1.0×2^{-3} in binary.

Different systems and software may use different numbers of bits for the mantissa and exponent. For example, we could choose to use four bits for the mantissa and four for the exponent in an eight-bit representation. One eighth would therefore have a four-bit unsigned mantissa value of 1_{10}, 0001_2, and a four-bit unsigned exponent value of 3_{10}, 0011_2, stored in eight bits by concatenating the bits together as 00010011. Of course, it would mean something totally different depending on your interpretation of the columns.

In computing, the interpretation of bits changes according to context. Bits can represent numbers but equally they could represent commands, text or the status of a device.

C.9 ASCII Strings

Letters and other characters can be represented using a common code. ASCII character code uses 8-bit unsigned values to represent 256 distinct characters. By storing a sequence of ASCII values we can represent a sentence. This is commonly called a text 'string'.

C.10 Hexadecimal

Hexadecimal (base 16) is a useful shorthand for binary. A sequence of four (binary) bits can be represented as a single hex digit, so a single byte can be a pair of hex digits. We only have ten numeral symbols so we extend our symbol set with letters (see Table C.8).

Hex notation is used extensively in MIDI syntax descriptions. eg. SYSEX F7 and F0 status bytes.

We also see it in representations of RGB/RGBA colour where we often see three or four bytes used to represent red, green, blue and alpha (transparency) components of a colour, eg. #FFFFFF is white, #000000 is black, #FF0000 is red.

Table C.8 Hexadecimal numbers represented in decimal and binary

Decimal	Binary	Hexadecimal
0	0	0
1	1	1
2	10	2
3	11	3
4	100	4
5	101	5
6	110	6
7	111	7
8	1000	8
9	1001	9
10	1010	A
11	1011	B
12	1100	C
13	1101	D
14	1110	E
15	1111	F

Appendix D

Pure Data (Pd)

Pd is a real-time graphical programming environment for audio and graphical processing. It resembles the Max/MSP system but is much simpler and more portable. For some time it sported a number of features not present in Max/MSP. With Mark Dank's GEM package, Pd could be used for simultaneous computer animation and computer audio. Additionally, an experimental facility was provided for defining and accessing data structures. Max/MSP has subsequently incorporated Jitter and Live and has grown considerably in size, in part due to its commercialisation.

Pd is extremely useful for creating signal processing tools that operate in realtime. Its graphic interface and flow diagram programming model make it relatively simple to learn and very intuitive if you are familiar with modular synthesisers. The flow diagram concept makes it very straightforward to visualise data and signal flow through your programs.

Perhaps its biggest disadvantages are apparent when you need to process complex structures of data in a very iterative way. In these situations other languages offer better control. Pd is best suited to real-time control and live performance and is certainly not the best tool for offline or batch processing of audio/MIDI data.

When we first load Pd we are presented with its main window. This window is the main area for creating new Pd files and setting up the devices that Pd will use. It also displays error messages and any information that you choose to send it.

In order to create programs with Pd we create patches. A patch is a like a blank canvas for you to add objects. Objects that you add to a patch can be connected together in different ways in order to describe the way that data will flow. This is somewhat akin to a flow chart or the physical wires between devices.

Pd responds to user-or device-generated information. These 'events' are such things as mouse clicks, key presses, incoming MIDI messages, OSC messages, etc. The various GUI object boxes and objects that represent devices generate messages. Other object boxes process and

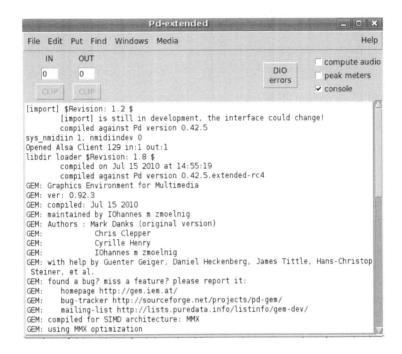

Figure D.I Pd main screen

sometimes generate new messages. The messages flow through the diagram and this is how we create programs. This processing model is therefore 'event based'.

D.I Basic Units of Programming Pd

Object boxes either do things to data, get data from physical devices or send data to physical devices. Objects are the main building blocks of programs in Pd. The available object classes are extensive and can be extended through libraries. If you are familiar with Max/MSP there is a particularly useful extension library called Cyclone which provides clones of many Max/MSP objects. The Pd extended version comprises many such libraries.

Message boxes let you specify commands or provide data to objects. It is very important to learn the difference between objects and messages. In essence: objects do things and messages provide data and control commands to objects.

Comment boxes let you make notes for yourself and others. It is a very good idea to comment complex sections of patches that you make.

Number boxes allow you to enter numbers with the mouse and keyboard. They are one of the GUI objects in Pd and they can be used to display numerical information as well as enter it.

D.1.1 Data types

integers (int, i): are whole numbers. In Pd (unlike Max/MSP), there is no specific integer data type, everything is in fact a floating point. However, it's useful to understand that many objects will expect whole numbers and may round values.

floating point (float, f): are real numbers. Pd uses a 32-bit floating point representation. The range is huge but as with any floating point representation precision is lost at extremely large or small values.

symbols (symbol): (in other languages these are normally called strings). You often define these in message boxes as a block of text surrounded by double quotes ("a bit like this").

bangs: In Pd there is a special data type that is often used to trigger the operation of an object. When you send a 'bang' to an object it performs its programmed task.

lists: A list is defined as a collection of any of the above data types. There are special objects for constructing lists but you can also define them directly in message boxes. For example, a message box containing (hello world 10 20 30 40.4 bang) would construct a list with "hello", "world", 10, 20, 30, 40.4, bang.

D.1.2 Numbers and range calculations

In Pd and any computer programming language, everything eventually boils down to numbers. One of the most useful skills in Pd is to understand the ranges of the numbers generated by objects and devices. Here is a quick list of common number ranges:

- MIDI notes: (0–127) (7-bit integer)
- MIDI velocity: (0–127) (7-bit integer)
- MIDI CC: (0–127) (7-bit integer)
- MIDI pitch wheel: (−8192–8192) (14-bit integer)
- Input range of audio: (−1.0–1.0) (32-bit floating point)
- Output range of audio: (−1.0–1.0) (32-bit floating point)
- Scaling audio: (0.0–1.0) (32-bit floating point)

- Oscillator frequency: (0.0–20000.0) (32-bit floating point) this is the range of human hearing.
- ASCII character: (0–255) eight-bit integer representing a letter, space or symbol.

Learning how to manipulate numbers from one range to another is a key skill in Pd programming.

D.1.3 Displaying values and messages using print

The print object is one the most useful objects in the Pd toolbox because it allows you to display the contents of messages. It can be connected to the output of an object and enables 'debugging'. Any messages arriving at the print object's inlet will be displayed in the Pd window. Specifying a name as the first argument (the first word after print) will cause messages to be prefixed with this name. This is useful to identify which particular print object is displaying a message. As a simple example, the following patch connects a number of different basic objects to the print object. Clicking on objects will cause some output in the Pd console.

Here we see the main window output that was produced by clicking on a number of different object boxes connected to a print object box.

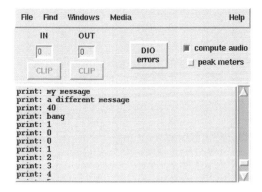

Figure D.2 Pd message output

D.1.4 Range mapping

In order to map a number range from one range to another we have a number of mathematical methods. Perhaps the simplest is to scale and offset using the multiplication object and addition object.

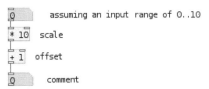

Figure D.3 Pd multiply offset

By setting the scaling factor and offset values appropriately we can perform a linear remapping of an input range. A simple method for understanding this range mapping is to perform the scale and offset on the minimum and maximum of your input range. So in the example our minimum is 0 and therefore the output minimum is $0 \times 10 + 1 = 1$. Our maximum is 10, so $10 \times 10 + 1 = 101$. This process is often also used in signal processing using `*~` and `+~` objects.

Often we need to perform a more complicated mathematical operation. The `expr` object allows complex mathematical equations to be expressed and performed on numerical messages. The `expr` object is very powerful and includes mathematical functions such as `sin`, `cos` and `pow` (raise to the nth power). This patch calculates the magnitude of a vector specified by two numbers and highlights some of the required syntax.

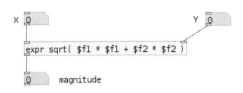

Figure D.4 Pd `expr` object example

There are also a number of musical range conversion objects that are particularly helpful. `mtof` converts from a MIDI note value in the range 0–127 to a frequency in hertz. This object is useful for creating traditional synths and for mapping linear controllers to logarithmic frequency scales. Its inverse, `ftom`, can be useful when converting analysed audio signals into MIDI. This example converts an incoming note number from a MIDI device to a frequency in hertz and uses the frequency to control the pitch of a sinusoidal oscillator.

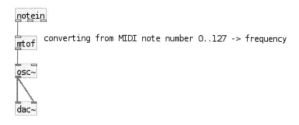

Figure D.5 Pd mtof example

D.1.5 Getting numerical data from MIDI controllers and keys

We can use the the notein, ctlin and key objects to grab incoming values from MIDI devices and the keyboard. The following patch shows how we can visualise the output using the print object.

With a combination of simple range mapping and some physical input we can start to make a real-time musical tool quite quickly. This example shows how we can use a simple range adjustment to map a physical slider into a range suitable for controlling the bpm of a metronome. A bleep is synthesised with a simple envelope generator line~ and signal multiplication *~.

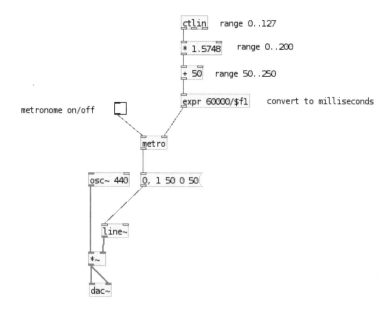

Figure D.6 Pd metronome using range scaling

D.1.6 Lists

The list data type is very important for controlling objects. It is vital to be able to construct and deconstruct lists of data using the objects that Pd provides. Lists can be manually entered into message boxes. In a message box the space character is used as the list element separator. We can use a number of special identifiers in a message box to insert data from an inlet into a message. If the message is formatted as a list then the output generated is a list message.

An alternative method of creating a list is to use the `pack` object. This object allows you to define the data types and number of elements to be packed together.

In order to deconstruct a list into its constituent elements we can use the `unpack` object. The following example constructs lists and then unpacks them further down the patch:

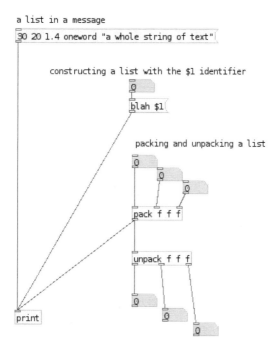

Figure D.7 Pd lists

D.1.7 Sending and receiving data without connections

Objects and data in Pd can be sent directly to objects without the need for connections. In fact, data can be sent from one patch to another if two are loaded at the same time. The send object allows data to be sent to a named receive object. You can have multiple receive objects and multiple send objects with the same names and all of them will intercommunicate. In addition, most GUI objects are able to send and receive data directly to named locations. This example shows some possibilities. Note the use of (r and s) shorthand for send and receive.

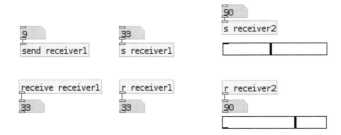

Figure D.8 Pd send and receive examples

D.1.8 Tips for exploring Pd

- Go through the tutorials.
- Use the browser; Section 1 is the manual for Pd.
- Use the help pages for objects (right click and select help). It's worth noting that the help is both interactive and editable so you can cannibalise help for patches in order to understand them.
- When reading the help page, the 'see also' section is also very useful for finding other interesting objects. Information is always given about the type and expected data ranges for each inlet and outlet. Details about creation arguments and optional arguments are also present. Try to identify the following keywords in the syntax information in order to understand an object:

  – Inlets: the messages and data expected at inlets, and what is done with it.
  – Outlets: the messages and data generated at outlets. What could you use the data for? What do you need to send in order for the data to be generated?

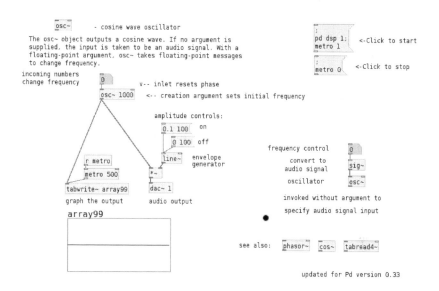

Figure D.9 Pd osc help file

- Arguments: the data that you put next to the name of the object. Arguments are creation-time parameters only. Could you use an argument to specify something without needing to connect another box? Some objects require arguments in order to be created.

D.2 Signal Processing in Pd

D.2.1 The audio signal data type

In Pd, audio signals are processed differently from events. An event is processed on demand: the event happens, Pd processes it then waits for more events. Signals are computed continuously once the 'compute audio' option is set. Real-time, host-based signal processing occurs in blocks and the size of the blocks is called the vector size or buffer size. A small vector size will allow the system to respond very quickly and a larger vector size will require the processor to wait for data and then process it all at once.

Our knowledge of sampling theory tells us that a signal is really a sequence of discrete samples. In Pd each sample is stored as 32-bit floating point numbers and the complete dynamic range of the audio device is mapped over the range −1.0 to 1.0.

Processing of signals only happens when the DSP system is enabled; the 'compute audio' option on the Pd main window allows enabling and disabling. However, there are other ways to do this directly from a patch. A special message box containing ; start dsp or ; stop dsp will do a similar job. This patch demonstrates some of the ways we can enable and disable signal processing and sets up a simple stereo amplifier from live input to live output.

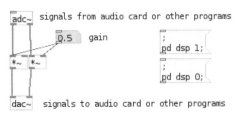

Figure D.10 Pd starting and stopping signal processing

D.2.2 Simple signal manipulation

Here are a few simple things we can do with audio. Adding together two signals has the effect of summing (mixing) the audio. The addition occurs sample by sample as the stream is processed. Pd automatically sums signals that are connected to a single inlet.

As well as this we can add a scalar value to a signal, which has the result of offsetting the signal by the specified value.

Multiplication is also performed sample by sample and a multiplication by a scalar value has the effect of scaling (amplifying) a signal. The multiplication of one signal by another results in a complex behaviour known as ring modulation.

D.2.3 Audio objects for generating signals

Here are some very useful signal-generating objects. osc~ generates a pure sine tone. phasor~ generates a ramp waveform. This waveform has a rich frequency content. noise~ generates white noise and is very useful for experimenting with filters. readsf~ is a soundfile playback object. It is relatively simple to use but needs some utility objects to provide a file selection dialog box.

D.2.4 Adjusting the range of signals

As with numerical data, you often need to adjust the ranges of signals. To do this we can use a similar linear range mapping by scaling and

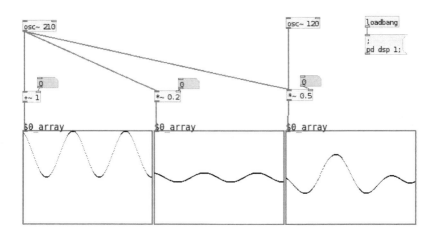

Figure D.11 Simple signal processing with +~ and *~ audio objects

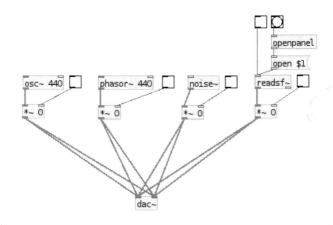

Figure D.12 Basic signal generators

offsetting using audio rate mathematical operators. As we are dealing with signals we use the signal versions *~, +~ and expr~. Figure D.13 uses two oscillators and some simple range adjustment to create an FM tone generator. One oscillator (the modulator) controls the frequency of the other (the carrier).

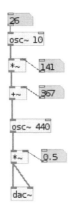

Figure D.13 Basic frequency modulation synthesis

D.2.5 Other simple manipulations on signals

Pd has a large array of filters to choose from and these are all relatively simple to play around with. The following example makes use of the vcf~ object but there are a number of others (hip~, lop and bp~).

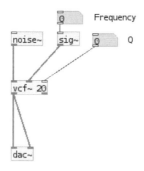

Figure D.14 Example of the vcf~ filter

We also have some very useful operators for creating multi-tap delay lines. Delay lines are one of the only places where Pd allows loops of signal processing objects. In the example, we are making use of this ability to create a feedback stage to the delay line.

Although it is perfectly possible to create a full implementation of a reverb unit with the basic operators in Pd, the algorithm tends to be

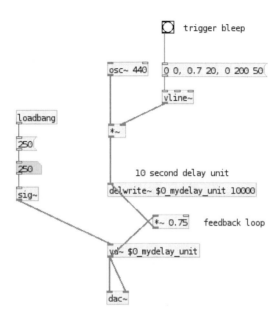

Figure D.15 Variable delay (vd~) with feedback

very complex and instead we can use a single external object to generate reverb very easily. Figure 2.25 uses the ready-made freeverb˜ object.

D.3 Sampling

Sampled audio (sections of prerecorded or algorithmically generated audio) can be handled in Pd with two distinct methods:

- Allocation of system RAM to store a fixed amount of audio that can be read from and written to extremely quickly (table/array based).
- Direct streaming of audio from hard disk (disk based, using the readsf˜ object).

D.3.1 Why do we need both types?

Buffers

- Buffers are important when random access within the audio is required.

- Buffers are always of a fixed preallocated size, limited by the amount of system RAM on the computer (approx. 10 Mb per stereo minute of audio at 44100 Hz).
- Buffers can be used as lookup tables for oscillators and functions.

Streaming

- Streaming is not limited by the size of your RAM so can allow playback of very large files.
- Streaming relies on the speed of your hard disk or storage medium and is slower to access randomly.
- Streaming to disk allows you to record for as long as you have storage space and the amount of time does not require preallocation.

D.3.2 Buffer objects: table and array

- The most important objects to understand are the table and array because they are the objects that are required by all other RAM-based playback and recording methods. We must always allocate a buffer with a certain name and specify an initial file, size and number of channels.
- Simple playback from a `buffer~` is achieved with `tabread~` or (for more complex pitch manipulation) `tabread4~`.

Glossary

acousmatic   A listening stance favouring sound over sight. Normally this means the perception of sound without trying to attribute source or cause (a very impersonal listening, quite scientific and relational). However, we are clearly going to bring our experience to bear upon any listening situation. The acousmatic stance asks that we 'listen in' and focus on the sound itself (its energy, motion, colour) and subsequently compare and contrast the meanings and emotions drawn from these perceptions.

acousmatic-potential   Normally the most audible characteristic of a sound that might best be modified. Acousmatic potential is how clearly a sound 'gives away' its characteristics. Consider a sustained ten-second sound that rises in pitch from C3 to C4 with some harmonic profile. Unless we want our piece to be going up and down like a roller-coaster, this sound is not going to feature in our work as 'the theme' but its acousmatic potential (sustained, harmonically pitched and rising) suggests a number of strategies. It is best to take these strategies separately.

ADSR   Attack, decay, sustain and release envelope shape. See Figure 1.3.

aiff   The AIFF format stands for Audio Interchange File Format and was developed by Apple, hence its suitability to Macintosh computers. Like the wav format it contains uncompressed pulse code modulated binary data.

ambisonic   A method of encoding sound which can then be decoded to present a three-dimensional field over any number of loudspeakers.

ASCII   American Standard Code for Information Interchange.

BEAST   The Birmingham ElectroAcoustic Sound Theatre is the performing wing of the postgraduate and staff composers at Birmingham University. Adrian Moore completed his PhD there under the tutelage of Professor Jonty Harrison.

bricolage   Construction drawn from a vast array of diverse objects. More commonly associated with the visual and sculptural arts.

Levi-Strauss and Boulez have used the term bricolage to denigrate sonic art made from manipulations of recorded sounds.

CCRMA   The Centre for Computer Research in Music and Acoustics was opened in 1978 at Stanford University and was founded by John Chowning. It is perhaps best known for Chowning's work on frqeuency modulation, research purchased by Yamaha who went on to put it in their now infamous DX7 synthesiser.

CDP   The Composers Desktop Project is a suite of programs running on desktop computers. Developed in the early 1980s, the CDP was innovative and experimental. One of its first pioneers and programmers was composer Trevor Wishart.

CEC   The Canadian Electroacoustic Community (http://cec.sonus.ca/), Canada's official national association for electroacoustic music, acousmatic and computer music and sonic art.

DAW   Digital Audio Workstation. Normally a software mixer that enables composers to edit and composite multiple soundfiles, craft volume curves, equalise sounds and send to effects. The finished mix is normally bounced down to a fixed stereo or multitrack master.

default-mode-network   The default mode network is a region of the brain which is active when we are at rest.

EMS   The Elektronmusikstudion is the Swedish national centre for electronic music and sound art. The research organisation started in 1964 and is based in Stockholm. Like the GRM in Paris it was originally associated with radio.

EQ   Equalisation is always associated with traditional filters such as low-pass, high-pass, low-shelf, high-shelf and notch. You cannot bring out or dampen frequencies that are not there in the first place, but EQ helps balance your sounds in the mix.

feedback   Feedback is simply the rerouting of the output back into the input. Normally this happens after the output signal has been attenuated. Care should be taken when using feedback as it can lead to your system overloading.

FFT   Fast Fourier Transform. A process where a sound can be broken into constituent sinusoidal waveforms. Computationally intensive, relying upon complex number theory, it used to be found only in non-real-time software. However, it is now prevalent in most pitch detection software.

flange   A delay-based manipulation where one sound is laid against itself after a small (often varying) delay. Additionally, the result is often fed back into the mix.

foldover   Often when a manipulation fails to do as you intend, frequencies go above 20 kHz and 'come back down again'. They are said to have been folded over back into the audible spectrum.

formant   A formant is a spectral peak. Formants are commonly referred to when describing characteristics of the human voice. It is the difference between the dark 'u' and the bright 'e'.

frequency-domain   The frequency domain takes a sound and analyses it into small segments called windows. Each window is further analysed to find out exactly what frequencies, amplitudes and phases are present. Normally, graphs of the frequency domain are drawn as frequency (X) against amplitude (Y) and do not show time. If time is to be shown, graphs are called sonograms and show frequency (Y) against time (X) with amplitude shown as a heat intensity shading.

fricative   Vocal sounds made by the close vibration of vocal articulators (examples are 'sss', 'zzz', 'thth').

Glitch   Glitches are precisely those sounds that would, under normal circumstances, appear unwanted. Often associated with low frequency amplifier hum and crackle or short noise bursts.

GRM   The Groupe de Recherches Musicales in Paris. A group of musicians and engineers under the initial direction of Pierre Schaeffer, later François Bayle. See www.inagrm.com/.

GRMTools   A selection of plugin modules for DAWs made by the Groupe de Recherches Musicales in Paris. A time-domain set was released in the early 1990s followed by VST plugins in 1997, a spectral set working in the frequency domain early in 2000 and a release of three new tools in 2010.

IRCAM   Institut de Recherche et Coordination Acoustique/Musique is a research and composition centre in Paris. Created by Pierre Boulez in 1973 and opened in 1977, IRCAM remains a cultural mecca for avant-garde instrumental and electroacoustic music.

LPC   Linear predictive coding is useful for speech processing as it models the voice and makes assumptions about future events based upon current data (linear prediction). As such, it is a highly efficient algorithm for predicting speech parameters (formants, intensities). Resynthesis works very much the same as a vocoder with voiced and non-voiced parameters being synthesised according to compressed LPC data.

micro-montage   Micro-montage is the construction of sound objects from very small (almost granular) portions of other sounds. Although montage suggests linear ordering of components, it implies mixing at a very detailed level. Micro-montage can be used to create fast-flowing passages of intense variety. It is a very time-consuming method of composition but often highly noticeable.

MIDI   Musical Instrument Digital Interface. A digital code that stores the essentials of a score (pitch, duration, timing) alongside a few musical parameters such as aftertouch. This code enables synthesisers to be linked together and eventually keyboards to become an input device to a computer.

OSC   Open Sound Control. Developed as but one of many 'sons of MIDI', Open Sound Control affords the communication of structured data between devices set up to send and receive information tagged in this way. Open Sound Control is common amongst many well-known hardware and software devices.

plosive   Vocal sounds made by first blocking the vocal tract so that airflow ceases. When air is released an explosive sound is produced. Examples are 't', 'd', 'k', 'b', 'p'.

post-fade   A tap on an audio channel after the fader, therefore affected dramatically by the state of the actual output fader.

pre-fade   A tap into an audio channel on a DAW that diverts a quantity of sound before it reaches the fader routed to the mix bus. Very useful when you want specific control of wet and dry outside of the effect plugin.

reduced listening   Reduced listening is the technique that allows us to adopt the acousmatic stance, listening to sound without reference to source or cause. The repetition of a sound or passage often tends towards the acousmatic as we are led to shift our attention from surface or superficial details to the interior qualities of the sound.

sound object   Normally a combination of sounds that have a strong beginning, short sustain and timely release.

space   From the physical space to the shape-spaces created by a gesture to the feeling of space suggested by reverberation or a sonic environment. Ultimately to an 'out there' space, in the imagination. Denis Smalley has written a conclusive text here.

SPL   Sound pressure level. Measured in decibels (dB), the sound pressure level is a relative measure of the magnitude of sound with reference to the threshold of hearing.

stereo   A stereo recording is taken with two microphones. Sounds arriving at each microphone may vary in terms of intensity and time of arrival depending on the stereo recording technique used. It is these small differences which, when played back over two loudspeakers, replicate the spatial position of the sound.

strata   Strata is a term we use to delineate spectral levels of sound. The most obvious strata are exemplified in the canopied and rooted texture setting where a low bass drone and a high frequency sustained sound 'encapsulate' the spectral space.

synaesthesia   Synaesthesia is activation of one sense by the perceptual activity of another. In music, most documented occurrences of synaesthesia occur between hearing and colour perception. Olivier Messiaen was known to have colour–music synaesthesia and it is identified in some of his works.

Syter   Syter stands for système en temps réel. It was a computer system begun in 1975 at the GRM. It is the forerunner of the GRMTools.

time   From tick-tock, tick-tock and the directness of the timeline in a DAW or the X axis on a time-domain waveform to the more global understanding of a period of time.

time domain   The time domain is our traditional view of sound as a moving waveform graphed as amplitude (Y) against time (X).

USB   Universal serial bus. An industry standard connection protocol connecting external devices to your computer. Most commonly seen in portable drives and memory sticks. www.usb.org.

WAV   The WAV file format normally holds uncompressed audio in LPCM format (linear pulse code modulation). Although files can be interleaved there is a maximum file size of 2 or 4 GB.

waveform   Normally a graph with the x axis representing time and the y axis representing amplitude.

Index

Max curriculem
www.darwingrosse.com/200bjects